FINANCIAL AND COMMERCIAL POLICY

UNDER THE CROMWELLIAN PROTECTORATE

FINANCIAL AND COMMERCIAL POLICY

UNDER THE CROMWELLIAN PROTECTORATE

MAURICE ASHLEY

D. PHIL

FRANK CASS : LONDON

Published by
FRANK CASS AND COMPANY LIMITED
67 Great Russell Street. London WC1B 3BT

First published in Great Britain by the Oxford University Press

First edition	1934
Second edition	1962
New impression	1972

ISBN 0 7146 1265 0

Printed in Great Britain by
Lewis Reprints Ltd.
member of Brown Knight & Truscott Group
London and Tonbridge

CONTENTS

INTRODUCTION

IT is extremely gratifying to me that this book, written more than a quarter of a century ago, based on my Oxford University thesis, should now be considered worthy of reprinting. Before it was first published I had left the academic world to make a living from journalism. But I always felt a pardonable pride when I saw my book quoted in works of mature scholarship and again when I heard later that it commanded a high scarcity price at learned booksellers'. Although the amount of time I have since had to pursue historical research has been limited, I have tried to keep up with the work done on seventeenth-century British history. For this edition I have made a number of factual corrections in the text, but I have not altered the style or the conclusions. Of course if I had my life to live over again, the book would have been written differently and the bold generalizations natural to a young man would have been modified. But alas! we none of us have that chance. In this introduction I draw attention to some of the work that has been done on the subject since the book was first published.

I have been criticized for underestimating the number of merchants in the Long Parliament in chapter I. The figure I published was only a very rough calculation, inspired by the then novel ideas of the late Sir Lewis Namier. D. Brunton and D. H. Pennington, *Members of the Long Parliament* (London, 1954) estimate the correct figure to be forty-five to fifty or seventy including 'speculators'. I do not myself see why 'speculators' should be classed with merchants. No member of parliament today, who speculates in stocks and shares, would automatically be classed as a 'tradesman'. Mary Frear Keeler, *The Long Parliament, 1640–1641: A Biographical Study of its Members* (Philadelphia, 1954) estimates that there were fifty-five 'men of trade' in the Long Parliament, but of these only thirty-one or thirty-two are given the general title of 'merchants'; the rest seem to have been members of City Companies, which may have meant as little then as it does now. Twenty-seven are said by Dr. Keeler to have been sons of tradesmen, which, curiously enough, was the number of my tentative estimate.

Important books on the economic history of the period preceding the civil wars are B. E. Supple, *Commercial Crisis and Change in England 1600–1642* (1957) and R. Ashton, *The Crown and the Money Market 1603–1640* (1960). Valerie Pearl, *London and the Outbreak of the Puritan Revolution* (Oxford, 1961) throws a flood of light on the attitudes of the City merchants: quite a number of them were Royalists. 'The Cost of the English Civil War' is discussed by D. H. Pennington in *History Today*, VIII (1958). Other contributions to this subject will be found in *Essays in the Economic and Social History of Tudor and Stuart England*, ed. F. J. Fisher (Cambridge, 1961).

Cecil Roth, *A History of the Jews in England* (2nd ed. 1948), pp. 157 *seq.* has something to add about the influences that induced Oliver Cromwell to re-admit the Jews, but he does not seem to differ much from my remarks. For Cromwell's own interest in economic affairs my friend Dr. G. D. Ramsay's article on 'Industrial Laisser-Faire and the Policy of Cromwell' in *Economic History Review*, XVI, no. 2 (1946) should be consulted. He wrote that there was little to suggest that Cromwell was tempted to pursue any distinct policy in the field of industrial regulation and that his policy showed the 'fundamental opportunism of a conservative mind'. On the whole, the administrative network of industrial regulation functioned much as it had done before the Interregnum. This conclusion chimes in well with my own conclusions about Cromwell's attitude to commercial policy.

A great many books about the Levellers and their friends have been written during the past twenty-five years. There are good books by Joseph Frank, by Christopher Hill, H. N. Brailsford and several others. On the whole, it seems clear that the Levellers were genuinely in favour of freeing trade by abolishing monopolies of all kinds.

To turn to public finance (chapters IV and V) a good deal has been added to our knowledge of Jacobean government finance in recent years. I would draw attention to R. H. Tawney, *Business and Politics under James I: Lionel Cranfield as Merchant and Minister* (Cambridge, 1958): this masterly book discusses *inter alia* the achievement of Cranfield as King James I's Lord Treasurer. Robert Ashton's article on 'Deficit Finance in the Reign of James I' (*Economic History Review*, second series X, 1, 1957) shows how at the end of the reign the public debt amounted to over a million pounds, despite Cranfield's efforts. Deficit finance was in fact the accepted thing in the forty years before the Civil War broke out. Political historians, as I argue in this book, have sometimes tended to attach too much importance to the significance of the public debt during the Cromwellian Protectorate.

Mr. Ashton has also published an article on 'Revenue Farming under the Early Stuarts' (*Economic History Review*, second series, VIII, 3, 1956). In this article he refers to his doctoral thesis at London University on 'Government Borrowing under the First Two Stuarts, 1603–42' (1953). He points out that the tax farmers were the first short-term lenders to the King. The rents paid by the farmers of the Customs were £120,000 a year at the end of King Charles I's period of personal rule. (Frederick C. Dietz, *English Public Finance 1558–1641*, New York, 1932, says that the farms of the great Customs in 1640 yielded £177,863 and in 1641, £169,388.) By comparison therefore the yield from Customs was substantially higher during the Protectorate when the Customs were administered on a commission basis. C. C. Crews wrote a thesis on 'The Last Period of the Great Farm of the Customs' for his M.A. degree at London University which is summarized in the *Bulletin of the Institute of Historical Research*, XIV (1936–7, pages 118–19). In this he wrote as follows: 'Unlike their successors of the Restoration the Interregnum customs commissioners were not state officials with a definite salary for their services. They had financial interests in the customs like their predecessors of the great farm. The only differences were that smaller advances and shorter periods of office weakened the incentive to profit and enabled the government to strengthen its control over the customs. The hybrid system thus established combined disguised farming with an arrested form of direct collection.'

On excise (chapter VII) reference should be made to Edward Hughes, *Studies in Administration and Finance, 1558–1825, with special reference to the history of salt taxation in England* (Manchester, 1934). Professor Hughes pointed out that excise was proposed about 1628 'but not allowed to hatch'; King Charles I is also said to have 'laboured to bring in excise, but it was distasted'. 'Excise,' wrote Professor Hughes 'by combining some of the experience of the hated patents with the principle of central assessment by shires successfully anticipated in the ship-money levies ultimately proved the key to the fiscal cupboard.' And at the Restoration the excise and customs were described as the 'pillars of the Revenue'. Professor Hughes's book contains some important facts about Martin Noell, the outstanding financier of the Cromwellian period. Mr. Hughes wrote a critical review of my book in *History* (June, 1935). I have embodied some of the corrections he then suggested in the present edition. Since I wrote my book both Professor Joel Hurstfield and Mr. H. E. Bell have written about the Court of Wards, to which I make a passing reference on pages 70–1 of chapter VII.

To turn to the subject of English commerce in the Cromwellian period: for a general introduction to this subject reference should be made to G. D. Ramsay's recent book *English Overseas Trading during the Centuries of Emergence* (London, 1957). He stresses there how embarrassing was British dependence on the Baltic for timber and other imports of naval supplies. The Dutch ships with their lower masts and rigging were much better suited to the Baltic trade than were ours. Violet Barbour's *Capitalism in Amsterdam in the Seventeenth Century* (New York, 1950) is also important for the background. On the trading companies we now have K. C. Davies, *The Royal African Company* (London, 1957), R. W. K. Hinton, *The Eastland Trade and the Common Weal in the Seventeenth Century* (Cambridge, 1959) and A. C. Wood, *History of the Levant Company* (Oxford, 1935). Mr. Hinton's book is most suggestive. Among other things he has pointed out that Benjamin

Worsley, who was the Secretary of the Council of Trade, appointed in August, 1650, was the author of two pamphlets, *The Advocate*, which deals with the Navigation Act of 1651 and a pamphlet on *Free Ports* published in 1652. Thus we have a direct insight into commercial policy as it was seen by the advisers of the Council of State. Mr. Hinton gives facts and figures which illustrate the decline of the Eastland trade during the Cromwellian Protectorate. A doctoral thesis by W. C. Palmer on 'The Activities of the East India Company in Persia and the Persian Gulf, 1616–1657' is summarized in the *Bulletin of the Institute of Historical Research*, XI (1933–4). Dr. Wood notes that three-quarters of the exports of the Levant Company consisted of cloth, that its business was hit by the Civil Wars, and that the Company claimed to experience poor trade in 1660. Dr. Wood's book is not however so valuable for the Cromwellian period as the thesis by G. P. Ambrose to which I referred in my original text.

A valuable general survey of 'Diplomacy and Trade in the Protectorate' by Menna Prestwich was published in the *Journal of Modern History*, vol. XXII, no. 7, in June, 1950. Mrs. Prestwich accepts my view that economic considerations did not play a great part in determining Oliver Cromwell's policy; on the other hand, she doubts whether the expansion of the Customs revenue in the later years of his Protectorate reflected an improvement in trade: she suggests that this expansion may have been owing to improved farming, but does not give any proof of this assumption. So far as her arguments over Cromwell's policy in the Baltic is concerned, these are questioned by Michael Roberts in an article on 'Cromwell and the Baltic' in the *English Historical Review*, LXXVI, no. 300 for July, 1961.

Articles dealing with English foreign trade before and after the Cromwellian period are F. J. Fisher's 'London's Export Trade in the Early Seventeenth Century', *Economic History Review*, 2nd series, no. 2 (1950) and R. Davis's 'English Foreign Trade 1660–1700' in the same journal 2nd series, no. 7 (1954).

The Navigation Act of 1651, which I discuss in chapter XIII of my book is a distinctly difficult subject. Everyone interested in this subject must now read Professor O. A. Johnsen's article 'The Navigation Act of 9 October, 1651' in vol. XXXIV of *History* (1949). From an examination of the surviving port books in the Public Record Office Professor Johnsen concludes that English commerce and shipping had 'made great strides at the end of the sixteenth and during the first half of the seventeenth century', increasing fourfold or fivefold between 1580 and 1640. So far as the carrying trade to England was concerned English ships ousted both Dutch and French vessels between 1600 and 1630. His opinion is that 'the testimony of contemporary and fundamental sources shows that the discontinuance of the Dutch transport of goods to England was not due to the Navigation Act: it was the result of a gradual development which continued all through the first half of the seventeenth century.' 'The Navigation Act,' he observes, 'can neither have had the object nor yet the importance generally attached to it.' L. A. Harper, *The English Navigation Laws* (Columbia 1939), which is subtitled 'a seventeenth century experiment in social engineering', has little to say about this Act, but quotes some figures of ships entered at English ports 'before 1651'. These show 674 entries of English ships against 281 entries of foreign ships. I find it difficult to know what importance to attach to those figures. R. W. K. Hinton, 'Dutch Entrepot Trade in Boston, Lincs, 1600–1640' in the *Economic History Review*, second series, IX, (1957), also quotes from port books and agrees with Professor Johnsen that the Dutch shipping declined enormously between 1628 and 1640. It seems that the Dutch decline set in catastrophically after the outbreak of the Thirty Years War in 1618. Mr. Hinton nevertheless adds: 'If port books survived for the years about 1650 they would probably show an even greater reversion to the Dutch entrepot than in 1615–1618 with a corresponding even more catastrophic decline in the English merchant fleet. *They would leave little doubt as to the purpose and justification of the Navigation Act of 1651*' (my italics, page 471). In his book, on the Eastland trade Mr. Hinton also attaches significance to the Navigation Act, but questions whether any pressure came from the trading companies as such, though he does not deny that some merchants as well as officials were in favour of it as a means of increasing English naval power. As between such eminent scholars who have studied the port books, I am not competent to judge. All I can say is that possibly Professor Johnsen overlooked the figures of seizures of Dutch ships for violating the Act which I quoted in my book from the exchequer rolls and owed to the kindness of Professor F. J. Fisher. Also there is clear evidence of Dutch ships carrying goods to the English colonies. Thirdly, one cannot, I think, entirely ignore the arguments of the contemporary merchants in the East India, Eastland, and Levant trades that their business had in fact been injured by Dutch competition. I suppose, however, it is possible that the Dutch brought in goods from the Far East, Near East, Baltic and elsewhere to their own free ports and that they were thence transhipped to England in English vessels.

To conclude, I would refer to two other theses summarized in the *Bulletin of Historical Research*. The first is 'London Merchants and Opposition Politics in Charles II's Reign' by Margaret Priestley (No. XXIX, 1956). In this she mentions the pro-Spanish tendencies of the London merchants and a claim that the 'underbalance' in the trade with France amounted to £1,000,000 a year. In 'The Part Played by London in National Affairs 1658–1660 with special regard to political and economic aspects' (*Bulletin*, No. 13, 1935–1936) Maureen Weinstock, M.A., observes that 'the attempt to produce further evidence of the trade depression of 1659 was only partly successful'. The late Godfrey Davies virtually ignored this trade depression in his book *The Restoration of Charles II* (San Marino, California 1955). There seems little doubt, however, that it happened. Incidentally, I should mention that Mr. Davies reviewed my book in the *English Historical Review* two years after it was first published and seemed to differ from some of my figures of Cromwell's debts. But he was then kind enough to say that my book was 'an extremely useful addition to our knowledge of the Puritan revolution' and that I had handled the complicated financial statements 'adroitly'. Finally I would like to express my gratitude to the selfless scholars who helped me in my salad days to master the difficult art of historical research and add the hope that students of this absorbing period of history who now read this second edition will find it of value to them.

Maurice Ashley

RUISLIP,
September, 1961

ABBREVIATIONS

The following abbreviations are used in the footnotes:

Letters and Speeches = Thomas Carlyle, *The Letters and Speeches of Oliver Cromwell* (ed. S. C. Lomas, 3 vols., 1904).
C.S.P. = *Calendar of State Papers.*
C.S.P. (*Dom.*) = *Calendar of State Papers* (Domestic series).
C.J. = *Journals of the House of Commons.*
D.N.B. = *Dictionary of National Biography.*
Firth and Rait = *Acts and Ordinances of the Interregnum* (ed. by C. H. Firth and R. S. Rait, 1911).

Except when otherwise stated, press marks are the present press marks in the Public Record Office. Carte, Tanner, and Rawlinson MSS. are in the Bodleian Library, Oxford; Additional (Add.), Lansdowne, Egerton, and Stowe MSS. are in the British Museum.

I

THE GOVERNMENT AND THE COMMERCIAL CLASSES

WHEN the beginning of the civil wars gave Oliver Cromwell the opportunity to take a leading part in the affairs of his country, he was already forty-three years old and had spent almost his whole life in a primarily agricultural county as the son of a landlord, as a landlord, and as a farmer. Agricultural progress and landed settlements were matters of profound interest to him,[1] and in his expressions of political ideas in later life the preservation of liberty and the security of real property were closely related.[2] All the members of his own family and of the families into which he married his children were landed proprietors, and excepting his wife's father, who was a merchant, so far as we know, none of the intimates of his youth or early middle age was interested in commerce.

It is curious to notice that the names of Oliver's mother, eldest sister, wife, and favourite daughter were all alike Elizabeth. Cromwell was himself an Elizabethan and emphasized on more than one occasion in his public speeches the deep respect he had for the wisdom of that great queen.[3] The careful student of Cromwell's speeches will not judge it fanciful to maintain that his attitude to matters of commerce and public finance was determined in no small measure by the fact that he was bred up to revere the striking success of the semi-piratical policy of Queen Elizabeth.

His education in the Elizabethan tradition and his upbringing in agricultural circles provided, it is reasonable to assume, two of the main prejudices given to Cromwell by heredity and environment and felt by him when, after his military genius had finally subdued resistance to the parlia-

[1] Cf. his part in draining the fens, the long and complicated negotiations over the marriage portion of Richard Cromwell, &c.

[2] See *inter alia* G. P. Gooch, *Democratic Ideas in the XVIIth Century* (1927), 127–40, and the remarkable speech Cromwell made to the army officers in 1657 (*Letters and Speeches*, iii. 487), wherein he couples together liberty and property as having been endangered by the Little Parliament.

[3] Cf. *Letters and Speeches*, ii. 513–14.

mentary Government in the three nations, he was induced to assume a position in which the supreme direction of public policy came into his hands. In this position he naturally called into consultation on economic matters men who were actually engaged in trade. The chief of these was Martin Noell, a scrivener by training, who was financially interested in Scotland, Ireland, the East and West Indies, and the Levant, besides financing the manufacture of salt to such an extent that he was called the 'Great Saltmaster of England'. The services which he performed for Cromwell in the way of financial administration and lending to the Government far exceeded in number and variety those of any other individual, and it cannot have been without significance that Richard Cromwell, in writing to his brother Henry in 1659, referred to Noell as 'our very good friend'.[1] After Noell, Thomas Vyner, the goldsmith, knighted by Cromwell in 1654, was probably the financier whose business for the Government was sufficiently large to make his advice next most influential on economic issues. The Venetian envoy in England records that it was to Vyner that Cromwell turned for help in the moment of his greatest financial stress in 1658, and when a month later he died, he was described as a 'good friend to his Highness'.[2] The names of these two men dart fitfully across the financial records of the Protectorate.

A well-known yet mysterious phase of Cromwell's career is the connexion between him and the Jewish colony in London. Post-Restoration writers and modern Jewish his-

[1] A summary of Noell's career is in C. M. Andrews, *British Committees and Councils of Trade, 1622–75* (1908), 49–50. His financial importance to the Government can be gauged from the indexes to the Calendars of State Papers and to the Exchequer Issue Rolls. Richard Cromwell's letter is in Lansdowne MSS. 822, f. 162. For Noell and salt see the same letter and *C.S.P.* (*Dom.*), *1654–5*, 36, for Noell's petition in which he says he employs 1,000 workmen and has many salt works.

[2] *C.S.P.* (*Venetian*), *1657–9*, 174; *Clarke Papers* (ed. Firth), iii. 147. Cf. also R. D. Richards, *Early History of Banking* (1929), 209–10, and various articles by the same author. Also the *D.N.B.*, s.n. 'Vyner'. F. Strong, in the *American Historical Review*, iv. 237, refers to Sir Ralph Maddison as the economic authority of the Protector. Maddison was the author of an economic tract called *England's Looking In and Out*, dedicated to Charles I (1640), reprinted without substantial alteration as *Great Britain's Remembrancer*, and dedicated to Cromwell in 1654. It is true that Maddison was a member of the Committee for Trade appointed by the Long Parliament in 1650, but there is no evidence that he had any more notable influence upon the policy of the Protector than any other pamphleteer.

torians agree in attributing his interest in it to economic motives.[1] Nor does this conclusion appear improbable. For while nothing in Cromwell's theory of 'liberty of conscience' had as its natural consequence the admission of the Jews to citizenship, the Elizabethan attempt made by his navy to capture Spanish treasure in order to ease his financial difficulties was greatly assisted by the wide knowledge possessed by Spanish and Portuguese Jews of the organization of bullion transport from the Spanish American colonies. Indeed, even before Menasseh Ben Israel came to England to plead for the return of his race, Cromwell was referring two petitions of an Andalusian Jew (Manuel Martinez Dormido alias David Abrabel) to the Council of State as being matters 'especially appropriate for their speedy consideration'.[2]

With the city of London, the heart of English commerce and finance, the relations of Cromwell were none too friendly. When in May 1653 an influential section of the City Council petitioned him to recall the Long Parliament, he told them angrily to mind their own business,[3] and when he visited the City to be dined as Lord Protector in the following year, his reception was not of the most cordial kind.[4] The behaviour of Fairfax's army in the City in the summer of 1647 long remained a bitter memory to the City magnates, and although, as may be gathered from the way in which strife immediately broke out between the City and the Government after the fall of Richard Cromwell, it is not unlikely that they preferred the Protectorate to a military republic, they seem to have looked upon Oliver's rule as at best a *pis-aller*. On more than one occasion Oliver in person harangued them on the necessity for their lending money as a corporation to his Govern-

[1] See especially various articles by Lucien Wolf: these are summarized in A. M. Hyamson, *History of the Jews* (1928), chaps. xvii–xx; Thomas Violet, *A Petition against the Jews* (1661); J. Bland, *Trade Revived* (1660).

[2] Egerton MSS. 1049, f. 7.

[3] The petition (British Museum, E. 697, 18) is dated May 20. Cromwell's response *qu'ils ne se meslassent que de leur commerce* is given in Bordeaux's report of May 24/June 3, 1653. All the government officials who signed this petition were dismissed from office, *C.S.P.* (*Dom.*), *1653–4*, 1.

[4] One should be cautious of accepting Edmund Ludlow's account of the unfriendly relations between the City and Cromwell in *Memoirs* (ed. Firth), i. 383, but his account of Cromwell's reception *en route* to the Grocers' Hall banquet on Feb. 8, 1654, is confirmed by other evidence; see Gardiner, *History of the Commonwealth and Protectorate* (1894), ii. 308–9.

ment, but they never repeated during the interregnum the enthusiastic efforts they had made for Parliament in the opening years of the civil wars. It is within the bounds of legitimate speculation to ask if the reliance which Cromwell's Government placed upon a man like Noell who, although an alderman, took no active part in the City government,[1] and the interest which it showed in the Jewish merchants, may not have been largely due to the fact that between the City authorities proper and the Protector the alliance of 1653–8 was of a tepid nature.

The very absence of a clear understanding between Cromwell and the City indicates how little mercantile interests were primary considerations to him. And even his financial advisers were possibly only consulted on matters of technical character and detail; Noell, for example, was definitely anti-Dutch,[2] but Cromwell came to the Protectorate with the deliberate design of bringing the Dutch war to an end, and actually offered in the negotiations commercial concessions in exchange for political pledges.

Cromwell's attitude to war in general was not by any means pleasing to the commercial classes. After the Dutch war ended the Protectoral Government concluded a number of maritime and commercial treaties and the mercantile community looked forward to an era of peace in which to develop the markets and trade routes thus thrown open to them. 'There is no greater enemy to trade than war', wrote a pamphleteer in 1644, 'be it in what country it will'.[3] But did Cromwell himself envisage the coming years as ones to be freed at all cost from renewed wars? His speeches and his actions have a superficial inconsistency. 'The greatest demonstration of [God's] favour and love appears to us in this: That He hath given us Peace', he announced on

[1] Noell was elected alderman for the ward of Aldersgate on Dec. 3, 1657, and was discharged from being an alderman on the payment of a fine on Dec. 15, 1657. City Rep. Book 66, ff. 15v., 21. He served on none of the City committees. Vyner was Lord Mayor when knighted by Cromwell, but he seems to have taken a back place after the expiration of his mayoralty. Cf. Sir Charles Firth in *History*, N.S. xi. 32: 'My conclusion is that the Protectorate had the support of the middle classes, and of traders and manufacturers in general, although the rich merchants of the London companies were increasingly hostile to it.'

[2] See his speech on Feb. 24, 1659, in W. Burton, *Diary* (ed. J. T. Rutt, 1828), iv, 480.

[3] J. B., *The Merchant's Remonstrance*, 2.

January 28, 1658.[1] Dryden wrote in commendation of Cromwell that 'He fought to end our fighting', and he compared himself in a phrase which reverberated in the ears of his contemporaries to a good constable who keeps the peace of his parish.[2] But all these arguments referred to internal peace only; the whole history of the diplomatic negotiations with the French and Spanish ambassadors which filled the summer months of 1654 bears witness to the fixed determination of his Government to re-engage in foreign war at no distant date and to do so with largely religious considerations in view. The repercussions of the wars of the Protector on commerce will be discussed later. It is sufficient here to say that, whatever part commercial considerations may have played in Cromwell's foreign policy (a question of much dispute among historians), when at length Cromwell's mind was decided he allowed no thought of economic interests to be otherwise than subordinate to the course on which he had decided.

Like Cromwell himself, the individual members of his Councils of State were not intimately connected with trade. They were sons of country gentlemen trained to be landlords, soldiers, or perhaps lawyers; a smattering of law was a part of a gentleman's education in those days (Cromwell himself was apparently a member of Lincoln's Inn), but for the most part the councillors came from a class which might reasonably be supposed ignorant of the principles of commercial policy.[3] On the other hand, it is probable that in some cases soldiering was the main livelihood of these statesmen; and among these a war policy may well have found more favour than one of peace. One fact we are fortunate in knowing concerns John Lambert, who was, after Cromwell, probably the most powerful man on the Council, namely, that his income depended on the price of wool in Yorkshire. May not his vehement opposition to war with Spain have been influenced by the knowledge that the Spanish Empire was then one of the principal markets for our cloth?[4]

1 *Letters and Speeches*, iii. 153. 2 Ibid., 63. Toland's *Life of Harrington*, xx.

3 The members of the different Councils of State of the Protectorate are all to be found in the *D.N.B.*, which is not, however, always very enlightening on their economic interests, possibly because they are unknowable.

4 'The most of my poor fortune their [there] depends upon the rate of wool', said

Writers on commerce frequently urged the English Government to seek the expert advice of merchants on economic questions, and the English Council of State was contrasted unfavourably with the Dutch States-General, in which it was said all the members were specialists in commerce and decided policy in terms of its needs.[1] That commercial affairs were in fact a far nearer concern to the Dutch than to the English governing classes is true for the whole century, but the existence of a specific military interest in Cromwell's Council is a factor which has to be borne in mind in discussing economic matters, more especially as many of them were referred to sub-committees of Council and not to committees of experts.

There is no reason to suppose that the trading classes had a more direct influence upon Parliament than upon the Council of State. Although we must await the result of the detailed researches of the official committee on the membership of the House of Commons before being in a position to give an exact analysis of the social structure of the interregnum parliaments, the general situation can be pretty clearly seen. The majority of the members of the Protectorate parliaments were country gentlemen, soldiers, and lawyers.[2] A contemporary royalist letter-writer asserted that Richard Cromwell's House of Commons contained one hundred and fifty lawyers,[3] and although this is no doubt

Lambert in introducing a Bill into the Commons 'for the better ordering and governing the makers and workers of broad mixed woollen cloths, within the West Riding of Yorkshire and for making them a body incorporate'. Burton, i. 127. Sir Charles Firth states in his article on Lambert in the *D.N.B.* that he advocated a war with Spain in common with Cromwell. Nevertheless, the French ambassador steadily called Lambert the leader of the anti-French party, and Gardiner speaks of him as favouring an alliance with Spain against France in 1654. Lambert was opposed to the West Indian expedition, Sir Charles Firth tells us in a supplementary note to the *D.N.B.*, so that it seems Lambert only advocated the Spanish war when it had become irrevocable.

[1] Compare, e.g., Samuel Lambe, *Seasonal Observations* (1658), 7, with Roger Coke, *A Discourse of Trade*, pt. ii (1670). It is needless to say that the English pamphleteers' views about the character of the Dutch States-General were fairly accurate.

[2] In this and the following paragraphs some use has been made of the W. D. Pink MSS. in the John Rylands Library, Manchester, notably vols. 296–306. Unfortunately Mr. Pink in these notes for his unfinished biographical dictionary of members of Parliament under the Tudors and Stuarts gives few or no references. Under the letters D, E, and F in his dictionary, taking the members of Cromwell's first Parliament, 1654–5, there were 20 country gentlemen, 8 lawyers, 7 soldiers, and 3 merchants.

[3] *C.S.P.* (*Clarendon*), iii (1932), 140.

an exaggeration, 'the gentlemen of the long robe' certainly formed a very powerful group both in this and the preceding parliaments. The representation of merchants and financiers, on the other hand, remained small.[1] There were at least thirty-two merchants and financiers in the Long Parliament, which was indeed described by contemporaries as 'a Trading Parliament',[2] but since this Parliament had a constantly changing membership and was frequently 'purged', that number must represent under 5 per cent. of the total membership. The Little or Nominated Parliament contained, apart from the representatives of the City of London, only two merchants, Edward Horseman of Rutlandshire and William Thompson, who represented the English merchants in the Anglo-Dutch arbitration over damages in the East Indies in 1654.[3] In the first Protectorate Parliament there were at least seventeen merchants and financiers (as compared with about forty officials and nine members of Cromwell's family). In the second Protectorate Parliament (1656–8) there were about the same number with the addition of Martin Noell, who was member for Stafford, and in Richard Cromwell's Parliament there were some twenty members, Martin Noell being joined by his business associates, Thomas Noell and Thomas Povey, while the famous Restoration merchant Josiah Child made his first appearance in Parliament as member for Petersfield. In 1761, roughly a hundred years later, we know that the House of Commons contained fifty merchants of whom at least fifteen were government contractors, while in 1933 there were over one hundred and twenty-five merchants and industrialists who were members of Parliament.[4] It seems to have been a fairly

[1] In the *Return of Members of Parliament* (1878) a few members are marked as merchants. I have supplemented these incomplete returns by various lists of M.P.s in the Thomason Tracts and have added therefrom the names of those members whom I know either from the Pink MSS. or other sources to have been engaged in trade or finance. In the Short Parliament there were at least 25 traders.

[2] W. Burton, *Diary* (ed. J. T. Rutt, 1828), i. xxv.

[3] I assume this was the same man, but it may not have been, for the name is common enough. Merchants during this period have an awkward habit of having identical names. It is not, I think, generally known that there were two Thomas Andrews, two Thomas Noells, and two Thomas Vyners.

[4] L. B. Namier, *Structure of Politics at the Accession of George III*, i. 70, and *England in the Age of the American Revolution*, ii. 255; Dod's *Parliamentary Companion* (1933).

general rule in the seventeenth century for London and the more important outports to be represented by men actively engaged in trade. Bristol, Plymouth, and Aldborough all returned merchants as members during the Protectorate. London, easily the largest port, was invariably so represented; but Newcastle, the second most important port, after having a merchant member in the Long Parliament, chose Sir Arthur Haslerig during the Protectorate. Kingston-upon-Hull had as its member from 1659 onwards Andrew Marvell, son of a clergyman and himself a poet. The numbers given above are probably not grossly underestimated, nor does the tone of taxation and certain other debates convey the impression that the mercantile interest was peculiarly strong in Cromwell's Parliaments.

Let us turn next to the administration. The separation of the legislative and the executive functions, which was reached in the nineteenth century, but has since tended to become obscure, was obscure enough under Cromwell. Higher officials like John Thurloe, Bulstrode Whitelocke, and William Roberts not only held more than one administrative post, but were also at times members of Parliament and of the Council of State. These men, though not perhaps themselves directly interested in commerce, were often connected with commercial people. John Thurloe, 'the little secretary', the Cromwells' right-hand man, who held in his grasp all the threads not only of domestic policy but also of foreign affairs, was the brother-in-law of Martin Noell and was engaged with him in more than one government economic enterprise. Nathaniel Manton, another big merchant of this epoch, interested alike in the French and Greenland trades, addressed Thurloe as 'much honn^red Cosen'.[1] William Roberts, who was a commissioner of the treasury and held other important administrative posts under the Cromwells, including that of commissioner for appeals in excise, was the grandson of a City alderman. Oliver Cromwell's intimate friend and one-time commissary-general, Henry Ireton, who died in 1651, left behind him a brother, John Ireton, a clothworker, who acted as excise commissioner

[1] J. A. Williamson, *The Caribee Islands under the Proprietary Patents* (1926), 125; S.P. 18/94, f. 120.

in 1657, became Lord Mayor, was knighted by Cromwell, and loaned him £2,500 in 1658. Another important official, John Barkstead, knighted by Cromwell in 1656, Keeper of the Tower, Major-General of Middlesex and an M.P., was a City alderman and a goldsmith by trade.

All these men must have had a real influence on the determination of policy. They formed a new class of government officials, distinguished alike by their single-mindedness and ability, who were appointed because their special knowledge made them suitable for the work. Commissionerships of the treasury, memberships of committees of appeal, and similar posts went mainly to lawyers; the actual collection and administration of taxes was assigned to merchants and financiers. But the key posts of treasurer of the army and navy were by Cromwell's time not in the hands of merchants. The joint treasurership of the army, held under the Long Parliament by two city aldermen, was taken over by army officers, Captains John Blackwell and Richard Deane, while the able Sir Henry Vane was replaced by his sub-treasurer, Richard Hutchinson, as treasurer of the navy.[1] The sale of the lands and goods confiscated by the Government after the civil wars was managed by London merchants, and the commissioners of customs and excise who under the Protectorate took the place of the royalist tax farmers were always eminent London merchants.[2] These commissioners differed somewhat in function from the old farmers, but all the smaller taxes were definitely farmed. That the tax-farming interest was particularly strong in London may be assumed from the fact that the amount of farming permitted steadily increased towards the end of the interregnum, despite the protests that arose against the system in Scotland, Ireland, and elsewhere not merely from the general public, but even from the Government's own representatives.[3]

[1] We know very little about these important officials. Perhaps it is worth while to notice that Hutchinson and Blackwell both invested in bishops' lands, the latter apparently speculatively. Rawlinson MSS. B. 239.

[2] See below, pp. 51 seq., &c.

[3] There is an interesting correspondence between Thurloe, Henry Cromwell, and G. Bodurda, chairman of the Customs and Excise Committee, in the *Thurloe State Papers* (ed. Birch, 1742) and Lansdowne MSS. 822.

Another definitely mercantile section among the higher officials were the contractors whose business was to arrange provisions and payments for the forces abroad and for those diplomatic representatives of the Government who were not paid for, as was, for example, the ambassador at Constantinople, by interested trading companies. At the beginning of the interregnum, we read of John Browne, the army ordnance contractor; but the Government evidently became dissatisfied with his tenders, and when in 1654 Cromwell took over Sir John Winter's ordnance works in the Forest of Dean, the army committee seems to have taken munitions largely under State control.[1] Apart from the ordnance and a number of small miscellaneous contracts, almost the whole of this business was in the hands of the Noell and Vyner groups.[2] Another semi-administrative group which included a number of City merchants was the 'purged' Trinity House committee which administered buoys and lighthouses, and whose advice was often taken by the Government on matters of naval and commercial policy.[3] Among the lower officials[4] we may distinguish two groups, the household group and the minor administrative group. The former consisted mainly of officers who had been employed about the court of Charles I and carried out similar functions at the court of the Protector. A list of their names, functions, and salaries can easily be drawn up from the records of the exchequer of receipt. One example may be given, John Embree, the court surveyor, who took from Cromwell in part satisfaction of arrears owed to him as a king's servant a Titian, a Tintoretto, and a Bassano.[5] The second group included officers appointed to look after the army and naval hospitals, auditors, minor customs officers, and the like. This

[1] Cf. *C.S.P. (Dom.)*, *1650*, 8, 331, 378; Ibid., *1651*, 16, 61; ibid., *1653–4*, 112.

[2] This is clear from the records of the exchequer payments. Captain Thomas Alderne, the contractor for victualling the navy, and a Portugal and West Indian merchant, was an associate of Noell.

[3] See the article on Trinity House in the *Encyclopaedia Britannica* (1929). I have to thank the secretary of Trinity House for giving me permission to consult its records. The prominent merchants who were elder brethren at this date were Samuel Moyer and Maurice Thompson.

[4] The difference drawn between 'upper' and 'lower' officials is a monetary one in terms of salaries.

[5] *Historical Manuscripts Commission Report*, vii. 92.

class is interesting because at least two well-known economic pamphleteers, Henry Robinson and Thomas Violet, belonged to it.[1] Robinson, the abler of the two, was the eldest son of a London mercer and held under the Protector the offices of auditor of the excise and of comptroller for the sale of the king's lands, and was a member of the committee for taking the accounts of the Commonwealth.[2] His writings are more valuable (although mainly derivative) than those of Violet, but seem to have been less influential. Thomas Violet, having acquired some knowledge of how to smuggle bullion by doing so himself, was appointed a searcher under Charles I. After being imprisoned in the Tower as a royalist plotter by the Long Parliament, where he occupied himself by writing various papers on currency and the exchanges, he was released to give his advice on mint questions and apparently resumed his previous post under Cromwell.[3]

Although the mercantile classes were not strongly represented in the actual executive and legislature, they formed by no means a negligible body in the community. It was calculated after the Restoration that there were nearly 1,800 merchants in London alone engaged in foreign trade.[4] From the Reformation onwards the City had steadily increased in size, and this was due in the main to the importance of its merchants and the activity of its port. The rate at which new buildings were put up in the suburbs became a source of alarm to politicians in the seventeenth century.[5] It was even said in Parliament in 1657, 'that this nation was falling into the rickets, the head bigger than the body. One nod of the head would command all the members.'[6] It is certain that the great City merchants, by means of the huge financial resources which they concentrated in their hands, had been able in a large measure to determine the result of the civil wars.[7] Few merchants were royalists, but some were

1 Sir William Petty, who was Henry Cromwell's secretary in Ireland, ought perhaps to be included in this class.

2 W. A. Shaw, *Select Tracts and Documents illustrative of English Monetary History, 1626–1730* (1896), 49–50.

3 To the account of Violet given in the *D.N.B.* should be added the information in his preface to his *Advancement of Merchandise* (1651).

4 E. Lipson, *Economic History of England* (1931), ii. 191, notes 6 and 7.

5 See below, p. 88.

6 Burton, i. 343.

7 This point is brought out by Mr. W. Harper in his 'Public Borrowing, 1640–60'

perforce Cromwellians.[1] The merchants were invariably members of the livery companies, and the leaders among them shared the offices in the City government. It is true that complaint was made in London, as elsewhere during the interregnum, that there were merchants who were not freemen of the City,[2] but few important names in this category have come to light. Perpetual cries arose from the outports at the predominant power of the London merchants, especially at the way in which they tried to exclude all others from their foreign markets, but there was nothing new about these, for they go back at least to the end of the fifteenth century.[3] It should, however, be noticed that it was alleged that the London tax commissioners and farmers abused their position to create a trading monopoly in their own favour. Newcastle, for example, asserted that Martin Noell manipulated the coal tax which he farmed to the detriment of the consumer generally and the town in particular.[4] Still, as some 80 per cent. of the total foreign trade of the country went through the port of London,[5] the Government did not need to treat these grievances very seriously.

It is an interesting problem how far the increase of foreign trade and widening of markets had accentuated division of labour among Cromwellian merchants. Henry Robinson divided trade into four classes, inland, import, export, and re-export. By the first he actually meant domestic industry, not retail trade; but let us substitute the latter. It is to be presumed that some merchants were still involved in retail

(1927), M.Sc. thesis in the Institute of Historical Research. I owe one or two of my following references to the appendices to this thesis.

[1] That the number of royalist merchants was small during the Protectorate is indicated by the Major-Generals' lists of royalists resident in England in 1655. These lists are pretty complete, but outside London name very few merchants; nor were they numerous in London itself. (Add. MSS. 34011–15.)

[2] City Common Journal, 41, f. 22v.: Committee of Trade appointed to consider 'how persons free of the several companies of Merchants who are capable may be drawn to take their freedom to this City'.

[3] *Newcastle Merchant Adventurers* (ed. Boyle and Denby, 1895), i. 165; W. G. Lingelbach, *Lawes Custome's and Ordinances of the Fellowshippe of the Merchantes Adventurers*, 205.

[4] *Newcastle Merchant Adventurers*, i. 195–6. Cf. R. Gardiner, *England's Grievance Discovered* (1655).

[5] This is a rough average figure of the percentage of the London to the total customs paid into the declared accounts.

trade from the constant complaints that were made against the shopkeeper-merchant on the basis of the recognized trade union principle of one man one trade.[1] But it is unlikely that the practice was widespread. The importing merchants generally sold their goods to a middle-man or a retailer who paid the excise duty on them after the first had paid the customs. It is, on the other hand, plain—to this the records of the trading companies bear witness—that the majority of merchants were equally interested in the import and export trades, although the re-export trade helped to make definite qualifications to this rule. Judging by the customs figures the re-export trade during the Protectorate represented about 4 per cent. of the total import and export trade, which meant possibly as much as 7 per cent. of the export trade.[2] The principal re-export trade was in the goods imported from the East Indies and from Turkey, with both of which we had a definitely adverse trade balance, the balance of payments being sent out there in the form of bullion. With Portugal and Spain the balance was the other way, so here the merchants must have specialized in exports.[3]

How far was there division of labour between merchants and financiers? In a number of cases merchants transacted financial business requiring knowledge of foreign bills and other financial instruments as well as the possession of ample credit and capital. Such men were Sir Thomas Andrews, the leather-seller, Sir John Dethicke, and Sir Christopher Packe (afterwards Lord Packe), but they were of course only three out of a number who engaged in financial work on behalf of the Government and the City. On the other hand, there was a considerable group of financiers who were not merchants but, for the most part, goldsmiths.

1 Cf. Bland, *Trade Revived*, 4, the City Journals, *passim*, and the petition of the Eastland Company, below, p. 127, n. 3. Bland was a royalist, a Virginian merchant, and a Dutch agent in London; these facts should be borne in mind when making use of his excellent pamphlet. Henry Robinson makes this division of trade in his *England's Safety in Treasures Increase* (1641).

2 See below, p. 150.

3 In 1663, these are the nearest available figures known at present: the City of London imported from the East Indies £384,671 worth of goods, exported to the East Indies only £24,051 worth of goods; imported from Portugal £86,961, exported to Portugal £145,061; imported from Turkey £373,595, exported to Turkey £167,661. (Add. MSS. 36785.)

According to post-Restoration pamphleteers (and there is some independent evidence in support of their statements) it was during the Cromwellian period that the separation of functions between the working goldsmiths and the goldsmith bankers began.[1] The discussion of the early history of banking has been somewhat obscured by the failure of historians adequately to define their terms:[2] but in any case it does not seem doubtful that Thomas Vyner, Edward Backwell, John Wollaston, William Gibbs, Thomas Noell,[3] William Leman, and one or two others were definitely specialists in financing trade and industry during this period.

How far was there specialization in foreign trade itself? To what extent did merchants tend to concentrate their activities on particular markets? A large part of the country's foreign trade was still in the hands of chartered companies with elaborate organizations, officers, and privileges.[4] But the uncertain position of the companies in the political circumstances of the interregnum made it very easy for merchants whose business was flexible to vary their activities. Really big men like Martin Noell; Andrew Riccard, who began life as the son of a labourer and became in turn Master of the Drapers, Governor of the Levant Company, and Governor of the East India Company; and Maurice Thompson, who traded equally busily in the East and West Indies, Virginia, and Guinea—these were able to seek out the most profitable enterprises as opportunity arose. But the organization of commerce even in those days was no simple matter, and the average merchant appears to have concentrated on one particular line of business. Specialization had not, however, reached anything near the state of perfection it had in the United Netherlands, where detailed knowledge of the quality of the goods and of the conditions of the world market

[1] *The Mystery of the New Fashioned Goldsmiths or Bankers* (1676); cf. Richards, *Early History of Banking*. Maddison (see above, p. 2, n. 2) does not mention the goldsmith bankers in his 1640 pamphlet, but does in his 1654 edition.

[2] e.g. I do not see with Dr. Richards why the treasury committees should be called banks, nor with Mr. Harper why the customs farmers should be called bankers. For a survey of the present position of this subject see the historical revision by Mr. A. V. Judges in *History*, N.S. xv.

[3] This Thomas Noell, who died in 1654, should not be confused with Martin Noell's brother who was sent to Jamaica in 1655.

[4] See below, Chap. XI.

enabled an entrepôt trade to develop, as was constantly admitted by contemporaries, far more rapidly than any similar trade in this country. But it is clear that certain markets were linked, notably, for instance, the trade with Portugal with that of the East Indies. The favourable commercial treaties which this country was able to conclude with Portugal, owing to the political disturbances in that country and the existence of a state of hostility between the Portuguese and the Dutch, threw open the Indian possessions of the Portuguese Empire direct to the English merchant to an extent hitherto unknown. Thomas Kendall, who was described in 1638 as 'the Chiefest and (because a merchant of great busynesse) of most sway among the refractious' at Lisbon was by 1654 a leading East India merchant, besides being interested in Barbados.[1] Another East India merchant, Richard Wylde, pointed out to Cromwell the importance of taking advantage of the situation in Portugal to establish an empire of trade in India.[2] Again, the specialization may not have been in markets but in commodities. It is probable that the group of which Kendall was a leading member was mainly interested in sugar, a big item of import, and one of the main products of the West Indies and Brazil.[3] Likewise those in the Eastland trade were most concerned in importing timber and naval supplies, those in the East India and Levant trades in silk, spices, and saltpetre, those in Spain in merino wool and silver. But the question of specialization is very difficult. It can only be stated with certainty that while there were a number of powerful merchants who were almost equally concerned in finance, industry, and commerce of various kinds, there were likewise specialist financiers, bullion dealers, commodity dealers, and merchants interested only in specific markets, and that therefore the variety of individual economic interests would not necessarily act harmoniously in recommending a course of policy to the Protectorate Government.

1 S.P. 89/4, f. 17v–18. Chandler, the consul at Lisbon, called Kendall refractious because he refused to pay consulage on the ground that the king could not levy taxes without consent.

2 See below, p. 147.

3 S.P. 89/4, f. 76 and *passim* for the Portuguese sugar trade. Sugar was first planted in Barbados about 1647, and by 1653 was said to be yielding £4,000,000 a year. R. Ligon, *A True and Exact History of the Island of Barbados* (1657), 95.

II

COMMERCIAL AND FINANCIAL PROGRAMMES OF GOVERNMENT AND MERCHANT

ALTHOUGH on June 10, 1654, the French ambassador wrote home[1]: 'il passe pour constant que les marchands ont tout crédit en Angleterre,' a short survey of the composition of the governmental and commercial classes in England has shown that the merchants were not at this time in a position to exercise a strong direct influence on policy and that the commercial interest itself was not homogeneous. Differing interests approached questions of economic policy from various points of view, and the actual policy pursued by the Government of the Protectorate was the result of a conscious effort to harmonize them. It had to give weight to two almost incompatible factors in arranging its fiscal programme. These were the necessity of maintaining efficient taxes, that is to say taxes which would produce a high yield for the exchequer, be easy to collect, and involve a low administrative cost, and the obligation to use any opportunity that arose to lower the scale of taxation so as to make the Government popular enough to avoid unrest. A high level of taxation was demanded by the cost of the army and navy, alike the guarantees of Protectoral power and the instruments of successful foreign policy; but the need to avoid irritating the tax-paying public by any oppressive form of levy was forced upon the governmental mind by the fate of Charles I.

The Venetian envoys resident in England under the Protectorate, consistent enemies to the Government to which they were accredited, remarked on Cromwell's practice in both these directions. On June 25, 1653, it was reported that General Cromwell was 'studying every possible way to obtain popularity' by appointing a committee to inquire into the repayment of forced loans, while Whitelocke, in his *Memorials*, describes how at the beginning of the Protectorate Cromwell attempted to frame ordinances 'to sweeten the generality of the people', and when his first Parliament met in September 1654 the Protector announced with pleasure

[1] Bordeaux to Brienne (Record Office transcripts).

a reduction of taxation by £360,000 a year.[1] But the outbreak of the war with Spain brought up again the problem of finding new fiscal resources; Venice was told, 'owing to the excessive expenditure incurred by the Protector for the maintenance of the fleet . . . they are considering how to raise money . . . the people complain . . . the Government lets them squeal'.[2]

In fact, however, Cromwell's ministers never found it easy to raise money in face of organized opposition. The country gentlemen in Parliament objected violently to an increase in the land tax, and the parliamentary constitutions under which Cromwell ruled contained express stipulations against this. Yet an army and navy regularly in arrears was as dangerous as a dissatisfied squire or merchant. The only solution which Cromwell seems to have conceived in face of this dilemma was that his vigorous foreign policy (for which even his great enemy, Clarendon, commended him) might itself be made a source of revenue. This was to be achieved by the encouragement of privateering, by licensing semi-piratic enterprises amid the colonies of rival empires and by instructing naval commanders during the Anglo-Spanish war to do everything in their power to intercept and bring home the bullion of the enemy. The policy of promoting privateering was a natural consequence of the naval war against the Dutch, a nation with a world-wide mercantile marine. The idea of establishing commercial companies was a by-product of the war against Spain, and there was little time to develop it during the Protectorate.[3] Thus the endeavour to emulate the successes of the famous Elizabethan pirates was alone given full opportunity. One other attempted method of using the armed forces of the country as collectors as well as consumers of revenue was an effort to revive the claim of James I to 'the tenth herring', a tax on foreign fishermen's catches in English waters; but Cromwell was no more successful in exacting this than had been his predecessors.[4] Finally a

[1] *C.S.P.* (*Venetian*), *1653–4*, 90; Whitelocke, *Memorials* (1682), 599; *Letters and Speeches*, ii. 245. [2] Cited in Guizot, *Cromwell* (English trans. 1854), ii. 245.

[3] See below, p. 137 seq.

[4] Whitelocke's Additional Instructions of April 7, 1654, mention the tenth herring (Thurloe, ii. 218). For some discussion of this see T. W. Fulton, *The Sovereignty of the Sea* (1911), chap. xi.

further expedient which remained available was a special tax on royalists. A capital levy had been exacted from the beaten side in the form of compositions (fines) by the Long Parliament. But after the passions of the civil war had begun to cool, royalist risings or the threat of royalist risings ceased to be productive of much revenue, and even the Roundheads called into question the justice of selecting their late enemies for special impositions.[1]

Turning from matters of finance to those of commerce, the ministerial approach was largely fiscal, that is to say, the question that interested the Government when examining any commercial policy submitted to it was how far that policy would increase the national revenue. A secondary factor, however, related to shipping. Throughout the seventeenth century European waters were infested with pirates, and the credit of a Government was much enhanced by its ability to deal with them. Moreover, since wars waged by an island State had necessarily to be largely maritime, its ship-building industry and seafaring profession were essential to it. It is true that the Government was less dependent upon armed merchant ships after the creation of a powerful navy by the Long Parliament, but the mercantile marine was also the school from which the navy drew (often forcibly) its recruits, nor could Cromwell afford to build so many frigates as his wealthier predecessors. Consequently any commercial scheme that might improve the efficiency of the navy, directly or indirectly, was looked upon very favourably by the Government.

These two considerations—the fiscal and the naval—invariably entered into controversies on commercial matters of the day. The question whether foreign trade should be open to all or closed to exclusive companies (which had been agitated since the beginning of the century) was affected by them. The problem whether certain commodities should be entirely prohibited from exportation or importation was affected by fiscal requirements and by the need to obtain munitions and war materials from the best markets available; indeed, the necessity of importing these latter commodities was allowed to qualify even the Navigation Act policy (the confining of the import-carrying trade to British vessels)

[1] See below, p. 95.

which was itself advocated as encouraging ship-building and the training of seamen.[1]

Between the ideas of Government officials and those of exporters there was little in common. For instance, although a few individuals or groups might benefit from a state of war with Holland or with Spain, the export trades as a whole could expect little but damage from wars which limited their markets and laid their cargoes open to confiscation by the enemy. Hence, while they might welcome a state of war between their commercial rivals—the Dutch–Portuguese war seems to have been fomented with the approval of commercial interests[2]—English exporters wrote in condemnation both of civil and of foreign warfare as detrimental to trade. Henry Parker, writing on behalf of the Merchant Adventurers, condemned in measured tones 'the piratical trade of war'. Another pamphleteer, writing on the eve of the Restoration, put a 'general peace' among his list of conditions for a revival of trade; and the author of *The World's Mistake in Oliver Cromwell* (1668), whose tract was intended especially for the trading public, reminded his readers that Cromwell 'indiscreetly neglected trade and chose war when he was at peace'.[3]

The only subject on which the exporters agreed with the military was on the necessity of an efficient system of convoy for merchant vessels, whether the country was at war or peace. Although there were numerous complaints about the provision of convoys and counter-accusations by the Government as to the failure of merchants to make use of them, yet on the whole, despite bickering, the two sides worked harmoniously in arranging the details of their administration. But otherwise the needs of war policy were completely antagonistic to the interests of exporters. Privateering was disliked as leading to retaliation, and towards the end of the Spanish war the City of London was petitioning Parliament that the seas should be so guarded in future 'that the trade,

[1] See below, Chap. XIII, for a detailed discussion of these questions and a fuller explanation of the Navigation Act of 1651.

[2] George Downing, the English ambassador at The Hague, received a bribe from the East India Company to look after its interests.

[3] H. Parker, *Of a Free Trade* (1648), dedicated to Alderman John Kenrick, Governor of the Merchant Adventurers; Bland, *Trade Revived* (1660); S. Bethel, *The World's Mistake in Oliver Cromwell* (1668) in the Harleian Miscellany, i. 287.

treasure and strength of the nation may not so often fall into the enemy's hands'.[1]

The Navigation Act policy probably increased to some extent the difficulties of export shippers. The frequent seizures of foreign ships for violating the Act cannot but have provoked their trade rivals into retaliation, and it also made it more difficult for them to obtain the foreign-built carrying ships which were essential for some of the bulkier export trades. Moreover, some exporters were injured by the Act, since they were unable to persuade Dutch ships to come over to fetch English goods unless they were permitted to bring freight with them.[2] There can be little doubt that those who were primarily interested in exports at the time of the Protectorate were opposed to the Navigation Act policy, but it is difficult to find direct evidence of this, since most of the references to that policy among contemporary pamphlets were criticisms of the existing Act which immediately concerned only one branch of the export trade, the export of fish. Section 4, which confined that trade to British ships, was merely an attempt to enforce a policy which had been accepted by English Governments for many years. But it had been steadily and naturally opposed by Yarmouth, the centre of the fishing industry, whose opposition was now again effective; and on June 9, 1657, the section was repealed by an amending Act on the recommendation of the Council of Trade. It seems certain, however, that an effort was originally made to include other exports in the trades which were to be confined to British shipping, that it was successfully resisted by the exporting interests and consequently no such limitation as appeared in the Act of 1660 formed part of that of 1651. The proof of this is a draft project of the 1651 Act submitted to the Council of Trade by Trinity House in which the list of goods to be confined to British ships included exports as well as imports.[3]

[1] City Journal, 41, f. 204v., petition to Parliament of May 31, 1659.

[2] Cf., e.g., Dec. 10, 1651, letter from the Merchant Adventurers of Newcastle to the Merchant Adventurers of York in which they say that it pays them better to ship back sugar from Holland in return for exports than to obtain money by exchange. *Newcastle Merchant Adventurers*, i. 170.

[3] 'Trinity House Transactions', 1613–61, 49. See these Transactions, *passim*, for numerous illustrations of the Yarmouth export-of-fish controversy.

Apart from opposition to the Navigation Act and the advocacy of a system of convoy, the export merchants urged upon the Government a national scheme of marine insurance. They complained of the excessive rates charged by private insurance companies which, they asserted, used every device to avoid paying when merchants suffered losses. A system of State insurance, combined with a proper distribution of frigates to guard the scattered commerce on the seas, would, it was urged, actually dispense with the necessity of convoys as well as immeasurably improve mercantile credit.[1] Finally, the sponsors of this scheme put forward an argument in its favour, especially calculated to appeal to Cromwell: if England is at peace, they said, insurance will be profitable to the State and should 'your Highness . . . think fit to settle the aforesaid busyness as propounded there will be raised greate Sums of money for Insurance and Custome towards the maintaining of severall fleets and Squadrons of Shipps of Warr. . .'[2]

Although exporters demanded that the Government should safeguard their trade by means of convoys and the nationalization of insurance, they were far from anxious to pay for these advantages. On the contrary, they insisted that the best way to increase their business was to reduce export duties as low as possible, and their demands were supported by semi-official writers like Henry Robinson. Arguments against high duties were largely based on an almost military conception of competitive salesmanship abroad. One writer said that, although it was of course desirable to sell as dearly as possible, they had first to oust their rivals. 'We must lade our cloth', said Robinson, 'as little as may be with customs, else other nations will be liable to under-sell and beat us out.'[3] Another author, who maintained that trade flourished when customs were low, as in the days of Good 'Queen Elizabeth', would have created a select council of merchants to 'direct

[1] This scheme is in Egerton MSS. 4395, ff. 149–57, and is written by Captain Lymbrey or Limbrey, who was engaged chiefly in the export trade to the West Indies. The original owner of the document dates it 1657. It is discussed by Professor Barbour in her article in vol. ii of *The Journal of Business and Economic History.* Lewis Roberts in 1641 favoured the nationalization of insurance.

[2] Egerton MSS. 4395, f. 150.

[3] *England's Safety in Treasure's Increase* (1641), 22.

how and where to weaken the Enemy in the course of Trade, which may be more useful than open Armes and hostility'.[1]

The enemy to be 'weakened' and 'beaten out' was invariably the Dutch, who were paid all the compliments of imitation. Export duties must be reduced because English commercial pamphleteers held wildly exaggerated notions of the lowness of the export duties paid by their competitors and did not take sufficient account of the other ways in which the Dutch export trade was burdened with taxes. Another advantage the Dutch were truly said to possess over English merchants was the lower rate of interest at which they were able to borrow money, and the English Government was constantly urged to reduce the rate by law again, as it had done before—from 8 to 6 per cent.—in 1651. London merchants were also firmly opposed to the admission of Dutch and other foreign merchants to settle and trade in England, on the ground that they caused the natives to lose foreign commissions, were exempt from local town duties, and had the unfair advantage of the lower interest rate at which they were able to borrow.[2] It was also alleged that the Dutch insured their cargoes in England so that their trading losses often had to be borne by Englishmen.[3] For these reasons the mercantile interest tried to persuade the Government to suppress foreign immigration. On the other hand, the native exporters attuned thenselves better with the progressive ideas of the time by advocating the free export of bullion. The leaders in this agitation were the East Indian merchants, whose trade depended largely on permission to export precious metals. Thomas Mun's *England's Treasure by Foreign Trade*, the best-known book on this subject, was not published until 1664, but its arguments were current long before the Restoration. Mun was a servant of the

[1] 'A Brief Discourse Concerning the Trade Bullion and Money of England' (1657 ?) (Add. MSS. 10402, f. 9.)

[2] Cf. *Reasons humbly offered to the Parliament by the Freeborn Merchants of England; shewing cause why the Sixty Merchants Aliens who pretended to be naturalized in the year* 1657 *and other Aliens trading as Merchants should not be admitted to Priviledges of Englishmen by Naturalization.* (No date, *c.* 1660), British Museum, 190 g 12/160; petition of the City to Protector and Parliament, June 13, 1657, on behalf of its right to exact portage and other dues from merchant strangers (Journal 41, f. 156v.–7).

[3] This is alleged in *The Advocate* (1651).

original East India Company, which obtained licences to export bullion so regularly that its rivals considered these were a means to cover systematic smuggling, and in 1657 the Council of State recommended for this reason that the ports from which bullion might be exported to the East Indies should at least be limited to London, Plymouth, Dartmouth, Bristol, and Hull.[1] It was, however, generally known at this date among practising merchants that the laws against the export of gold and silver were ineffective, and this very fact was put forward as an argument for abrogating them. In addition the exporters urged that the wheels of trade were oiled by complete freedom to send bullion abroad, and that what went out came back increased many-fold, since the sole means of accumulating a surplus of 'treasure' for the nation was a balance in value of exported over imported commodities.[2] Not only were all exporters in complete agreement upon the question of bullion, but also upon the desirability of the Government's establishing colonies which would buy provisions, clothes, furniture, and other necessities exclusively from the mother country.[3] When Sir George Ayscue sailed out to subdue Barbados or Penn and Venables went forth to conquer San Domingo, the privilege of accompanying and victualling the fleets was fiercely competed for by merchant groups, and from long before the Protectorate it was a commonplace among exporters that the setting up of 'new plantations' was one of the surest means by which 'merchant statesmen can improve traffick'.[4]

Although, of course, all mercantile interests had much in common in the programmes which they put before the Government, there were certain questions of policy on which sharp divergences or differences of emphasis were demonstrated. The most remarkable of these is to be seen in the fiscal question. The exporters were naturally anxious that the revenue derived by the Government directly from trade should not be raised by high export duties, but as much of

1 March 11, 1657, *C.S.P. (Dom.), 1656–7*, 308.

2 For this well-worn economic doctrine see Roberts, Maddison, Mun, &c.

3 Especially recommended by Bland the Virginian merchant and by Povey the West Indian merchant.

4 L. Roberts, *The Treasure of Traffike* (1641), 67.

the customs revenue was in fact so obtained they were driven to advocate the alternatives of heavier import duties and excise. But as it was claimed by at least one writer that the excise also was paid by the importers, contrary to the letter of the law,[1] the importers under this scheme would have had to pay almost the whole of the indirect taxes. The author of this pamphlet, which condemned the excise as an undue burden on importers, not only sought its abolition, but asked for a reduction of customs and a return to the 'good old way' of 'taxing estates at high rates'.[2] Other taxes which were proposed to the Government as substitutes for the foreign excise and import duties were an increased excise on native manufacturers and a general raising of strangers' duties, i.e. the customs paid by foreign importers.

It must be remembered that the importer in all his writings about his trade had, unlike the exporter, to be perpetually on the defensive. To import goods was considered less beneficial to the community as a whole than to export them, and thus while the merchants who were primarily interested in importing tried to shift some of the taxes they had to pay on to the landed proprietor or the foreign importer, they did not hesitate to justify their calling to the Government as 'beneficial to the revenue'.

Another example of conflicting interests between importers and exporters was over the question of the export of bullion. If bullion is freely exported, said the importing merchant, domestic prices will be low and foreign prices will rise, and since high prices are good for trade and low prices bad for it, the foreigner is benefited at the expense of the native importers and retailers. Indeed, the seventeenth century fully grasped the position that a depreciated currency favours the man who has to sell abroad and injures the man who has to buy abroad, and Sir Ralph Maddison realized the obvious solution when he saw that what the country needed at all costs was stability of exchange.[3]

Another difference in attitude between exporter and importer relates to the Navigation Act. We have seen that the

[1] W. C., *Trade's Destruction* (1659), 6.

[2] R. Baker, *The Merchant's Humble Petition* (1659), 9.

[3] See Maddison, Violet, &c.

exporter was only indirectly interested in the question, as exports were not included within the scope of the policy until after 1660, but importers were immediately affected since they were obliged according to the Act of 1651 to use ships belonging to Englishmen or to the actual producers of their imports. Professor Violet Barbour, in a recent article,[1] has pointed out that this Act caused greatest difficulty in the bulky carrying trades, particularly those with the Scandinavian countries,[2] since most English ships were unsuited to their freighting requirements. It is interesting to observe that, in the draft plan drawn up by Trinity House for the 1651 Act, the trade in masts, deals, wainscots, rafters, clapboards, and timber of all sorts was to be exempted from the importing monopoly given to English-built ships, while special arrangements were to be made about the Scandinavian export trades.[3] It was largely because of this difficulty that the importers urged modification of the Act, but some of them liked to convey the impression, especially during the war with Spain, that its only result was to benefit the Dutch. They therefore argued that instead of a total prohibition the Government should forbid Englishmen to freight foreign ships, and should give English shippers preferential treatment by making foreign importers pay additional customs and excise when bringing in goods other than those made in their own countries.[4]

1 'Dutch and English Merchant Shipping', *The Economic History Review*, ii. 261.

2 Often referred to as 'the lost trades'.

3 See n. 3, p. 20. A much earlier scheme of exemptions from a Navigation Act propounded by James I's customs farmers and the Masters of Trinity House (*c.* 1617) includes the same list of commodities. Transactions, 9.

4 See Baker, Bland, &c.

III

COMMERCIAL AND FINANCIAL PROGRAMMES OF POLITICIAN AND PURITAN

THE author of 'The Libel of English Policy', a fifteenth-century poem which has been called one of the earliest tracts on commerce in the English language, pressed upon his readers the desirability of exploiting the geographical situation of their country to levy a toll on the trade of other countries passing through the 'narrow seas', guarded by Dover and Calais, then in English hands. By the middle of the seventeenth century trade had become a little more civilized and commercial writers had different ideas as to how to derive profit from an island position. We should, they said, endeavour to create a large entrepôt trade. Ships from the north of Europe could unload their cargoes at London, Dover, and other convenient ports whence they would be re-shipped to the south and to the New World; similarly goods from the south for the north would be unloaded and reshipped in English harbours. The establishment of these centres of exchange would be made easy by the fact that differing kinds of commodities and of ships were found in the two areas separated by the English Channel. The advantages of creating and encouraging an entrepôt trade were obvious for English shipping, warehouses, and customs revenues. These arguments occurred all the more simply to independent economic thinkers because they had before them a first-class example of how such a scheme could operate in their neighbours' country across the North Sea. The United Provinces had ever since the foundation of the Dutch republic derived a large part of their national income from shipping, fishing, warehousing, international finance, and the other constituent factors in a world-centre of commerce and trade. Peter de la Court, whose treatise on *The State of Holland* was written about 1662, but not translated into English until forty years later, attributed the origin of the Dutch entrepôt system mainly to the existence of special duties on aliens in England which had discouraged Protestant merchants from settling there and had driven them to Amsterdam, where equal taxes, religious toleration, and a favourable geographical situation made the capital of Holland the most prosperous city in Europe.[1] Modern historians confirm and enlarge de la Court's description of the Dutch achievement. The merchant statesmen of Amsterdam with their watchword of free trade, with low duties, enabled their city to outstrip by the time of Cromwell the older entrepôts of Antwerp and Hamburg.[2]

The English commercial public, therefore, really needed no further persuasion than the example of their neighbours to convince them of the advisability of taking steps to establish an entrepôt trade; the pamphleteers had only to stress the superior navigability of our harbours, the more prolific character of our fisheries, the greater size of our population and the prescriptive right to all things conferred by the puritan deity on his chosen people. What were these steps to be? In the first place, the Government must reduce customs duties and raise revenue by means of excise. As the excise was only paid on imported commodities and native manufactures, it could not fall on goods brought in solely for re-export. In the second place, even though customs duties were low, they should be entirely rebated on re-exports. At least some writers said entirely rebated; the more realistic ones said that they should be largely rebated. Actually during the greater part of the interregnum half the customs and all the excise was rebated on re-exports, but half was thought by the advocates of entrepôt to be far from sufficient, especially as in Holland only 2 per cent. duty was charged on the average on this class of goods. The term re-exports, they thought, should also be widened to include goods which were not directly re-exported but were manufactured or semi-manufactured before being reshipped. Such commodities were wool, sugar (refined), linen, canvas, copper, calicoes (dyed), and tobacco (dried).[3]

[1] John de Witt [*sic*—really de la Court], *Political Maxims of the State of Holland* (1702), chap. xvi. Violet was a great protagonist of the entrepôt scheme; he had various Dutch associates, e.g. Giles Vandeput.

[2] See a good description in P. Blok, *History of the People of the Netherlands*, iii, chap. iv.

[3] See T. Violet, *The Advance of Merchandize* (1651); *Free Ports* (1652); R. Maddison, *Great Britain's Remembrancer* (1654); H. Robinson, *Certain Proposals* (1651); *Short Notes on the Decay of Trade* (1662); R. Coke, *A Detection of the Court and State of England* (1697).

Besides using these methods to encourage the importation of foreign merchandise, the Government was urged, in pursuit of the entrepôt ideal, to induce foreign merchants to settle in England, since they would engage in the re-export trade and employ Englishmen and English shipping in it. De la Court in his book was to write that even Roman Catholics should be permitted to settle in Holland for the purpose of trade, and although none of the Puritan pamphleteers of the interregnum went to this extreme, Thomas Violet was not ashamed to say that a good Dutch merchant was as beneficial to the country as a good Dutch cow.

On the whole, the supporters of this policy were the most consistent 'free traders' that the seventeenth century knew.[1] They favoured religious toleration, were opposed to discriminatory taxes on aliens, and were the especial sponsors of a Court of Merchants (similar to those in existence in France and Italy), where merchants of all nationalities could have their differences decided by an expert tribunal less dilatory in its proceedings than the court of chancery. But further than this, they were for the most part enemies of monopolistic companies (as were de la Court and the majority of Dutch commercial writers) and they supported the abolition of all restrictions on the free flow of the precious metals. Their argument against the restriction on export is best summed up by the report of the Committee of Trade in 1660, which recommended the final abolition of these restrictions[2]:

> It [the prohibition of export] evidently gives a great interruption to the English merchant and keeps foreigners (upon the same account) from lodging their money here as otherwise they would, this being a place so much more convenient than Amsterdam doth consequently lose the great benefit that would arise to Your Majesty in your Mint and Revenue.

Finally, these writers strongly favoured the creation of free ports where commodities destined for re-export need not go through the customs house at all, but might be deposited in special warehouses whence they could be taken out and reshipped at any time up to six months on the payment of

[1] That is to say, in theory. In practice, as it appeared in later years, one of the most immediate results of their policy was the 'enumeration clauses' of the Navigation Act.

[2] Add. MSS. 25115, ff. 42–53, esp. f. 44.

a small composition fee. Violet in his declamation in favour of free ports reminded his readers how when there was a composition trade at Dover (after London clearly the town best suited to be a free port), the town and townsmen grew rich, the poor were employed, and £50,000 a year was raised in customs. It is certainly true that as early as January 1634 Charles I authorized the customs farmers to compound with foreign merchants at Dover, although the sum mentioned by the town itself as raised by its special privileges was £16,000. The Dover composition trade existed at least till 1640 and foreign merchants of various nationalities had their agents in residence there. The local histories of Kent contain no description of this interesting example of the entrepôt ideal in practice; it is a valuable piece of local history that awaits writing.[1] Violet devoted many pages of his voluminous writings to the subject of free ports, but Maddison, a more trustworthy writer than Violet, produced an argument in their favour which would especially appeal to Cromwell. Free ports, he wrote, will keep our monies at home, and will encourage the Dutch to settle here; our ports will become their storehouses, and they our huxters; they will find the calm Thames more inviting than the stormy Texel; and many Dutch merchants will become our subjects, '*the next best thing to their being incorporated into one nation with us*'.[2]

It is generally held that there was no necessary connexion of ideas between the policy of free ports and the opposition to the Navigation Act policy. Certainly many pamphleteers expected those who made use of English ports also to employ English shipping. But it is plain that this would hardly have been feasible in all cases, as, for example, the Scandinavian timber trade. And it is curious to read how Roger Coke in his *Detection of the Court and State of England*,[3] published as late as 1697, criticizes the Rump for making the Navigation Act of 1651 which, he said, was a direct cause of the decay of the English coast towns; and adds that instead of promoting the Act they should have made the ports of England free to

[1] Violet, *Advance of Merchandize* (1651); *Free Ports* (1652); 'Trinity House Transactions', 1613–61, 66–7; *C.S.P.* (*Dom.*), *1633–4*, 441; *1640–1*, 367. For the Dover composition trade after the Restoration, see below, p. 151.

[2] *Great Britain's Remembrancer*, 38–9, my italics.

[3] pp. 365–7.

all foreigners especially to import timber, pitch, and tar, and reduced their taxes below those paid in Holland.

Besides the entrepôt programme, which was that of independent writers rather than of professional merchants, there was another old and popular line of thought on economic questions which should perhaps be described as essentially political in its outlook, namely, the idea of 'self-sufficiency'. It used to be a commonplace among writers on medieval history that the early European village and urban communities tended to live an economically self-sufficient life which towards the sixteenth century became extended into a nationally self-sufficient life, and was glorified into the ideal of making one's own country relatively richer and stronger than the rest of the world.[1] Although modern research has to some extent qualified this view,[2] it is at any rate certain that sixteenth-century statesmen became anxious to accumulate vast stocks of bullion, munitions, and corn supplies to be ever-ready provender for national military enterprises. In England this was the aim of the great Tudor kings; in France of Henry of Navarre.[3] And clearly such a policy appealed with inordinate strength in Cromwell's time to the military classes, who thought, as many 'protectionists' of later generations were to think, largely in terms of preparations for war.

The principal method of procedure advocated by this school of thought was the State control of imports and exports for the purpose of obtaining the desired store of necessities within the boundaries of the nation-state.

We have seen how the importing merchants had to be perpetually on the defensive in justifying their profession; and it was against this line of nationalistic economic thought that they had to defend themselves. 'There is no time for dallying,' wrote Henry Robinson,[4] 'we must whilst we are able make our own laws and conditions, still keeping ourselves stronger, as no nation may ever have power or ability

[1] Cf. W. Cunningham, *Growth of English Industry and Commerce* (1903), i. 478–9, &c.

[2] Cf. N. S. B. Gras, *The Evolution of the English Corn Market* (1915).

[3] Cf. G. Martin, *Histoire économique de France* (1927), 201.

[4] *England's Safety*, 22 seq.

to spurn against us'. To this end, he urged, we must lessen our importations and reduce our consumption of foreign goods at home. Therefore the Government was advised to impose high taxes on all foreign imports. But to this rule there must be a few exceptions. Raw materials of essential manufactures, munitions (including horses), and corn when the domestic harvest was poor must not be heavily taxed. An English writer of 1662 indeed recommended that all raw materials should be tax free, while Violet pointed to the United Netherlands which, lacking corn, wood, and most raw materials, was yet a magazine of the native commodities of all countries.[1] In compensation for its loss of revenue the Government was recommended, again in accordance with medieval tradition, to levy very high or prohibitive import duties on all 'luxury' goods. The practice of 'some princes', who prohibit the importation of commodities that 'tend to riot or excess' was especially praised.[2] The activities of the East India and Levant Companies came under grave suspicion on the ground that they imported silks and spices and other things which were only judged desirable national acquisitions if re-exported promptly at a profit. But all companies and merchants who engaged in the so-called 'rich trades' were sharply criticized, and even the Greek currant trade was scolded for encouraging the nation to spend money on puddings and cakes 'whereas in other countries they eat none'.[3] The foreign excise—that is, the excise duty on imports—was generally approved by the protagonists of self-sufficiency because it was believed to fall mainly on these luxuries.

Turning to exports the advocates of self-sufficiency urged that those commodities only were to be exported of which the country had an abundance; munitions should not be exported, and necessary foodstuffs only by special licence. In effect corn could then only be exported with parliamentary permission, and we find in October 1654 the City of London petitioning Parliament likewise to prohibit the export of butter unless the price at home was less than 4*d*. a pound.[4]

[1] *Short Notes on the Decay of Trade* (1662); Violet, *Advancement of Merchandize* (1651).
[2] Roberts, *Treasure of Traffike*, 38.
[3] Violet, 9.
[4] City Journal, 41, f. 109v. Control of exports was the first of Lewis Roberts's

In theory if not in practice the idea of prohibiting the export of essentials like food and raw wool had long been deeply engraved on the official mind.

It followed also from the premisses of this school of thought that every possible means had to be sought to accumulate a vast quantity of gold and silver in the country. Its export had of course to be strictly forbidden and high prices should be offered at the mint to induce merchants to bring it into the country. At the same time a Council of Mint Affairs should be established to buy and sell silver and gold so as to prevent an unequal ratio driving either metal out of the country.[1] Self-sufficiency was always a *raison d'être* of 'bullionist' thought.

The attitude of those who believed in self-sufficiency towards the policy of the Navigation Act was not, as might at first be imagined, one of unqualified approval. For they held that it was more important in some cases to obtain raw materials and munitions by the assistance of foreign carriers, than to enforce a total prohibition of alien shipping in the interests of the English mercantile marine. This exception applied particularly to the imports of naval stores from the Scandinavian countries.[2] Otherwise the Navigation Act policy was welcomed by them.

While it was held to be vital to the nation that the Government should ensure an ample supply of 'necessaries' from abroad, the consideration that this class of goods should in future be derived as far as possible from British territories was not overlooked. Some such commodities were already so obtained: saltpetre, the raw material of gunpowder, was imported in large quantities by the East India Company, which could not re-export it until the Government had exercised its option of buying.[3] But for the greater part of their supplies the army and navy were dependent on other than British sources, and it was not until a century later that New

four 'considerations' in his *Treasure of Traffike*. Ordinances against the transport of wool were frequently enacted during the interregnum, as before and after it.

[1] See Maddison for the functions of a Council of Mint Affairs.

[2] This was emphasized by Bland in both his pamphlets.

[3] There are innumerable references to the sale of saltpetre in the Court Minutes of the East India Company; see especially *1655–9*, 155, for a report of the Council of State, July 23, 1657.

England was able to furnish the full complement of timber, pitch, tar, cordage, and other raw materials required by the forces. There are some indications of attempts on the part of Cromwell's Government to encourage the production of these commodities in the colonies and in Great Britain, although it was recognized that the amount would not immediately be sufficient. On the same principle certain manufactures were stimulated at home, for example, efforts to set the poor to work upon the manufacture of hemp were frequent throughout the century.[1] Finally, in support of this policy the Government was advised to establish new and essential manufactures in England by offering high rewards for useful inventions, as was the practice in Holland.

In some of the pieces of advice that they offered to the Government all writers were in agreement.[2] This may be said of the proposals for the establishment of a Court Merchant, of an executive Trade Committee, and of a Council for Mint Affairs. But there was nothing about any of these three suggestions which made them notably characteristic of the Cromwellian period. On the other hand, the advocacy of banking projects became increasingly common at this time and is to be found in such differing publicists as Gerbier, Potter, Chappel, the author of *The Advocate* (1651), Robinson (1652), Hartlib (1653), Maddison (1654), Lambe (1658), and Cradocke (1659). Robinson's proposals were recommended to the notice of Oliver Cromwell by no less a person than the future first Earl of Shaftesbury.[3] Of course these writers differ considerably in their opinion of the exact type of bank that was needed, but most of them had in mind a rival institution to the Bank of Amsterdam, which had been successfully functioning under the direct control of the government of that city since 1609, that is to say, they envisaged a State bank with branches at home and abroad administering

[1] e.g. *C.S.P.* (*Col.*), *1675–6*, 87–8. For an example of this line of policy see Trinity House Transactions, *1613–61*, 55, under December 9, 1650.

[2] It does not seem desirable to enter into a detailed discussion of banking theories. Dr. Richards in his *Early History of Banking*, chap. iv, surveys some of these writers and refers to other surveys.

[3] *C.S.P.* (*Dom.*), *1653–4*, 364. 'Sir A. A. Cooper to move the Protector to put Hen. Robinson's proposals concerning a bank into speedy consideration.'

deposit accounts and making advances to traders.[1] These writers seem to have recognized that the private banking institutions which were beginning to prosper in London at the time they wrote could not hope to achieve the successes that would come to a bank sponsored by the Government, while some of them, notably Maddison, went so far as to assert that private bankers were not only less efficient than the employees of a State bank would be, but that their policy was directly contrary to the common good. A bank, guaranteed by Act of Parliament, it was maintained, would attract bullion from abroad (Amsterdam paid 5 per cent. on deposits of bullion), would reduce the rate of interest by having a large supply of money to lend, and would induce foreigners to invest in London. Robinson suggested that the governors of the bank should be chosen by the several City companies, Lambe explained somewhat obscurely that a bank would prevent the evasion of the Navigation Act, and Hartlib favoured a land bank.

Such suggestions, although they bore little fruit in Cromwellian policy, were to have prolific results at the end of the century. They seem, however, to postulate a flourishing condition of English trade demanding more plentiful credit.

To complete the survey of programmes of commercial and fiscal policy submitted to Cromwell by various sections of public opinion, it is necessary to consider whether any of the religious sects had any contributions to offer. The relationship between puritanism and economic life generally has been widely discussed by great scholars like Professors Weber, Sombart, and Tawney, and is still a disputed academic battle-ground. But a few things stand out beyond dispute. One is the attitude to commercial companies of the Levellers, a democratic party drawing support mainly from sectaries inside and outside the army. This group regarded all companies whose membership was in any way limited as monopolies, and in *The Case of the Army*, one of their principal manifestoes, they laid it down that the Government must abolish all trading companies and make trade completely

[1] Adam Smith, *Wealth of Nations*, Bk. iv; H. Baasch, *Holländische Wirtschaftgeschichte* (1927), i, vii.

free, especially of excises, while in another manifesto, *The Agreement of the People*,[1] they stated that a Parliament which granted monopolies or levied taxes on food would be violating the fundamental laws of a free state. Proposals for the suppression of all companies with exclusive markets had been brought before King and Parliament ever since the beginning of the century, and the successful attacks on James I's and Charles I's grants of industrial monopolies had strengthened the open trade or, as it was more commonly called, 'free trade' party. The published attacks on the commercial companies during the interregnum came largely from Levellers, and were particularly irritating to the Presbyterian magnates of the City, strongly entrenched in their livery companies. One attack on foreign trading corporations of exceptional interest remains still in manuscript and was written by the Leveller William Walwyn.[2] In their pamphlets these writers stress first the fact that monopolies, which were allocations of exclusive trading rights to a limited number of men, were obviously opposed to any notion of individual liberty. 'Free Trade' was claimed by them as an Englishman's right: 'we look for a new heaven and a new earth in which dwelleth righteousness. . . .' But they were not lacking in practical economic arguments. Monopolistic prices benefited only a few individuals; at lower prices more goods might be sold with a bigger total profit to the nation. The costs of merchants who were compelled to enter companies and pay heavy fees to obtain markets necessarily increased the price at which they had to dispose of their goods in competition with foreigners. On the other hand, mariners, workmen and even landed proprietors would find themselves benefiting by an opening of trade; for 'trade is like dung which being close kept in a heap or two stinks, but being spread abroad, doth fertilize the land and make it fructify.' Open trade would give rise to a spirit of adventure and enterprise creative of

[1] *The Case of the Army* and *The* [*First*] *Agreement of the People*, both published in 1647. For the Levellers, generally, see T. C. Pease, *The Leveller Movement* (1916).

[2] Walwyn, 'Conception for a free trade' (1652); S.P. 105/144, ff. 68–74. It is Dr. Gooch's opinion that Walwyn was probably a communist. S. Bowtell, *A Discourse for Free Trade* (1644); T. Johnson, *A Plea for Free Men's Liberties* (1646)—Johnson was a man with a personal grievance; *The Golden Fleece Defended* (1646); G. P. Gooch, *Democratic Ideas in the XVIIth Century*, chap. v.

wealth—and this would be a wealth to be diffused among many instead of among the few who are 'born rich' and add 'wealth to wealth by trading in beaten roads'.

In one part of their onslaught on monopolies the Levellers were especially supported by the Quakers, namely, in their attack on oaths, which the companies demanded from their members so as to enforce their rules.

On another economic issue all the Puritans, and not merely the democratic element among them, were agreed; this was in a firm antagonism to luxurious living. In the Middle Ages the sumptuary laws against the consumption of luxuries were imposed by the rich upon the poor, but with the advent of puritanism the middle classes and the poorer classes all came to believe with religious fervour in the desirability of their revival. The sugars and silks and spices brought over from the Near and Far East met with their sternest disapprobation. How could these obnoxious imports be kept out of the land? A pamphlet called *A Mite to the Treasury*, published in 1653, and well adorned with religious texts, considered the excise only justifiable in so far as it fell on luxuries; the subsidy was a fairer tax. The author of an earlier pamphlet showed much greater enthusiasm, for he laid it down that a fair excise would repress riots, abate luxury, abolish class envy, and inspirit all trades![1] It would hardly be an exaggeration to say that to the Puritan taxation was not so much a necessary adjunct of efficient government as an instrument of social justice. 'To raise taxes on the vices of a people,' wrote John Bland in recommending a tax on taverns, 'is most approved of by wise men.' But it would be wrong to suppose that the excise was universally commended by interregnum pamphleteers; the question of its social inequalities had to be probed; and undoubtedly many Puritans would have agreed with the author of *Excise Anatomized* (1659) that the farmers of the excise (and of other taxes) were 'monopolizers of freedom' who exacted oaths 'impossible to be taken'.

There is an interesting proof that the result of the Puritan revolution as stabilized by Cromwell was hostile to the luxury trades. Among the Thurloe Papers in the Bodleian library is one headed 'Some Observations on the Decay of Trade'; it is

[1] *The Standard of Equality* (1647) in the *Harleian Miscellany*, iv. 119–20.

undated but certainly belongs to the period of the Protectorate. It explains how 'mechanics and retailers' are maintained chiefly by the expenditure of the gentry on superfluous garments and ornaments, and shows in what manner the wealth of the country is divided between the Roundheads and Cavaliers:[1]

> The treasure of these dominions is chiefly divided between the well-affected and the adverse party; it should at home be continually spreading; for parsimony may advance particular families, but stops the revenue and destroys the peace of the state. The former party hath a private thrift . . ., the second an open expensiveness; which since it maintains the people, contributes much to tax and excise. That party . . . resolve to live no more in the City . . . and will likewise further repair their estates by reducing garments and ornaments. If this . . . exodus from the city . . . proceed the livelihood of retailers and mechanics will be lost and native excise and customs on imports be reduced.

It will be shown in a later chapter that the strength of the commercial companies was definitely damaged under Cromwell, so that if the above story is true it would seem that the two specific suggestions in the way of economic policy offered to Cromwell by the Puritans—abolition of trading monopolies and restraint of luxury expenditure—were to a large extent made effective by his Government. It may well be that he was more interested in an appeal to Bible economics than in the conflicting ideas of the various merchant groups and military parties.

[1] Rawlinson MSS. A. 45, f. 293.

IV

PUBLIC FINANCE

INTRODUCTORY

DURING the debates on the recognition of Richard Cromwell as Protector in the early part of 1659 the Republican speakers took the opportunity to defend the financial administration of the Long Parliament and to contrast it favourably with that of Cromwell. They asserted that the Long Parliament had left the State free from debt and in possession of £600,000 in cash besides; and they maintained it was only when Cromwell attained supreme power that the Government's financial difficulties began to arise by means of regular deficits which accumulated until an unmanageable debt was left at his death.[1] This accusation was repeated by the Republican Edmund Ludlow in his *Memoirs*, who put Cromwell's cash in hand at £450,000;[2] and Mrs. Hutchinson, wife of a republican colonel, also related how

> the parliament . . . by the blessing of God, restored the commonwealth to such a happy, rich, and plentiful condition, that it was not so flourishing before the war, and although the taxes that were paid were great, yet the people were rich and able to pay them: they were in a way of paying all the soldiers' arrears, had some hundred thousand pounds in their purses, and were free from enemies in arms within and without, except the Dutch, whom they had beaten and brought to seek peace upon terms honourable to the English. . . .[3]

Finally, Slingsby Bethel, 'that irreconcileable republican' as a Restoration bishop called him, asserted in 1668 that when the Long Parliament was turned out the 'public stock' was £500,000 in ready money, £700,000 in stores and the whole army paid in advance, some six and none under four months ahead.[4]

Cromwell, on the other hand, in his speech of September 17, 1656, stated:

> When the Long Parliament sat [ceased to sit] this nation owed £700,000. We examined it; it was brought unto that—in that short

[1] Burton, iii. 45 seq.

[2] Firth's ed., i. 379.

[3] *Life of Colonel Hutchinson* (ed. 1906), 362.

[4] *The World's Mistake in Oliver Cromwell*, 3.

Meeting that was within half a year after the Government came to our hands. I believe there was rather more than less[1]

and his Secretary of State, Thurloe, speaking in debate after Cromwell's death, claimed that he knew nothing of 'the great treasure' left by the Long Parliament, but did recall that in April 1653, there was a debt of £500,000 on the navy,[2] a statement which, incidentally, is confirmed by surviving contemporary financial records.[3] Nevertheless, there was no real discrepancy between the assertions of Cromwell and those of his political opponents. For an exact appreciation of this problem, it is essential to examine briefly the financial history of the Long Parliament.

When the civil war broke out the system of the King's exchequer was naturally completely dislocated, and the whole fiscal machinery of the country fell to pieces. Parliament had to find new methods of raising the money necessary for the war.[4] Its first steps were simply to borrow and appropriate. On November 26, 1642, a committee was appointed to sit in the Haberdashers' Hall to raise loans, pledging the 'public faith' of the kingdom for their repayment at 8 per cent. Assessments, based on the subsidy, were levied, sometimes compulsorily, sometimes voluntarily, on the adherents of both parties, the rates being one-twentieth of real and one-fifth of personal property. The public faith was also pledged to all who lent sinews of war in kind. On September 13, 1644, the committee at Goldsmiths' Hall, first instituted to raise loans for the Scottish army, was ordered to compound with delinquents, i.e. vanquished royalists, who had to pay a fine proportionate to the value of their estates on penalty of total forfeiture. The fines varied considerably in amount from about one-third to one-tenth. The number of compounders was large, and 'would possibly have been larger, but for the fact that, as soon as a person made a composition at Goldsmiths' Hall, he was sent straight to Haberdashers' Hall to pay his fifth or twentieth'. In April 1650, the functions

1 *Letters and Speeches*, ii. 545–6.

2 Burton, iv. 365–7.

3 Cf. Rawlinson MSS. A. 223, f. 127.

4 See *C.S.P., Compounding, Advance of Money and Domestic*, especially the introductions; W. O. Scroggs, 'The Finances of the Long Parliament', *Quarterly Journal of Economics*, xxi. 463; S. Dowell, *History of Taxation and Taxes in England*, chap. i, App. VIII, iii. 72–81.

of these two committees were combined. In 1643 Pym had introduced the excise. In 1644 there came the monthly assessment which has been described as the link between the Tudor subsidy and the property tax of William III. Other funds assigned to the payment of the war were derived after the final defeat of the King from the sale of crown lands and property (including Charles I's wonderful collection of paintings), church property, bishops' and dean-and-chapters' lands, the property of the royal family, the lands of delinquents and recusants (Roman Catholics).

For the purpose of administering these resources the Long Parliament had instituted particular funds of receipt, with trustees and commissioners and officers situated in London; in 1650 there were ten such treasury funds, and expenditure was charged more or less indiscriminately on one fund or another. But most of the payments out were made through committees equivalent to modern departments, e.g. the Admiralty Committee, the Public Debt Committee, &c.; these departments had treasuries and treasurers who paid out for the purpose of administration the moneys received from the receipt funds. These two sets of different treasuries were co-ordinated by means of a committee originally known as 'the committee of inspection' or 'inspectors of the treasuries', and ultimately simply as 'the treasury commissioners'. The business entrusted to these commissioners was very considerable; their main duty was to find supplies when ordered to do so by the Council for any specific charge payable out of any fund available at the time. From a very early period their instructions contained the phrase 'to consider how all the revenues can best be brought into one channel', but it was not until the establishment of the Protectorate that active steps were taken to unite the different funds in one exchequer. Thenceforward the powers of all the treasury committees were gradually curtailed and one by one they ceased to exist. Among the papers of Edward Montague, later Earl of Sandwich and the hero of Pepys's *Diary*, who was one of the treasury commissioners under Cromwell, are some notes on the offices of Lord Treasurer and Chancellor of the Exchequer which evidently belong to the year 1654 and bear witness to the importance attached at that date to the reinstatement of the royal system.[1] The ordinance 'for bringing the revenues of the commonwealth into one treasury, viz. the Exchequer at Westminster' which was to be put into execution by the treasury commissioners was passed on June 21, 1654, but it was not carried out fully until Parliament met in September;[2] actually, however, the monthly assessments were kept by Cromwell in the hands of the treasurers of the army, and thus the exchequer never saw all the sources of revenue.[3] Moreover, some of the revenue committees, e.g. the Sequestration Committee, lingered on half-moribund throughout the entire Protectorate.

On account of the multiplicity of treasuries thus set up by the Long Parliament it is impossible to arrive at anything like annual balance-sheets of the national accounts during the civil wars. But, taking into account the fact that Parliament decided to live on its capital during the latter part of the civil war and, as victory was achieved in England, to utilize confiscations from the defeated parties for further expenditure, we can reach a fairly accurate general estimate of the financial situation in 1653. The following is a summary of what the special sources available to the Long Parliament had raised by the end of that year:[4]

Sale of King's Goods	108,990
Bishops' Lands	675,603
Dean-and-Chapters' lands	503,179
Fee Farms (gross)	1,469,087
King's Lands	1,993,951
Compositions	1,304,957
	£6,055,767

This list does not take into account the confiscations of royalists' lands which were not merely sequestered for composition but actually sold outright.[5] We may therefore reckon

[1] Carte MSS. 74, ff. 241–4.

[2] *C.S.P. (Dom.), 1654*, 215–16; Firth and Rait, ii. 918, 1016.

[3] See below, p. 81.

[4] *Historical Manuscripts Commission, Report*, vii. 91–2; Rawlinson MSS. B. 239; Shaw, *A History of the English Church, 1646–60*, ii. 517; E. 351; Shaw, *Cambridge Modern History*, iv. 457; *A Catalogue of the Lords . . . that have Compounded* (1655).

[5] Confiscation Acts were passed on July 16, 1651, Aug. 4 and Nov. 4, 1652

a minimum sum of £6,000,000 as having been raised from sales of capital and royalist fines up to 1653. As it is safe to assume an annual revenue of at least £2,000,000 from ordinary sources[1] and a maximum annual expenditure of £3,000,000[2] it is evident that the Long Parliament was still solvent when Cromwell dissolved it.

But the war with the Dutch which had begun in May 1652 had a damaging effect on the national finances. Thurloe said that it cost two million pounds, but this was an underestimate of at least half a million.[3] By the end of the Dutch war the special resources at the disposal of the Government were almost exhausted and the annual debt on the navy rose in an alarming way. In other words, Cromwell, who was no financier, accepted the responsibilities of government at precisely the moment when public debt was increasing and by the time of his formal investiture as Protector he was faced with a series of financial problems that were to prove an unyielding embarrassment to him throughout the remainder of his life.

With the close of both civil and foreign wars in 1654 most of the powerful classes in the country sought peace, economy, and retrenchment, and looked to Cromwell to provide it, even as the French were to seek it from their successful general on his return from Egypt in 1800. Cromwell at first did his utmost to meet the popular demands.

In the period preceding the assembly of his first Parliament on September 3, 1654, the Lord Protector contented himself with appointing a new treasury commission, adding to its members Robert Tichborne, a leading member of the London City Council, Gervase Bennett, the reputed inventor of the word 'Quaker', and Colonel Edward Montague.[4] Ludlow described the commission with little justice as consisting entirely of Cromwell's creatures.[5] During 1654 a few unim-

(Firth and Rait, ii. 520, 591, 623), but they were not all enforced; cf. S. R. Gardiner, *History of the Commonwealth and the Protectorate*, i. 417; ii. 141, &c.

[1] The assessments, customs and excise alone averaged about £1,800,000.

[2] Various writers greatly exaggerate the amount of the national expenditure during the interregnum. The figures during the interregnum never reached £3,000,000, but those of 1652–3 nearly did; cf. Pepys's *Diary* (ed. Wheatley), iv. 52.

[3] Burton, iii. 482; but the navy alone cost £1,410,312 in 1652; £1,059,382 in 1653 and £569,512 in 1654. Rawlinson MSS. A. 195A, f. 241.

[4] *C.S.P.* (*Dom.*), *1653–4*, 317–19.

[5] *Memoirs*, i. 372.

portant ordinances were promulgated relating to the settlement of assessments and excise and the sale of church lands, arrangements were made to restore the exchequer course, and on the eve of the summoning of Parliament Cromwell reduced the assessments by £30,000 a month.

When Parliament met it tried to force wholesale economy on the Protector. A sub-committee was appointed under the chairmanship of Colonel Thomas Birch, one of Cromwell's most consistent opponents, to discover how much would have to be provided by taxation to meet the expenditure outlined in the Instrument. The committee reached the conclusion that by allowing £840,000 for customs and excise, £29,000 for Scottish and Irish revenues and £60,000 for the yield from the sequestered estates, in addition to the various revenues derived from the post office, wine licences, &c., and adding to these £150,000 from customs and excise on French wines, the importation of which was then prohibited, £9,000 a year from an excise to be imposed on Scotland, and a further £124,000 a year from various other new taxes, a sum of £1,210,000 could be raised which they thought sufficient to cover the cost of the stipulated number of ships and soldiers and the £200,000, allowed for civil government.[1] Edward Montague, on behalf of Cromwell, denied the accuracy of the committee's calculations and presented a balance-sheet which showed a revenue of £2,250,000 to meet an expenditure of £2,611,532.[2] Parliament, however, was satisfied with Birch's report, especially as it envisaged the total abolition of the assessments, and attempted to limit the protectoral revenue by resolution. However, Cromwell promptly dissolved Parliament and propounded two 'orders and declarations' for assessments and excise with which to carry on his rule. But he accepted the parliamentary recommendations to the extent that he lowered the assessments by a further £30,000 a month, cut down the army by ten thousand men and reduced the pay of the remainder. He also reduced the salaries of his Council and from the end of the Dutch war

[1] Burton, i. cxx–i; Carte MSS. 74, ff. 60–2. The report of the sub-committee of the revenue, Dec. 4, 1654, is to be found in Stowe MSS. 322; Add. MSS. 28854 and Carte MSS. 103. It corrects and amplifies Gardiner's account, iii. 80–3.

[2] Carte MSS. 74, ff. 63–5.

he enjoyed a considerable saving on the fleet.[1] In order to facilitate the finding of employment by his disbanded soldiers, Cromwell issued an ordinance dispensing with the requirements of the apprenticeship laws, and allowing them to exercise any trade.[2]

It has been calculated that by his economies on the army Cromwell saved £300,000 a year, but to meet the requirements for policing the country, he took advantage of the royalist rising at Salisbury in May 1655, to institute a highly organized militia under his Major-Generals which was to be paid for by a new capital levy of 10 per cent. on the defeated royalists.[3] In the winter of the same year Cromwell dispatched a fleet to the West Indies which was expected to capture for the exchequer a portion of the celebrated wealth of the Spanish empire. In both these ways war was envisaged as self-supporting. A fond delusion!

The West Indian expedition involved the country in war with Spain and the financial stress forced Cromwell to permit the election of another Parliament in September 1656. This Parliament, when properly 'purged', submitted a new constitution for the approval of the Protector, known as 'The Humble Petition and Advice'. According to this document Cromwell was to be given a revenue of £1,300,000 a year which at his suggestion was later increased to £1,900,000.[4] To supply the immediate necessities for the war an additional assessment to yield £215,000 in three months and a tax on new London buildings was imposed. Some slight adjustments were made in the customs rates and an excise rate book was issued before Parliament was prorogued on June 26, 1657. When Parliament met again on January 20 Cromwell announced that although 'we have been as good husbands as we could some supplies have not come in as expected', and after a certain amount of fumbling he produced a paper which made his financial situation tolerably clear:

The debts of the Commonwealth with arrears to the armies and

[1] Firth and Rait, ii. 1029, 1035; *Clarke Papers* (ed. Firth), iii. 38 seq.; C. H. Firth, *Cromwell's Army*, chap. viii; D. Masson, *Life of Milton* (1860), v. 87.

[2] Aug. 11, 1654; *C.S.P. (Dom.)*, *1654*, 295.

[3] For some further mention of the decimation see below, p. 95.

[4] Cf. Cromwell's 'Paper on the Revenue' endorsed in his own hand 'the debts the Parliament hath already undertaken' (*Letters and Speeches*, iii. 493–4).

fleets to October, 1656, as given in to Parliament, were between £800,000 and £900,000. The charge for the following year ending October last (1657) would be £2,400,000. The provision suggested was the Excise and Customs and Exchequer revenue, estimated at £1,300,000 and £50,000 a month taxes, which came to £1,900,000 and they (parliament) ordered the raising of three months taxes over again at £60,000 a month in England and Ireland instead of £20,000 and in Scotland £15,000—total £225,000 and the buildings were to make up the other £300,000 to complete this £2,400,000. But only £3,000 is come in by the new buildings, and the Exchequer revenue is fallen short £200,000 which causes the armies to be in arrears £300,000 and the navy £540,000, beside former debts, and now there is half a year's salary due to all the militia forces in England.

But no further help was forthcoming from Parliament, which Cromwell dissolved on February 4, 1658, and he had to carry on the Spanish war as best he could with the burden of a debt of at least a million and a half pounds.[1] After his advisers had discussed various expedients throughout the summer of 1658 they reached the conclusion that the recalling of Parliament was the only possible solution to his financial difficulties. It was apparently about to be called when Cromwell died.

The new Protector, Richard Cromwell, was left about two million pounds in debt and made desperate efforts to borrow the meagre sum of £50,000 to cover the costs of his father's funeral and institute his own régime.[2] Before discussing the significance of this situation we shall survey in detail the expenditure of Cromwell's Government and the various taxes levied to meet it; and also examine the facilities at its disposal for public borrowing during the Protectorate.

1 *C.S.P., 1658–9,* 80; *Letters and Speeches,* iii. 502; cf. Thurloe to Downing, Jan. 28, 1658: 'The Commons asked for "the State of the Revenue" that they might provide better.' (Add. MSS. 22919, f. 11.)

2 See below, pp. 150 seq.

V
GOVERNMENT EXPENDITURE

WRITERS on public finance generally teach us that the difference between public and private expenditure is that whereas an individual determines his outlay by his income, a government raises its income to meet its outlay. The historian is, however, obliged to notice that political considerations invariably place a limit upon the size of a government's income; and Cromwell's income was no exception to this rule.[1] Indeed so pronounced was public resistance to the payment of heavy taxes at the end of the civil wars that the Protector was forced, like any private individual, to reduce his expenditure to meet his income.[2] But even then his budgets were markedly higher than those of either Charles I or Charles II.

Although it is undoubtedly true that external pressure limited Cromwell's spending power, this fact is no proof that taxes were unduly injurious to trade or were directly responsible for the depression of 1659–60.[3] The depression was partly due to political and financial causes, but the conclusion to which a number of political historians have leapt, that because there were protests, and effective protests, against the level of Cromwellian taxation, this must have been the primary cause of the trade depression, is much too facile;[4] for the resistance to taxation on political, constitutional and personal grounds was just as violent under Charles I as under Cromwell, although the amount of taxes paid was on the whole smaller. But in all cases the Government was forced to cut down its expenditure rather than to increase its income to balance its budget.

The character of Cromwell's expenditure is not the most interesting part of the economic history of his time. The bulk of it went to the army and navy and varied in accordance

[1] See above, p. 43.

[2] See above, p. 44, for Cromwell's reduction of the army and navy.

[3] See below, p. 176.

[4] Cf. the just observation of Sir William Petty on the Dutch: 'No country in Europe have paid so much by way of tax in Holland and Zealand this last hundred years, yet no Country hath in the same time increased their Wealth Comparably to them'. *Works* (ed. Hull), i. 271.

with the needs for their services on military enterprises. Some idea of the proportion of the national revenue that was spent upon warfare can be gauged from the figures for the year 1653–4 when, out of a total of £2,877,079, the army was reckoned to cost £1,566,705, the navy £1,059,382, the ordnance £50,000 and the civil expenditure £200,992, out of which Cromwell's household cost £50,000.[1] During most of this year the country was at peace, but the total amount devoted to the forces in this budget was relatively high even by the standards existing in Britain before 1939.[2]

Owing to the fact that the army accounts did not go through the exchequer, we do not possess the complete and exact annual figures of army expenditure. Various estimates are, however, available and give a total expenditure on the army during the Protectorate of over seven millions.[3] We know from the accounts of the treasurers at war that between June 24, 1653, and February 2, 1659, they actually paid out £4,757,370,[4] but as the army was partly paid with money that did not go through the treasurers' hands the deficit was not nearly as large as might appear from these figures. Nevertheless, there was certainly an annual deficit and the army was regularly in arrears.

The figures of naval expenditure on the other hand are fairly complete. There are various detailed accounts among the Bodleian MSS. and notably a paper compiled by Sir George Carteret, the treasurer of the navy at the Restoration, and given by him to his subordinate, Samuel Pepys. At the Restoration the navy was still three quarters of a million in debt.[5]

[1] See especially Carte MSS. 74, f. 56 seq. Estimates of income and expenditure in this year are to be found in Add. MSS. 4156, 28854, 32471; Stowe MSS. 322; Lansdowne MSS. 323 and the Goddard MSS. printed in Burton, i. cxx–ii.

[2] The population for the three kingdoms may be reckoned at $7\frac{1}{2}$ millions, the weekly wages of artisans at 7*s.* 8*d.* Using the change in the general wage level as a price corrector, and taking the cost of armaments per head of the population, the expenditure on armaments in 1933 expressed in seventeenth-century standards comes to $£110{,}000{,}000 \times \frac{7\frac{2}{3}}{60} \times \frac{7\frac{1}{3}}{44}$ or £2,300,000 approx.

[3] These are collected in W. R. Scott, *The Constitution and Finance of English, Scottish, and Irish Joint Stock Companies to 1720* (1912), i. chap. xiii.

[4] E. 351/305. See below for a discussion of army payments.

[5] A. W. Tedder, *The Navy of the Restoration* (1916), 41.

The civil expenditure can be divided into two main categories: salaries, which include the pay of administrative and law officers, and household expenditure, which consisted in the cost of Cromwell's court and the upkeep of the royal palaces. Contemporary republicans and post-Restoration writers have dwelt maliciously on the extravagance of Cromwell and 'his numerous family',[1] but in fact the eighty or ninety thousand a year he was allowed was a mere ripple (3 per cent.) on the total stream of national expenditure, and very much less than the corresponding sums spent by the Stuart kings. During the Dutch war Cromwell actually offered to give up part of his emoluments towards the expenses of the Government.[2] Thurloe was likewise accused of pouring out money on his famous spy system to the extent of £60,000 a year, but there is good reason to believe that the figure was actually about a twentieth of this, for in the year 1658–9 there is among the issue rolls only one entry, of £2,999, paid out for this purpose.[3]

A rough estimate of the annual budgetary expenditure during the Protectorate is as follows:[4]

	Army	*Navy*	*Civil and Ordnance*	*Total*
1654	1,566,705	1,059,382	250,992	2,877,079
1655	1,508,000	569,512	250,000 (?)	2,327,512
1656	1,057,819	768,538	250,000 (?)	2,067,357
1657	1,900,489	742,034	235,652	2,878,174
1658	1,346,706	599,108	252,179	2,197,985

1 Notably Slingsby Bethel in *The World's Mistake*.

2 'Le Parlement est tousjours occupé à faire des fonds pour les despenses de la guerre. Il a commencé par un retranchement de la moitié des appointemens, pensions et recompenses de tous ceux qui reçoivent quelque chose de l'Estat, et M. le General a voulu donner bon exemple.' Bordeaux to Brienne, Sept. 8, 1653, Record Office Transcripts.

3 Under Dec. 5, 1659, E. 403/1757; cf. 'List by Thurloe of 66 acquittances for moneys paid by his order for public intelligence, from April 3, 1656, to April 9, 1657' = £2,234 3*s*. *C.S.P. (Dom.)*, *1656–7*, 362.

4 The army accounts come from Carte MSS. 74, f. 63; Add. MSS. 4156, f. 89; Carte MSS. 74, f. 7; Thurloe, vi. 596 (adding £58,000 for Scotland and Ireland), and *C.J.* vii. 628–30. The naval accounts are from Rawlinson MSS. A 195, f. 241, figures which correspond roughly with those of the Declared Accounts, E. 351/2292. The civil and ordnance come from Carte 74, f. 56 and *C.J.* vii. 628, those for the middle years are not discoverable, but all figures published suggest that they did not vary much from year to year; cf. Richards, 'The Exchequer in Cromwellian Times,' in the Economic History Supplement to the *Economic Journal*, ii. 213.

VI

TAXES

I. CUSTOMS

FROM the earliest times customs duties or, in medieval parlance, the subsidy of tonnage and poundage, had been one of the most staple and lucrative items of the royal revenue.[1] They were levied at the ports on all merchandise as it was carried to and from the country; for by the beginning of the seventeenth century internal customs duties or 'tolls' had practically disappeared, and the organization of customs on sea-borne goods had been welded into a centralized national system. The immediate control which the parliamentary forces were able to exercise over London and the out-ports at the beginning of the civil wars secured to the opponents of the King that revenue which had long been regarded as his peculiar prerogative. On January 21, 1643, an ordinance was promulgated to legalize the levying of tonnage and poundage for one year and this was renewed at regular intervals throughout the entire interregnum.

It was the Tudors who were responsible for centralizing the customs administration, but neither they nor their direct successors could decide which was the most profitable and least difficult way of collecting these taxes. There were two main alternatives: either to let the customs as a whole or in parts as a farm for a specified sum after the Government had first settled the rates, or to appoint managing commissioners who had to render a fuller account of their transactions to the exchequer and receive in return a percentage on each sum they raised. The ministers of state demanded that farmers and commissioners alike should directly they took up office advance large sums of money out of what they might expect to realize; yet there was seldom any lack of business men ready to bid high for the posts.

The Elizabethan treasury officials experimented in both these methods, but towards the end of the reign definitely

[1] The best book on medieval customs is by N. S. B. Gras, *Early English Customs System* (1918); there is as yet no good general book on the sixteenth and seventeenth centuries.

preferred farming the customs by sections;[1] in this they were followed by the officials of James I until the consolidation of all the customs in one great farm in 1605; this farm was leased to the same group of business men for twelve years, but, owing to constitutional disputes, the final book of rates was not produced till 1610–11.[2]

Charles I found the customs one of the most convenient sources of revenue during his eleven years of non-parliamentary government; a new book of rates was framed in 1635, and in 1638 there was fierce competition between two rival groups of financiers, one including Sir Nicholas Crispe and the other Sir Paul Pindar, for the royal farm. In a short time the two groups coalesced, but the venture was to prove a most unsuccessful one; when the war began they had lent the king £276,146, and despite the most elaborate plans and projects submitted to the Commonwealth Governments, they did not even obtain a recognition of this debt until the Restoration twenty years later.[3] Tax farmers were never popular, and when the Long Parliament met, it at once appointed a committee to investigate the abuses practised by the royal customs farmers, who were fined £150,000 for their 'illegal' conduct in raising taxes without parliamentary authority. This sum they chose to pay in the hope of being retained in their places and thus having their debt recognized; but such was not the intention of the committee, henceforward to be known as that of the Navy and Customs, which, after calling on advice from all parties concerned,

[1] See especially an article by Prof. F. C. Dietz on 'Elizabethan Customs Administration' in the *English Historical Review*, xlv. 35, reprinted in his *English Public Finance, 1558–1641* (1932).

[2] There are in the Goldsmiths' Library, South Kensington, books of rates, dated 1610, 1635, 1642 (3), 1653, 1657. The former two include in parallel columns rates of 'subsidy' and of 'impositions'. The latter three only include subsidy, since what Parliament itself levied could not be an imposition. The differences in the subsidy rates are accounted for in part by this fact. See below, p. 57, n. 2 for some further discussion of the latter books.

[3] For the adventures of Charles I's customs farmers see Stowe MSS. 185; the *Fanshawe Memoirs* (ed. 1907); *C.S.P.* (*Dom.*), *1732–62*, *passim; C.S.P.* (*Treasury Books*), *1660–7*; an article by W. P. Harper in *Economica* (1929), 'A Remonstrance of the Case of the late Farmers of the Customs', 1653, 669, f. 17 (55); &c. The wealth of this group was very considerable. Pindar offered £19,000 for the rebuilding of St. Paul's Church in Laud's time (Whitelocke). At the beginning of the Protectorate they offered to lend a further £100,000 to the Government if their debt was secured to them. At the Restoration they at once lent £200,000.

drew up a new book of rates, framed a bill for the 'legal' levying of customs, and reverted to the old commission system. The commissioners appointed were leading financiers of the city which was proving itself so faithful to Parliament; at first Thomas Andrews, John Foulke, and four others were chosen, and later they were superseded by another group which included Samuel Avery and Christopher Packe (February, 1645).[1] There was, however, some dissatisfaction with the way in which the Navy and Customs Committee did its work, and on August 8, 1649, an Act was passed 'For taking the accounts belonging to the Navy and Customs', ordering them to be audited and in future to be declared before the Barons of the Exchequer. Henceforward this committee decreased in importance and was dissolved in 1654.[2] In the original ordinance for the levying of tonnage and poundage the only way in which the commissioners could enforce collection was by summoning recalcitrants before the justices of the peace. This was obviously a most inadequate backing of State force for the most obnoxious of State functions, as the commissioners rapidly discovered. Hence a Committee for the Preservation of the Customs was appointed before whom offenders could be summoned by the officers of the commissioners; this committee worked well and continued to exist till the reconstitution of the exchequer in the first year of the Protectorate.[3]

Such was the position of the administration of the customs when the Cromwellian régime began. The organization of the customs revenue, which must have been relatively easy if over three-quarters of it were raised at the port of London,[4] was entrusted to five or six commissioners and their officers who were appointed for short periods, not longer than eighteen months at a time. Exactly how much the commissioners received for their services is difficult to discover.

[1] Maurice Thompson, the East India merchant (see pp. 114, 115 below), was a member of the former group. The names of the groups are in the books of rates and the *C.S.P. (Dom.)*.

[2] For this committee see especially a pamphlet by a member of it, Giles Greene, M.P., *A Declaration* (1647); and M. Oppenheimer, *A History of the Administration of the Royal Navy, 1590–1660* (1896).

[3] See the Tonnage and Poundage Act of June 26, 1657, in Firth and Rait; *C.S.P. (Dom.), 1655*, 51.

[4] See above, p. 12, n. 5.

Nominally they were paid 4*d.* in the pound on what they raised gross, but in addition they were paid the current rate of interest on all money they paid out in advance of its receipt. And for a time all other merchants who paid cash in advance were allowed a 'defalcation' of 15 per cent.

On the dissolution of the parliamentary Customs Committee at the beginning of the Protectorate, instead of the money being paid directly by the commissioners to the treasurer of the navy or the appropriate supplies, they were ordered to pay the money into the exchequer every week, deducting therefrom the salaries of their officers, and to have their accounts audited annually. To these instructions Cromwell added an order to appoint an accountant-general to act as a check on the commissioners.[1] These rules seem to have been strictly kept. Dr. Bruno Ryves, an eminent Royalist divine, requested the customs officers in September, 1655, to allow him to import a thousand reams of paper customs free to print the Bible, but they replied regretfully that they would gladly do so 'but now we can permit no goods to pass free, for we are ordered to pay all moneys on imports and exports every Monday into the Exchequer'.[2] But clearly Cromwell and his Council were dissatisfied with the amount produced by the customs under this system. They probably hoped to increase it by renewing the commission at intervals and improving the yield by creating competition for the office. But even those business men who assured them that they

[1] This view of the office of the customs commissioners under the Protectorate is derived mainly from the contract reported by Desborough for the Committee on Moneys on March 26, 1656, *C.S.P.* (*Dom.*), *1655–6*, 241, 230, &c. Here it is clearly stated that the commissioners were to receive 4*d.* The matter of the defalcations is complicated. The first ordinance on the subject printed in the books of rates of 1653 said 'That although the said last Bill of Tonnage and Poundage hath not yet had the royal assent, and therefore the Subject by the Law is not compellable to pay . . . yet the Lords and Commons doe declare that it shall be taken as an acceptable service to the commonwealth' for merchants to pay by loan to the commissioners as advance receiving an allowance of 15 per cent., by way of defalcation. The commissioners themselves lent £30,000 in 1643 which they repaid themselves plus 15 per cent. (see the book of rates for 1653 under the ordinance of 1643). According to the Tonnage and Poundage Act of June 26, 1657, the commissioners were still allowed a defalcation of 15 per cent. Apparently the Convoy Act of 1650 which took away the 15 per cent. from merchants was only temporary and possibly was not fully enforced —see p. 156.

[2] *C.S.P.* (*Dom.*), *1655*, 351. Actually the exemption was allowed later by Cromwell.

could easily raise the receipts by £100,000 a year cautiously demanded 2*s.* in the pound for their pains and a guarantee that they would be continued as commissioners for three years.[1] If the existing commissioners were told that they were making far less than they could, they naturally replied that they did not possess the means of enforcing their claims upon the taxpayer under the existing administration. The Government attempted to remedy this defect by reviving the Committee for the Preservation of the Customs in 1655 or, more accurately, giving the treasury officials, including Sir William Roberts, the auditor of the receipt, the coercive powers the old committee possessed.[2] This committee may also have been established to keep a watch upon the customs commissioners. In November 1655 one of the latter, Colonel Harvey, who had acted in this capacity from 1649, was thrown into the Tower for embezzling £30,000 committed to his charge.[3] But the revenue did not improve, and it was decided to revert to the Caroline practice of farming. When the Bill for the renewal of tonnage and poundage was read for the third time in Cromwell's second Parliament, a clause was added to permit the farming both of the customs and of the excise. Mr. Burton, the author of the diary which recounts the debate on the subject, moved the rejection of this clause, observing 'You will destroy the revenue by it, and discontent the parties that pay it'. He was opposed by Alderman Sir Christopher Packe, who told the House that 'never were the customs so well paid, nor with so much quiet, as when they were let out to farm. It was both more satisfaction to the merchants, and did advance the revenue.'[4] The House may well have been impressed with Sir Christopher's views, as he was not only a great merchant, but had himself been a commissioner. In any case three days after this debate, on June 26, 1657, a bill 'for the improvement of the revenues of the customs and excise', appointing a parliamentary committee to farm both, received the assent of the Lord Protector.[5] A month later the Secretary of State wrote to Henry Cromwell in Ireland describing the success which

[1] Ibid., *1655–6*, 41.

[2] Firth and Rait, ii. 1127.

[3] *Clarke Papers*, iii. 61; Thurloe, iv. 177.

[4] Burton, ii. 272.

[5] Firth and Rait, ii. 1268–9.

attended the efforts of the parliamentary committee thus appointed:

Severall citizens of London of good account doe offer £800,000 per ann. for the customs and excise of England and Scotland (excepting ale and beare); which sum is accepted, and they are to advance part of £800,000 . . . in hand, and to pay their money weekly, that is a part of £800,000 every weeke. For the ale and beare other persons offer £300,000 and upwards. If these rates be made good, it will be a very brave revenue, and will induce you to thinke of farming these duties in Ireland too; it being certeyne that wee here could not have made soe much of the excise and customs in England by some £100,000 in the hands of the commissioners (tho honest and careful).[1]

We are not surprised to find that the man who was responsible for this gigantic financial coup was Martin Noell, the long trusted and favoured Government contractor and reputed intimate of the Protector. In July details of the farm were printed in the news-letters and on August 20, Noell's business associate, Thomas Povey, wrote to his brother, 'Noell has become a much greater man now he has become Farmer of the Customs and Excise'.[2] Actually the farmers drew back from their contract and the customs remained in the hands of commissioners until the Restoration, but the coal customs established under a separate Act in 1650[3] together with a large block of the excise came into Noell's hands and justified his title to be 'a greater man'.

As an indirect and as an old tax the payment of the customs was felt to be far less burdensome by the general public, who ultimately paid most of it, than other heavy taxes. Since it was paid insensibly there were few complaints of its incidence. But the shipper, knowing how severely he would be punished if he attempted to evade it by smuggling, naturally watched to assure himself that the levy was a legal one. Hence *Bate's Case* in James I's time; and hence

[1] Thurloe, vi. 425.

[2] Add. MSS. 11411, f. 39. The purchase of the farm is noted in a news-letter among the *Clarke Papers* (iii. 114) dated July 25, 1657: 'The excise and customs of goods imported into England (excepting ale and beare) are farmed at £800,000 per annum by Ald. Dethwicke, Ald. Fredricke, Ald. Tems, Mr. Martin Noell, Mr. Ford, Mr. Banks, and others'. *Historical Manuscripts Commission, Report*, v. 165; cf. C. H. Firth, *The Last Years of the Protectorate*, ii. 262.

[3] For the coal customs, see below, p. 156.

Cony's Case under Cromwell. This latter case aroused great public excitement in the first year of the Protectorate.[1] On November 6, 1654, the deputies of the customs commissioners charged George Cony, the elder and younger, before the Committee for the Preservation of the Customs with having received goods not entered in the Customs House. They were fined £500, but refused to pay on the ground that Cromwell had no right to levy customs by mere ordinance. Yet the 'Instrument of Government' was perfectly clear on this point; for it said that to defray the necessary charges the revenue should be raised by customs and other means, and that until the first meeting of Parliament the Lord Protector and Council should have power to do so. But the case dragged on for seven months and led to the imprisonment of three lawyers and indirectly to the dismissal of the Lord Chief Justice. In the end apparently the younger Cony was persuaded to give way and the matter was compromised out of court. But after the 'Humble Petition and Advice', Cromwell did not repeat his mistake; for he immediately obtained the confirmation of his power to raise customs by means of the Act of June 26, 1657, which instead of referring to the innumerable customs ordinances which had been made during the previous ten years preferred to treat the question simply as a renewal of the last Act passed by the Long Parliament.

We now approach the difficult question of the actual value of the customs under the Protectorate. There are three main sources from which information can be drawn:

1. Estimates made by treasury commissioners and other officials of the probable yield from the customs during a given year; some of these figures appear in the *Journal of the House of Commons*. Their value depends upon how good Cromwell's officers were at budgeting.

2. The total 'charges and receipts' and the total 'payments and allowances' enrolled in the Declared Accounts of the customs commissioners and available almost complete in the

[1] The best secondary account is in Godwin's *History of the Commonwealth* (1828), iv, chap. xiii. The main sources are Samuel Selwood, *A Narrative*, Ludlow, and *Perfect Proceedings*, June 7, 21. It is curious to compare the emphasis laid on the case by Guizot and Gardiner.

Record Office. Only a detailed analysis of these enables one to arrive at the actual amount ultimately available net for the State.

3. The actual amounts of cash paid into the exchequer of receipt by the customs commissioners throughout the year. From the point of view of public finance the third class, the net figures, are most useful and are those used by Dr. Shaw in his survey of the equally scanty records of the early years of Charles II.

The following are the figures belonging to this class (M. = Michaelmas, E. = Easter):

	£
M. 1627—M. 1628 . . .	131,465[1]
M. 1641—M. 1642 . . .	217,269[1]
M. 1654—E. 1655 . . .	116,637[2]
E. 1655—M. 1655 . . .	151,245[2]
M. 1655—E. 1656 . . .	150,963[2]
E. 1656—M. 1656 . . .	166,189[2]
M. 1656—E. 1657 . . .	156,398[2]
E. 1657—M. 1657 . . .	152,615[3]
M. 1657—E. 1658 . . .	156,643[3]
E. 1658—M. 1658 . . .	166,421[4]
M. 1658—E. 1659 . . .	152,566[3]

Dr. Shaw estimates £228,730 for the net customs revenue in the first year of Charles II's reign and an average of £285,000 for the first seven years of his reign.[5]

An estimate of 1653 makes the customs of England £350,000, but for 1654 and the rest of the Protectorate period £400,000 is the sum always reckoned. The same amount was the estimate accepted by the first Parliament of Charles II.[6]

[1] 'The Receipts and Issues of the Exchequer during the reigns of James I and Charles I', by F. C. Dietz, *Smith College Studies*, vol. xiii, No. 4.

[2] 'Collection out of Accompts remaining before the Lord Comes. of his Highnes Trea^ry^ what the severall Branches of the Revenue hereunder mentioned have clearly produced . . .' June 4, 1657, Carte MSS. 73, f. 67; Add. MSS. 32471, f. 1 gives the identical figure for M. 1656—M. 1657.

[3] Record Office, E. 405/289, 390–1.

[4] This figure is found by subtracting that for M. 1657—E. 1658, £156,643, from that for M. 1657—M. 1658, £323,064 given in 'A Briefe Declaracon of monies Received . . . as the receipt of His Highnesses Exchequer' in Add. MSS. 32471, f. 15.

[5] Shaw, intro. to *Calendar of Treasury Books, 1660–7*, xxxv seq.

[6] Carte 74, f. 123, 78v.; Lansdowne 232, f. 36; Add. MSS. 32471, f. 53, 28854; Stowe, 322; Appendix A to this essay; Shaw, intro. to *C.S.P.* (*Treasury Books*), *1660–7*, xxxv seq.

We now give the gross and net figures taken from the commissioners' account audited in the exchequer; these are not merely the totals as recorded on the rolls, but by eliminating the arrears on both sides of the account and with certain other adjustments they are made roughly comparable with the figures previously given. Thus they become fairly reliable as indications of general trade movements and are therefore given for the entire interregnum:[1]

	Gross £	*Net* £
Jan. 21, 1643—Dec. 30, 1643	165,690	140,774
Dec. 30, 1643—Feb. 24, 1645	226,229	181,243
Feb. 25, 1645—Dec. 25, 1645	192,867	174,273
Dec. 25, 1645—Dec. 25, 1646	267,680	239,702
Dec. 25, 1646—Dec. 25, 1647	262,785	230,785
Dec. 25, 1647—Dec. 25, 1648	203,054	163,073
Dec. 25, 1648—July 21, 1649	146,856	136,923
July 22, 1649—June 24, 1650	290,355	253,127
June 25, 1650—June 24, 1651	267,776	211,857
June 25, 1651—June 25, 1652	239,949	187,592
June 25, 1652—June 25, 1653	272,189	240,537
June 25, 1653—June 25, 1654	364,443	317,251
June 25, 1654—Sept. 29, 1655	455,411	384,788
Sept. 29, 1655—Mar. 30, 1656	155,564	128,974
Mar. 30, 1656—Mar. 30, 1657	375,296	314,939
Mar. 30, 1657—Mar. 30, 1658	352,704	?
Mar. 30, 1658—Sept. 29, 1659	603,526	502,558

The approximate annual figures of gross receipts at the ports were therefore:[2]

	£		£
*1643	165,690	1652	266,070
1644	231,440	1653	328,317
1645	227,278	1654	364,486
1646	267,680	1655	364,328
*1647	262,785	*1656	338,728
1648	203,054	1657	375,296
1649	292,034	1658	352,704
1650	276,066	1659	482,820
1651	250,863		

1 These figures are taken from A.O. 1 and E. 351; unfortunately some are burnt and torn and no complete roll survives for 1657–8. I have neglected the Scottish and Irish customs which do not appear in the rolls and were always very small, about £10,000, see below, pp. 90 seq. On the other hand, from 1650 the 15 per cent. convoy tax is included, see above. These figures correct and supplement those given in Hall, *History of the Customs Revenue*, i. 184. Rogers gives the completely wrong figure of £500,000 for 1642 (*Agriculture and Prices*, v. 188).

2 The years marked with an asterisk are those in which the rates were changed. The most notable differences between the book of rates of 1643 and the earlier is an

Before making any remark upon these figures it is well to recall that we possess a valuable estimate of the yield of the Dutch customs during the same period. A table of the annual yield (January–December) of the Dutch convoys and licence money, which by this date had become equivalent to import and export duties, was published by Dr. Becht[1] in 1908, and although these figures are open to certain qualifications they are useful for the purposes of a general comparison with the English figures:

	Gulden		Gulden
1643	2,828,212	1652	1,524,173
1644	2,561,539	1653	1,150,345
1645	2,374,528	1654	1,170,741
1646	2,513,010	1655	1,701,446
1647	2,704,534	1656	1,945,223
1648	2,796,103	1657	1,686,604
1649	2,206,050	1658	1,665,282
1650	2,363,387	1659	1,757,182
1651	2,145,873		

As £1 was equivalent to 11 gulden, it is clear that the Dutch customs were lower than the English. The Dutch customs were raised on account of the English war by a third, and a new book of rates, a revenue tariff, was imposed in 1655. The above figures are so constructed to disregard these changes in rates.

The most remarkable fact about these two sets of figures is that whereas there is a considerable rise in the English figures in 1653-4, the Dutch customs were lower during these years than at almost any other time in the course of the century. We may partly attribute the size of the English figures to the economic recovery at the close of the war, but it also seems very probable that English trade actually gained at the expense of the Dutch. After the sea battle between the

increase in the export duties on food-stuffs (e.g. beef) and raw materials (e.g. tin). For alterations in rates on wines, see below, p. 60. Other alterations after 1643 were unimportant. A few new export duties were imposed by the Act for Transportation of Nov. 26, 1656, but the export of most of these commodities had already been permitted under licence, see below, p. 149.

[1] H. Becht, *Statistische Gegevens betreffende den Handelsomzet van de Republiek der Vereenigde Nederlanden, 1579–1715* (1908). Amsterdam always contributed 50 or 60 per cent. of these taxes. The Amsterdam figures have been published separately by Pringsheim, *Beiträge zur wirtschaftlichen Entwicklungsgeschichte der vereinigten Niederlande*, 13, and show the same trend. For some observations on Becht's figures see W. Sombart, *Der moderne Kapitalismus*, ii. 2. 947.

two nations in June, 1653, we are told that 'the English could now blockade the Dutch ports, reduce to a standstill such trade as remained', and 'cause an immense shrinkage in the volume of Dutch sea-borne trade'.[1] After the conclusion of peace in April, 1654, the English and Dutch figures follow much the same trend until 1660 in which year there is a considerable rise in the Dutch (1,757,182 to 2,048,254 gulden) and a huge fall in the English (£482,820 to £285,000) which suggests that the Dutch benefited from the political dislocation of the Restoration year. In the intervening years the English net revenue is high from Easter, 1656, to Easter, 1657; the subsequent fall may have been due in part to the active prosecution of the Spanish war from the time of the military alliance with France which was ratified by Cromwell in May, 1657, while the surprising rise in 1659 may have been to some extent due to the close of the war.

As to the division of the receipts from the English customs between export and import duties, no indication is provided by the Declaration Rolls. There is, however, at least one account among the State Papers which gives an idea of the proportions. This belongs to the year 1650 unfortunately, but there was probably no substantial change during the interregnum:[2]

	£
Subsidy inwards (English)	51,052
Subsidy inwards (strangers)	4,732
Wines	8,924
Currants	5,841
Subsidy outwards	11,324
Cloth	5,530

On this basis the yield from import duties was about four times that from export duties.

Various other suggestions may be drawn from these figures, incomplete though they are. Firstly, it is interesting that while there was no heavy increase in the customs rates between 1642 and 1654, there was yet an enormous increase in their yield. Although the books of rates of 1643 and 1647 did raise the rates to some extent this would not sufficiently account for the big difference between the revenue collected under James I and Charles I and that raised by Cromwell.

[1] *Cambridge Modern History*, iv. 476.

[2] *C.S.P.* (*Dom.*), *1650*, 315.

The civil wars were therefore not damaging to foreign trade. Secondly, the great differences, averaging £50,000, between the charges and receipts of the customs commissioners, which included their own profits, and the actual amounts paid into the exchequer, show what a wasteful system it was. Thirdly, the difference between the net revenue and the payments and allowances made by the commissioners in a given year shows that the accounts were never properly balanced and the commissioners always expected to lend considerably more than their actual receipts to the Government; and this no doubt was the justification for their profits. Finally, in considering the customs estimates, one notices the curious fact that equally in the years of the Protectorate and in the early years of Charles II, the customs actually yielded to the exchequer about £300,000 and were calculated at £400,000. The later history of Charles II's reign suggests that this may have been partly due to inefficient administration.

In no country in modern times has customs policy been entirely dominated by the 'fiscal view of taxation'. Perhaps it cannot be. Political considerations invariably influence statesmen in determining the character which this form of taxation shall take, and even if they do not do so, tariff changes inevitably have unexpected repercussions. In the seventeenth century alteration in customs policy was a recognized method of achieving political ends. The success or non-success of the policy of controlling importation in foreign ships in order to encourage the British carrying trade—the Navigation Act policy—was mainly dependent on the honesty of the customs officers; but that must be discussed later. In addition to this form of prohibition, during the wars a somewhat crude form of attack on the enemy was attempted through the customs rates. When during the second civil war the royalist sympathies of France led to attacks on Parliament-protected merchantmen an additional 6*d*. per tun was imposed on the importation of French wines. This meagre addition to the existing duty of £6 could have little effect, and so in the August after the execution of Charles I the French wine trade was entirely prohibited; but this was possibly merely an excuse for a really considerable addition to the existing rates.[1] In November 1653, an English merchant wrote to a friend: 'I understand that the Council of State, by Act of Parliament, grants licences for importing French wines, upon petition and a payment of £2 more per tun, since the prohibition.'[2] During the Spanish war exactly the same policy was adopted in relation to the sweeter Spanish wines; for the duty was raised £2 per tun upon them in the Tonnage and Poundage Act of 1657.[3] The policy of 'making the foreigner pay' could only work on the assumption that the inelasticity of supply of luxuries would force the producer to continue importing and himself bear the double duties.[4] But it was more probable that if the rate on one class of imported wine were raised much above that of another either the former would cease to be imported or the consumer would have to pay for his expensive preference. An attempt was made to meet this difficulty by fixing the retail price of wines. At £5 a tun and excise duty of £6 on top of that, the retailer was ordered to sell at 1*s.* 6*d.* a quart; but the fallacy of the 'making the foreigner pay' theory was exposed when no one could be found to sell at that price.[5]

The third instance that occurs during the Protectorate of the use of customs rates for political purposes is the granting of preferential duties on some of the goods imported from the English plantations; preferential rates were allowed on ginger and sugar, two main exports from the West Indies.[6] This was granted partly to compensate for the losses caused to the colonists through the enforcement of the Navigation Act.[7]

[1] On Dec. 16, 1647, £4 10*s.* per tun was the customs duty on native importation, £6 on foreign; on Oct. 19, 1648, an additional 6*d.* was imposed on imported French wines; on Aug. 28, 1649, their importation together with other French goods was prohibited. Firth and Rait, i. 1033, 1224; ii. 239.

[2] *C.S.P.* (*Dom.*), *1653–4*, 241.

[3] On Dec. 16, 1647, £2 5*s.* was the duty of native importation, £3 on foreign per tun or 30*s.* and 45*s.* a pipe. By the Act of June 26, 1657, it was raised 15*s.* and 20*s.* a pipe; 90 : 45 = 40 : 20. Firth and Rait, i. 1034, 1123.

[4] This argument can be found in Henry Robinson, *England's Safety in Treasure's Increase* (1641).

[5] An Act for limiting and settling the price of wines June 9, 1657, Firth and Rait, ii. 1057; A. L. Simon, *History of the Wine Trade in England* (1906), vol. iii, chap. iii.

[6] *C.S.P.* (*Dom.*), *1657–8*, 16.

[7] Cf. Add. MSS. 11411, f. 13.

VII

TAXES

II. EXCISE

THE excise was a commodity tax paid indirectly by consumers as a contribution to the expenses of national defence.

Historically the idea of its payment was probably the same as the payments in kind by the tenant of a medieval farm to his lord for protecting him and his crops from external enemies. The derivation of the word 'excise' is disputed, but it has been popularly supposed to mean a portion 'cut off' from movable property and paid into a common fund. Such a tax was to be found in Italy, Flanders, and the United Netherlands in the fifteenth and sixteenth centuries, and was often suggested as a financial expedient in England from the time of Elizabeth. It was thought of in connexion with the 'Great Contract' of James I in lieu of feudal dues, and decisively rejected in 1628 by the second Parliament of Charles I. But the exigencies of the civil war, so fruitful of financial experiments, once more brought the matter forward, and the first ordinance for the levying of excise was passed to take effect from July 22, 1643.[1] The effect of such a tax was to raise commodity prices, and it has been argued convincingly that the country was prepared for this by the almost universal system of monopolies that prevailed during the previous twelve years; although the only case quoted where a monopoly tax directly became an excise is that of soap.[2] So far as articles manufactured at home were concerned the tax was paid by the manufacturer, was levied by counties and has been described as 'a kind of universal octroi'.[3] The excise on foreign imports was payable by the first buyer, and did not otherwise differ materially from an additional customs tax on imports. The excise officers were ordered to take care that the real importer signed the entry at the customs house and were encouraged

[1] Harleian MSS. 164, f. 346v.; cf. Dowell, vol. ii, chap. i; Leftwich, *History of Excise*; Baasch, *ut supra*; W. Kennedy, *English Taxation, 1640–1799* (1913); Firth and Rait, i. 202.

[2] W. H. Price, *English Patents of Monopoly* (1906), 131–2; Scott, 215; &c.

[3] Rogers, v. 159. The analogy is perhaps a little far-fetched.

to act in co-operation with the customs officials, the two being regarded as a check on each other.

Under the ordinance of July 22, 1643, eight commissioners were appointed to administer the collection of the new tax, one of whom was made treasurer. Three of the commissioners were aldermen of the City of London, their office was situated in the city and two auditors were appointed to whom their accounts were to be rendered annually. The commissioners were empowered to examine on oath, to enter cellars and to punish insubordinate officers. They received for their pains 6*d*. in the pound on what they raised gross, and in 1647 the cost of administration was said to be 2*s*. in the pound.[1] An Act of September 20, 1650, adopted a new policy. Six commissioners instead of eight were named, of whom one only, the then Lord Mayor of London, Foote, was the same; they were only paid 3*d*. in the pound, but were empowered to farm the excise by sections. In 1654 a new group of commissioners was only allowed 2*d*.

In the United Netherlands the excise had always been farmed, and it is clear that an inland excise was a far more difficult tax to levy than the customs duties at the ports, and hence might more reasonably be left to private enterprise. The principal service which the excise commissioners were expected to perform was the advancing of money to the government on the security of the excise revenue. But they were not given the exclusive right to this security. For, however rich they were, they could not advance a sum equivalent to the entire yield anticipated, and consequently all who were prepared to advance money were given this form of security.[2]

The difficulties involved in collecting the inland or 'native' excise were aggravated by the undoubted unpopularity of the tax. In 1647 there were serious riots against it at Smithfield, and during the same year, Parliament, in exhorting

[1] Firth and Rait, i. 202, 709. All the pamphleteers agree to the 2*s*. in the pound figure. One of the auditors later became comptroller.

[2] 'The Common Council of London propounded for the security of the two hundred thousand pound to be advanced for the Scots, that all who had contributed upon the propositions for Flax, Money and Plate, may contribute the like sum upon this proposition for the two hundred thousand pound, and be secured both sums out of the Excise.' Whitelocke, 226.

justices of the peace to assist the commissioners in their duties, took notice of 'the many Tumults and great riots which have of late happened, and been privily fomented in several parts of the Kingdom against the Receipts and Collections of Excise'.[1] Three years later there were reports of serious anti-excise riots in Worcestershire and Lancashire.[2] In 1652 a typical piece of Puritan humour was published bearing the title *The Excize-Men's Lamentation or Their Strange Creed and Letany*,[3] a blasphemous parody of the Anglican general confession and litany beginning, 'O God the Father have mercy upon Us, miserable Excize-men'.

Five years later a broadside entitled *A Dialogue between an Excise Man and Death* again reflected this view of the sinfulness of the levy and the popular hatred of the interfering methods of the excise officers.[4] The excise man is made to conclude the dialogue with this awful thought:

Oh! that my conscience were but clear within,
Which now is racked with my former sin:
With horror I behold my secret Stealing,
My Bribes, Oppression, and my graceless Dealing;
My Office—sins which I had clean forgotten,
Will gnaw my soul, when all my bones are rotten;
I must confess it, nay grief doth force mee,
Dead or alive, both God and Man doth Curse mee.

And this is the moral:

Let all Excise-men hereby warning take
To shun their Practice for their Conscience Sake.

The consequence of this quite widespread feeling against excise was that the Government had continually to introduce new legal means of enforcing its levy. On June 6, 1645, an ordinance for regulating the excise appointed a parliamentary committee to imprison those who hindered its collection, and in August 1649, the commissioners were given additional powers for removing obstructions to the Acts. Finally, after the establishment of the Protectorate, six Commissioners for Appeals and Regulating the Excise were appointed, all of whom were trusted treasury officials.[5] This committee super-

[1] Gardiner, ii. 216; Firth and Rait, i. 916.
[2] *C.S.P. (Dom.), 1650*, 12, 23.
[3] By G. Horton. British Museum, E. 683 (9).
[4] British Museum, 669, f. 21 (58).
[5] Act of March 17, 1654, Firth and Rait, ii. 846. There is in the Customs House

vised the administration of the various farmers.[1] The sectional farming of the excise from 1650 onward did not add to the popularity of the tax although it considerably increased its yield.

By 1654 over thirty-one counties and towns were in the hands of farmers, while Martin Noell was given the whole of the excise farm for salt, glass, wire, copperas, and alum.[2] By the end of the interregnum well over half the excise was administered by farmers. In 1657 the greater part of London and Middlesex was let out in one farm, and the London farmers were especially unpopular.[3] They met with powerful opposition in the pursuit of their work, and they claimed that they had to deal with organized opposition from the brewers and connivance at tax evasion by the justices. They urged that previously the coercive powers had been in the hands of the commissioners themselves, and sought the same privileges. Finally, they threatened that they would be unable to fulfil their contract. The Government issued a proclamation concerning excise on March 9, 1658, calling upon the justices to do their duty, and supplemented this on June 1 with an order that the Commissioners for Appeals were to issue warrants for the forcible entry of breweries and the confiscation of instruments of manufacture until such time as the brewer should see fit to pay his excise.[4] On the other hand, when in Richard Cromwell's Parliament there were numerous complaints at the failure of the London and other excise farmers to pay their money into the exchequer punctually, the House of Commons was by no means convinced that it was entirely the fault of the brewers.[5] So far as administrative

Library a warrant book of these commissioners, the sole surviving record of this period from Somerset House, which shows that the commissioners were acting as early as 1652.

1 Cf. Th. Broome to Ed. Marston, Aug. 29, 1653: 'What is the committee for regulating the excise doing with reference to the many complaints against the farmers of the excise?' *C.S.P. (Dom.), 1653–4*, 112.

2 The value of this farm was £65,000: see a list of excise farms in Add. MSS. 4107, f. 256.

3 The amount of excise administered by farmers and sub-commissioners respectively can be traced in the Declared Accounts. The excise was never entirely farmed during the interregnum.

4 'Petition of the farmers of the beer excise', Feb. 1658 in Stowe MSS. 185, ff. 117–18 for farmers' complaints. *C.S.P. (Dom.), 1657–8*, 262, 322, ibid., *1658–9*, 42–3.

5 Burton, iv. 140–2.

policy was concerned the Government was prepared to offer every reasonable assistance to the excise farmers, but at the same time determined to keep in its own hands full control over the right of search and power to confiscate which the administration of this new tax involved.

The preamble to the first excise ordinance stated that its purpose was to raise money for the better security of trade, the maintenance of the forces and the payment of the national debts. When it was introduced, the excise was regarded as a last resort to obtain funds for the civil warfare. It was at once charged with all the miscellaneous expenses incident upon this; for example, in July, 1645, an ordinance was passed for charging upon the excise £500 for the prisoners who were taken at Naseby and were willing to serve the Parliament against the Irish; in the same month an ordinance was passed to reimburse the excise commissioners for money lent by them to pay for the siege of Oxford.[1] After the civil war was over, the large increase in the size of the armed forces caused its continuation, and naval charges were regularly allotted to the excise; but the army also had its share; and since neither the customs sufficed to meet the cost of the navy nor did the monthly assessments pay for the army, there were probably often disputes between the treasurers of the two forces as to which had prior claim upon the excise.[2] It is arguable that the fact that there was no one definite form of expenditure with which the excise was associated contributed in some degree to the break-up of that sectional financial system of which customs duties had been a characteristic part.

The anticipation expressed by 'old Mr. Caye', M.P. for Ipswich, when Pym first brought in the excise bill, that the tax duty would not only fall on 'superfluous commodities' was speedily realized.[3] It was first imposed on tobacco, wine, cider, beer, groceries, silks, hats, lace, linen, and furs. Within

[1] Whitelocke, 143, 157.

[2] e.g. on July 6, 1658, the Commissioners of the Admiralty told the council that of the customs and excise nominally set apart for the navy, half was diverted to the army, £2,000 a week to the Protector, and the salaries of judges and others paid out of it. Quoted from S.P. 182, f. 18, 8 by Oppenheimer, 319.

[3] Harleian MSS. 164, f. 346v.

three months it was found necessary to make a considerable reduction in most of the rates, e.g. the duty on tobacco fell from 4*s*. to 2*s*. a pound, but in the following year it was extended to meat and salt, alums, copperas, hops, starch, &c. Indeed there was little difference between the articles charged with excise and those charged with customs, and by the Protector's ordinance of March 17, 1654, there was a revision of rates, in which tobacco was again reduced—from 2*s*. to 1*s*.—but most of the existing duties were raised and all saleable commodities brought under the excise. The Dutch ambassadors noted the arbitrary character of this ordinance, issued concurrently with the customs ordinance, the legality of which was called into question by *Cony's Case*, for they wrote home that his Highness had 'continued the excise, and settled the proportion thereof, without any limitation of time, which formerly was always regulated by the Parliament, as we are informed, and was never in the power of the king'.[1] Indeed the celebrated Puritan pamphleteer, William Prynne, went so far as to imitate Cony by refusing to pay excise on hops on the ground that it had not been legalized by Parliament and indeed was contrary to Article 36 of the 'Instrument of Government'. It was, he said, 'an arrogation of a supertranscendant jurisdiction'; but he deigned to accept after the Restoration a post as collector of the arrears of excise which had not been paid during the interregnum![2]

With a new tax of this kind it was inevitable that there should be frequent changes in the rates. For instance, originally the tax was entirely remitted on re-exports, but by Cromwell's 1654 ordinance 'half the impost and all the excise' were rebated, but only to the actual importers. The tradesmen, however, demanded that as the first buyer paid the impost (the foreign excise) he also should be allowed the rebate; and the matter had to be put right by another ordi-

[1] Thurloe, ii. 193–4. The ordinance is in Firth and Rait, ii. 846; cf. *C.S.P.* (*Dom.*), *1654*, 118, for a report of the Council advising the reduction of duties on Spanish tobacco on the ground that the increased import would more than offset the reduction.

[2] Prynne, *A Declaration and Protestation against the Excise* (1654); his resistance to payment only seems to have been just sufficient to enable him to write this pamphlet. A note of his being paid a salary as collector of arrears is in a record in the Customs House, which the librarian, Mr. Leftwich, kindly showed me.

nance.[1] Again, there were elaborate differentiations of duties between ale brewed at home and manufactured ale, the former being exempted for administrative reasons,[2] also between plantation-grown tobacco and tobacco imported from the Spanish colonies; complaints and criticisms had perpetually to be dealt with by committees of Council or of Parliament.[3] The second Protectorate Parliament appointed a committee especially to consider the subject of excise rates. They chiefly concerned themselves with the subject of Spanish wines. They considered that the vintners made excessive profits, and Sir George Downing, true to his principle of taxing 'superfluities' as highly as possible, stated that we did not charge taxation upon wines nearly as heavily as the Dutch, and desired that an additional excise should be paid by the retailers. The excise was duly raised from £6 to £9 a tun and on Spanish raisins from 1*s.* 6*d.* to 3*s.* the cwt.[4]

Bearing in mind these frequent alterations in excise rates, for which it is almost impossible to make allowances, we turn to an estimate of the sums raised in this way under the Protectorate.

The following are figures of the net receipts from the excise commissioners paid into the exchequer during the Protectorate:

	£
July 1654—Dec. 1654	206,362[5]
M. 1654—E. 1655	162,659[6]
E. 1655—M. 1655	171,254[6]
M. 1655—E. 1656	176,070[6]
E. 1656—M. 1656	177,185[6]
M. 1656—E. 1657	182,062[6]
E. 1657—M. 1657	192,453[7]
M. 1657—E. 1658	238,024[7]
E. 1658—M. 1658	211,150[8]
M. 1658—E. 1659	215,902[7]

[1] *C.S.P. (Dom.), 1654*, 115–17, 151.

[2] The excise on home brewing was abandoned on Mar. 28, 1650. Firth and Rait, ii. 368–9.

[3] Cf., e.g., the Petition of the London Soap-makers, *C.S.P. (Dom.), 1654*, 17.

[4] Burton's *Diary*, i. 321–30, gives an account of the debate in the committee. *C.J.* vii. 453–4, Captain Baynes's report from the committee. For Downing's views on indirect taxes, see *Clarke Papers*, iii. 177.

[5] Carte MSS. 74, f. 232.

[6] Carte MSS. 73, f. 67. Exactly the same figure for the year E. 1656—E. 1657 is given in ibid., f. 69.

[7] Record Office, 405/289, 391.

[8] This figure is obtained by subtracting from £447,544, a figure given in Add. MSS. 32471, f. 15, for M. 1657—M. 1658, that given above for M. 1657—E. 1658.

At the Restoration only the beer excise and foreign excise were retained, which yielded in the first year (1661–2) £261,052, and on an average 1661–7, £307,463.[1]

The following are some figures of the gross charges of the excise taken from the audit office; the charges and receipts include arrears owed and exclude rebates:[2]

	Charges and receipts	*Payments and allowances*
	£	£
M. 1653—E. 1654 . .	334,176	187,498
E. 1654—E. 1655 . .	531,991	431,255
E. 1655—E. 1656 . .	506,980	407,459
E. 1656—E. 1657 . .	534,027	432,420
E. 1657—E. 1658 . .	517,119	392,615

In order to make the comparison clearer, we may add the net receipts paid into the exchequer for the three years of the Protectorate during which a comparison can be made with the above figures:[3]

	£
E. 1655—E. 1656 . . .	347,324
E. 1656—E. 1657 . . .	359,227
E. 1657—E. 1658 . . .	428,659

For the years 1655–6 and 1656–7 we see therefore that the cost to the public of the excise was over £500,000, the actual receipts at the exchequer were about £350,000, while the amounts paid out by the commissioners exceeded this by about £50,000. The reason why the receipts at the exchequer in 1657–8 exceeded the amounts paid out by the commissioners was that the commissioners had surrendered the rich revenue from the farm of the London inland excise which had been let separately at £128,400 for each six months. The excise commissioners had been most reluctant to consent to this separate farm, and had reported in July 1656, that such farms were disliked by the people and would be unpopular with the brewers, that the judicial powers given to themselves could not be delegated, and that the receipts

[1] Shaw, intro. to *Calendar of Treasury Books, 1660–7*, xxviii.

[2] A.O. i. 889–90. The annual figures from 1643–53 are not available among the Declared Accounts. According to a report to Parliament in 1650, the Treasury received between Sept. 11, 1643, and June 24, 1650, £1,915,705, and according to a declared account of 1650–3 (E. 351/1296) in three years there was a net yield of some £1,034,860.

[3] Taken from the half-yearly totals given above.

were rising in value, and hence the Government would lose by it.[1] But so pressed for resources was Cromwell at this time that he let it go for £10,000 cash down, and consequently the receipts from the London excise farm of beer and ale read:[2]

	£
E. 1657—M. 1657 . . .	10,700
M. 1657—M. 1658 . . .	205,135
M. 1658—E. 1659 . . .	121,920

We have already read the complaints of these farmers about their difficulty in exacting the revenue, which explains their failure to keep their contract;[3] but the experiment of making London into one farm proved a success, the total revenues were increased and the farm was continued at the Restoration. Before leaving these figures, it should be noticed that they were always higher than the corresponding customs figures, and that the estimates of their yield (£400,000–£440,000) were somewhat nearer the mark. Because of the number of changes in the rates and the peculiar character of the foreign excise, these figures are probably not a very reliable index of commercial activity, but it seems reasonable to suppose from them that the years 1654 and 1658 were the best.

Note on the Abolition of the Feudal Dues.

The excise was introduced partly and implicitly as a fruitful substitute for the feudal dues of the Crown. An Act of February 24, 1646, abolished the Court of Wards and Liveries, all wardships, liveries, primer-seizin and ousterlemains. Ten years later this Act of the Long Parliament was confirmed by the Protector and his Parliament who added that all tenures in capite and by knight's service were to be turned into common socage. On the other hand, all rents and certain heriots and reliefs (e.g. mortdancester) due to manorial lords had still to be paid, and have continued, unless compounded for, until this day. Finally an Act of June 9, 1657, abolished the royal right of purveyance, the right of pre-emption by the king on certain goods, a matter which no doubt came under consideration as the result of Cromwell's effective essay in limited monarchy.[4]

In connexion with the Court of Wards the Government evidently

[1] *C.S.P. 1656–7*, 41–2, 66–7; ibid., *1657–8*, 262, 322.
[2] E. 405/289, 390–1; Add. MSS. 32471, f. 15.
[3] See above, p. 65.
[4] Acts in Firth and Rait, i. 833; ii. 1043, 1057.

had in mind some scheme for making legal provision for orphans to be properly cared for by their nearest of kin.[1] All these acts and schemes were combined in Charles II's Act abolishing feudal dues. This refers in its preamble to how the late intermission of the Court of Wards and the abolition of knight's service had brought into being a series of new legal practices, and concludes by substituting for the royal feudal dues an excise 'to be paid to His Majesty and his successors for ever after'.[2]

[1] Draft of an Act for 'registering and preserveing the Discent of heirs and Orphans', Add. MSS. 32093, f. 395.
[2] *Statutes of the Realm*, v. 259 seq.

VIII
TAXES
III. THE MONTHLY ASSESSMENTS

THE parentage of Cromwell's principal source of public revenue and only general direct tax belongs to two highly criticized taxes of the early Stuart period, namely ship-money and the forced loan.[1] Partly because the old direct taxes, the subsidy and the tenth-and-fifteenth, had ceased to yield more than a small stereotyped amount, and partly on account of constitutional difficulties, the advisers of Charles I had decided upon the expedient of demanding a large sum of money (the equivalent of three of the old subsidies) for building ships, and had divided it up among all the towns and counties of the land. It was generally admitted that this ship-money assessment of 1636 was extremely fair, 'to the end', it was said, 'that the equality might take off the illegality', and in the course of financial debates in the Commons under the Protectorate it was often urged, despite reprimands from Government officials, that no assessment could be found so equal as that of ship-money.[2] The use of forced loans stretches far back into the history of the English kings, and, when the civil war came, both sides used this method to obtain money when it was found that voluntary contributions would not suffice. In November, 1642, Parliament appointed a committee, which included John Pym, to arrange such a loan from the City of London, real property contributing 5 per cent. and personal 20 per cent. of their assessed value, those assessed under £100 being exempt; the lenders were promised 8 per cent. interest on the guarantee of the public faith.[3] But soon after this Committee for the Advance of Money had been established, an ordinance 'for the speedy raising of money for the maintenance of the army raised by Parliament' was promulgated, which imposed a direct weekly

[1] Mr. Harper says in his thesis that 'under the name of assessment the forced loan became a tax pure and simple' and that the assessments were 'forced loans in democratic guise'. It will be seen from the text that I consider this view one-sided. For the history of subsidies and ship-money see Dowell, Dietz, &c.; also Rogers, *Agriculture and Prices*, v, chap. vi.

[2] Burton, ii. 214, 218, 227–8 &c.

[3] Intro. to *Calendar of the Committee for the Advance of Money*, i.

tax for a period of three months.[1] As with ship-money the sum aimed at was first decided upon and then divided up proportionately among the towns and counties over which the parliamentary forces exercised control. London was heavily assessed at £10,000, but was promised a 60 per cent. repayment on the public faith and that the rate should not be regarded as a precedent. A second weekly assessment was levied in August from which London was omitted, and the first monthly assessment, which demanded the sum of £21,000, was introduced for the payment of Fairfax's army on February 21, 1645, and henceforward the monthly assessment became a regular tax used by the interregnum governments.[2]

Professor Cannan has justly observed that, although the monthly assessment is generally described as a land tax, it was also a local rate.[3] The Government finally settled the proportions to be paid by each county at the end of 1649; county committees of local magnates—till he became Protector, Cromwell was always a member of the Ely and Cambridge county committees—were nominated to supervise the raising of the money. These committees appointed assessors who valued the local property, making £20 of personalty equivalent to £1 of rent, and then the commissioners decided how much the correct pound rate would be to obtain the required sum from their district. In the case of rents this tax was paid by the occupier, who was allowed to transfer part or all of it to his landlord. The collectors, after 1647 the receivers-general for the counties, paid the money thus raised to the army treasurers at the Guildhall, and received a poundage on the amount they collected. Professor Cannan, who lucidly describes this process, is surprised to find among the provisions for the first Restoration levy a clause in the Act which allows the commissioners to cause the assessment to be made by the 'most just and usual ways of rates held and practised' in their area, and comments on the roughness of the administrative methods after twenty years. As a matter of fact this particular provision dates at least from 1650, was to be found in the Protectorate Acts,

[1] Firth and Rait, i. 85–100.

[2] Ibid., 958, &c.

[3] *History of Local Rates*, 114–15.

and probably merely signifies the fact that the Government was uninterested in the character of the local rating so long as the sum assessed to the county was produced by the collectors. What is more significant is that after the Restoration the tax gradually ceased to be levied on personalty and went the way of previous direct taxes by becoming a pure land tax.[1]

So long as the civil wars lasted and a large standing army had to be maintained little opportunity arose for criticizing the tax. But the Little Parliament proceeded to discuss its inequalities, and its dubious conduct in this matter is said to have been one of the causes of its dissolution by the supporters of the army.[2] It was at first hoped that the Government under the 'Instrument' would not require assessments at all, and a committee was set up under Colonel Thomas Birch to study the possibilities of economy, especially in the army; but after some discussion the rate was not abolished, but reduced by £30,000 a month. 'It was in every man's sense', wrote the author of Goddard's diary, 'to go as low as it possibly could consistent with our safety; for certainly, this was that which was so much desired and expected by the people from us. This was that which would render our government acceptable and amicable'.[3] Mr. Secretary Thurloe wrote off to Switzerland that he expected far greater stability in the realm from this reduction of taxes.[4] It may be noticed here that Cromwell later claimed credit for taking off this taxation, as being one of the initial benefits derived from his Protectorate.[5] But this second reduction was forced upon him by his Parliament, who would have abolished the tax altogether if he had not threatened them with free quarter as an alternative.[6] Parliamentary expression of grievances was thus postponed until the meeting of the second Protectorate Parliament in 1656–7. Here it was represented that the rates assigned to the different counties were unjust, more so than those of ship-money, and that it was absurd that a

[1] Dowell, iii. 81.

[2] See a brief summary of the Little Parliament's proceedings in *Somers Tracts*, vi. 273–4; Firth, *Cromwell*, 336.

[3] Intro. to Burton, lxxxiv seq.

[4] Vaughan, *Protectorate*, i. 126–7: an interesting letter to Pell.

[5] *Letters and Speeches*, ii. 358.

[6] Gardiner, *History*, iii. 60, 64–5, quoting French transcripts in the Record Office of Dec. 11, 1654.

national tax should involve a different rate being paid by citizens in accordance with the district in which they happened to live. Major-General Whalley, supported by Major-General Desborough, moved for a national rate of 6*d.* in the pound. The opposition said that it was plausible but not practicable; rents differed in character, while close investigation of personal estates would involve inquisitorial methods. It was clear that this proposal could only be carried out on the basis of an elaborate survey of the entire property of the kingdom. The suggestion was ultimately dropped. One member said that the thing looked like a 'court project' but Desborough denied this.[1]

In the course of these debates Sir Christopher Packe complained of the excessive charge which fell upon the City of London. In the earliest levies the district of London and Westminster ('the Bills of Mortality') had contributed the bulk, and in the later assessments the share of the City alone was 15 per cent. of the total. What was considered their undue share of national taxation[2] exercised the minds of the City Common Council throughout the whole of the Protectorate. In the early years of the civil war the City had lent generously to the Government and later it had organized an elaborate credit system whereby it advanced large sums of money to the Government on the basis of the assessments. But on April 28, 1654, the Court of Aldermen, 'sensible of the great decay of trade within the Citie', appointed a committee to draft a petition for the remission of arrears in the monthly assessments and to reduce their proportion. On October 20, a second committee, including Packe, about to become Lord Mayor, was set up for the same purpose, and later it decided to omit all mention of arrears from the petition. The petition was finally drawn up and complained that 'though the City stretches only from Temple to Aldgate and from Bridge to Bishopsgate, it pays one-fifteenth of the total assessment of England and Wales'. Four aldermen were to present it, but after much coming and going, it was again

[1] This interesting debate is in Burton, ii. 229 seq.

[2] Ibid., 208. The speaker after Packe said: 'Make it an universal case, all the nation over, for other parts have as much cause to complain as the city.' Cf. Rogers, loc. cit. When the assessment was £120,000 a month, the city paid £8,000; when £90,000, £6,000; when £60,000, £4,000.

altered. Its ultimate fate was presumably determined by the rapid dissolution of Parliament. When the second Protectorate Parliament was in session a new petition was carefully prepared, and this time the request for the remission of arrears was put at the forefront. This petition was referred to a committee, and representatives of the City were ordered to attend with a full explanation of why they had failed to pay their arrears. At the same time the City prepared further petitions and its Council held discussions which showed the other side of their picture, for claims were laid to public-faith debts which had never been repaid by the Government.[1] For the City of London, however, as with other towns, the problem of assessment payments was probably quite a simple one. The alternative was always free quarter for the soldiers. A declaration of the army had announced this when it approached London in 1647,[2] and the Acts and Ordinances, the decisions of the Council of State and the speeches of the Protector all indicated the same issue. We may even reflect that ship-money would have been paid more easily if the alternative had been the quartering of the navy. In this sense, Professor Cannan is right in saying that, like ship-money, the assessments were naturally unpopular. All direct taxes are unpopular; yet surprisingly little mention is made of them in the pamphlets of the day. Generally speaking the pamphleteers show more interest in commercial affairs, and it was the great innovation of the excise and the heightened customs which primarily disturbed them. One writer, it is true, preferred the excise to the assessments on the ground that the assessors tended to spare themselves,[3] but on the whole it appears that the country was so used to paying a land tax of some kind that a system which meant that the apportionment was handed over to commissioners who really knew the economic situation of the neighbourhood was almost as good as could be expected from a government. Finally, in criticizing the monthly assessments, one may recall a piece of constitutional history that is not always

[1] Journal of the City Council, No. 41, ff. 98v, 107v, 109v, 110, 110v, 113v, 129v, 130–6v, 141, 142.

[2] British Museum, E. 476. *A Declaration of the Army's General Survey of the Income of England*; cf. *C.S.P.* (*Dom.*), *1654*, 284, &c.

[3] Bland, *Trade Revived*, 25.

remembered; namely, that the seventh article of the 'Humble Petition and Advice' (1657) laid down the willingness of Parliament to grant a yearly revenue of £1,200,000, 'no part thereof to be raised by a land tax'. Yet a Parliament of landowners continued the assessments; which at least shows how inevitable a part they formed of the national budget.

We have seen that the first ordinances for a weekly and a monthly assessment announced that their purpose was to pay for the upkeep of the parliamentary armies. The first monthly assessment was actually administered by the Committee for Scottish Affairs and used to pay Leslie's army in England. Preambles to subsequent Acts stated that the taxes were raised to pay for the land forces in various places, in Ireland as well as in Scotland, in Flanders as well as in England. The Act of December 10, 1652, which raised £120,000 for six months, announced that its aim was to pay for the navy as well as the army, but the whole of the tax always went through the hands of the army committee, and was varied in amount in accordance with the size and scales of pay that were maintained in the army at the time.

The following are the sums which were demanded per month during the Protectorate; the proportions paid by the different counties, differing considerably from those of the ship-money assessments, were those fixed in 1649, which were not altered, despite many complaints, till the Restoration:[1]

	£
Dec. 25, 1653—Mar. 25, 1654 . .	120,000
Mar. 25, 1654—Sept. 25, 1654 . .	120,000
Sept. 25, 1654—Dec. 25, 1654 . .	90,000
Dec. 25, 1654—June 24, 1655 . .	60,000
June 24, 1655—Dec. 25, 1655 . .	60,000
Dec. 25, 1655—June 24, 1656 . .	60,000
June 24, 1656—Dec. 25, 1656 . .	60,000
Dec. 25, 1656—June 24, 1657 . .	60,000 (*payable in advance*).
Mar. 25, 1656—June 24, 1657 . .	60,000 (*for Spanish war*).
June 24, 1657—June 24, 1660 . .	35,000

The Scottish assessment was first (1653) £8,500, then £10,000 (1654) nominally, although it only raised £7,300,

[1] The assessment Acts are either printed or referred to in the index to Firth and Rait; there are also copies of all the Acts among the Thomason Tracts. For a comparison of the ship-money assessment with that of 1649, see Rogers, loc. cit.

finally, at the request of General Monk, in 1657 it was reduced to £6,000.

In Ireland the Adventurers had contracted to raise £10,000 a month in assessment, but in 1657, at the request of General Fleetwood, Cromwell reduced the charge to £9,000.[1]

From the end of the civil war to the establishment of the Protectorate the figures of £120,000 a month or £1,440,000 a year had been demanded from the monthly assessments, a sum which alone exceeded the total revenue of Charles I. In June 1654, Cromwell had promised a reduction by £30,000 a month in September, the time significantly when Parliament was to be summoned, and then, as we have seen, Parliament forced a further reduction of £30,000.

The finances of 1656–7 are distinctly curious. On May 29, 1656, Cromwell issued as usual an ordinance for the raising of the following six months' assessment of £60,000 from June to December, but on July 24—a committee having been first appointed to prepare it[2]—a second ordinance was published for the *following* six months' assessment from December to June, 1657, and this was ordered to be collected and paid before it fell due, actually by November, 1656; in other words, the country was again paying an assessment of £120,000 a month in the latter half of 1656. By this time Parliament had once more met, and Cromwell, by dint of explaining to it the heavy charges of the Spanish war and the inadequacy of the sums allowed to him in the 'Humble Petition' persuaded them to authorize an additional three months' assessment of £60,000 specifically for the purpose of the Spanish war.[3]

What was the actual yield of the assessments? Did this new method of raising direct taxation produce the amounts demanded in the Acts? The cost of administration was not unduly heavy for those times. The county commissioners, who were for the most part justices of the peace, were unpaid, and the assessors and collectors were given at first 3*d*., then 1*d*., in the pound, according to the size of the sum they

[1] Burton, ii. 207–14; Firth, *Last Years*, ii. 114–18, 164–9, and references there given.

[2] *C.S.P. 1656–7*, 14, 121–2.

[3] *Letters and Speeches*, ii. 546—'we laboured to pull off the common charge, as you see, £60,000 a month', &c.

collected. The treasurers of war, who also acted as receivers-general for the money, and endorsed every receipt sent up from the counties, were paid an annual salary of £520 each. From their accounts we are able to estimate the nature of the return from the assessments. There is in the Bodleian library an abstract of the accounts of the treasurers of war from 1645–51.[1] According to this:

From March 25, 1647, to Dec. 15, 1648, they received £1,133,071, when the gross yield should have been £1,260,000.

From March 25, 1649, to Dec. 25, 1650, they received £1,644,496, when the gross yield should have been £1,770,000.

From Dec. 25, 1650, to Jan. 25, 1651, they received £1,514,445, when the gross yield should have been £1,560,000.

These figures do not, however, include the costs of administration. Over the whole period covered by this paper, February 1, 1644, to January 25, 1652, I estimate that the gross yield should have been £5,598,720, the actual yield was £5,228,873, or, less the cost of collection and the treasurers' own fees (£28,534 + £80,203 = £108,737), £5,120,136—that is, about 91½ per cent. of the sum authorized to be collected by the Ordinances and Acts. No such useful abstract exists for the later period, and the figures have to be discovered from two rolls among the declared accounts in the exchequer of receipt.[2] From these it appears that from December 25, 1651, to June 25, 1653, the assessments raised £2,417,483 and the gross yield should have been £2,880,000. From the former figure, the local administration but not the central administration costs are deducted, and similar figures of the amounts raised from individual levies are available for almost the entire Protectorate:

	Demanded £	*Received by treasurers* £
June 24—Sept. 24, 1654 . .	360,000	351,676
Sept. 24—Dec. 24, 1654 . .	270,000	262,266
Dec. 24, 1654 for 6 months . .	360,000	349,870
June 24, 1655 ,, ,, . .	360,000	346,865
Dec. 25, 1655 ,, ,, . .	360,000	348,825
June 24, 1656 ,, ,, . .	360,000	353,376
Dec. 25, 1656 ,, ,, . .	360,000	350,947
Mar. 25, 1657 for 3 months . .	180,000	175,083

[1] Rawlinson MSS. A 195, f. 243.

[2] E. 351/304–5.

For the rest of the period of the interregnum the assessments fell in arrears; nevertheless, from June 24, 1657, to December 25, 1658, at the rate of £35,000 a month, or £630,000 for 18 months, the army treasurers received £571,465, and an additional £448,816 to the date of the Restoration. In Scotland and Ireland it is clear that the actual yield of the assessments did not approach nearly so closely the amounts expected. But, if the above calculations are correct, the English Commonwealth assessment must have been one of the most ably managed and most prolific taxes in the whole history of seventeenth-century public finance.

Of course the fact that under pressure the taxpayer sooner or later paid his full contribution was not incompatible with his falling continually into arrears; and that this was then the case is amply clear from the army treasurers' accounts. But a more curious illustration survives of these two facts. We have seen that the City of London complained bitterly and continuously of the assessment imposed upon them, and begged Cromwell to excuse them their arrears. From this it might be assumed that they found much difficulty in producing the money. But this does not appear to have been so. The account book of the receiver-general of the City of London from June 24, 1657, to June, 1659, is in existence and gives the amounts which were paid to him without deductions.[1] Admittedly the national rate had by this time been reduced to £35,000 a month and that of the City to £2,333 6*s.* 8*d.*; yet it is surprising to discover that the receiver-general actually obtained a little more than the amount he was supposed to collect in accordance with the terms of the Act.[2] Nor is there any reason to suppose that the City assessments were unique in this respect. The figures for Middlesex tell exactly the same story. According to the

[1] S.P. 28/334. Account Book of Robert Barrett.

[2] The figures are:

	£
June—Dec. 1657 . .	13,594
Dec.—June 1658 . .	14,613
June—Dec. 1658 . .	13,623
Dec.—June 1659 . .	14,134

The amount assessed was £14,000.

From June 24, 1659, for twelve months this book gives £27,294 as collected instead of £28,000, which shows that the arrears were gathered in under Charles II.

accounts of Francis Sanders, the receiver-general of the monthly assessments for the county, the charge from December 25, 1651, to June 24, 1659, was £176,330 and his receipts, which he paid over to the treasurers of the army, amounted to £173,323.[1] Miscellaneous accounts of the assessments in Worcestershire, Cambridgeshire, Suffolk, Cornwall, and Surrey are also extant among the Commonwealth Exchequer Papers and all of these seem to indicate that the yield of the tax fell very little short of the sums assessed.

It has been pointed out by Dr. Shaw that the monthly assessments never went through the exchequer course.[2] When the committee system held sway the receivers-general in the counties paid the money to the treasurers of the army by whom it was paid out on the instructions of the Army Committee. According to the Act of September 2, 1654, which reconstituted the ancient exchequer, the assessments together with the other sources of revenue were to be paid into the Exchequer of Receipt;[3] but there is no doubt that this was never done. Not only does no account of the assessments appear among the general exchequer records, but various mentions of how this came about are to be found among the State Papers.[4] Moreover, none of the accounts of the treasurers at war were inspected by the treasury commissioners or received an audit until the Restoration, when they were submitted to Anthony Ashley Cooper, and in this they are in marked contrast with the accounts of the treasurer of the navy. What apparently happened in the administration of the tax was this: the assessments were considered the fund out of which the army was paid, but as the cost of the army diminished, other expenses were charged on them, and then the treasury commissioners directed to whom the money should be paid. For example, in the event of part of the

[1] S.P. 28/334.

[2] *Cambridge Modern History*, iv. 456.

[3] Dr. Shaw, loc. cit., is mistaken when he says this Act (first issued on the authority of the Protector and Council on June 21) was 'significantly silent' on the subject of the assessments. On the contrary, it specifically names them.

[4] *C.S.P.* (*Dom.*), *1655*, 99, 123–4; ibid., *1657–8*, 8, 33–4. Dr. Richards who, like myself, has recently gone through the exchequer records of receipt, accepts Dr. Shaw's conclusions unreservedly.

assessments being allotted to the navy, the army treasurers paid it directly to the treasurer of the navy, but whether they did this or kept it for their own expenditure they would obtain tallies from the exchequer, one-half of which would be given to the county receivers-general and the other would be kept as their own warrant for paying out the money. This the treasurers at war were enabled to do by the simple expedient of being appointed also as central receivers-general for assessments. So Blackwell and Deane took in the assessments with one hand, gave themselves a receipt and paid it out with the other hand. Furthermore, as it would have been absurd for the pay of troops which was raised from the counties in which they were stationed to be brought up to the Guildhall, and then back to the county again, a special order of the Protector and Council permitted the receivers-general to pay appropriate sums direct to the paymasters in the regiments concerned, while their receipts and any surplus money raised by them were handed over to themselves as treasurers at war and were entered in their accounts, acquittances for the transaction being then obtained from the exchequer. It seems that Dr. Shaw has not exaggerated the significance of this matter. It is true that the direct payment of the assessment moneys by the county officials saved a great deal of time and was a more efficient administrative method than the exchequer course which brought with it an annual audit, but it also is very likely that Cromwell was determined to keep the army fund under his own control.

But public and Parliament were jealous of so-called constitutional rights. On February 13, 1655, a news-letter writer recorded that in publishing the three months' assessment as an ordinance 'his Highnesse hath modestly denied to assume the Legislature of the Nation'; and two years later Thurloe wrote to tell Henry Cromwell that an Act of assessment had been passed by the second Protectorate Parliament and that to the vote it had added, 'that in the Act to be passed for this money, the right of the people should be asserted, viz. that no money was to be levied but by consent of Parliament'. And the essential keynote of the debates on the financial clauses of the 'Humble Petition' was the fear that too generous a vote of assessments would enable

Cromwell, through the army, to get beyond parliamentary control.[1]

The monthly assessment, then, was not a remarkably new kind of tax nor was it administered in a very revolutionary manner. Nevertheless, it contributed to the break-up of the medieval financial system. It was much more efficient than the subsidy and, under Cromwell, it appears even to have solved to a large extent the problem of how to tax other income than that derived from land. At any rate Sir Christopher Packe gave as one of his reasons for not substituting a pound-rate in its stead that the City contained 'some that have only trades . . . and yet are able to afford something to the Commonwealth'.[2] The system was continued sporadically by Charles II, who in 1661 approved an Act for eighteen months' assessment at £70,000 a month. Various heavy monthly assessments were also levied under William III, still on the basis of the surveys made in 1649, but in 1692 Parliament turned to a national pound-rate of 4*s*. in the pound, and thus began the land tax of the eighteenth century.

1 *Clarke Papers*, iii. 22; Thurloe, vi. 53; Burton, ii. 28 seq.
2 Burton, ii. 232.

IX

THE REMAINING SOURCES OF REVENUE

PRIZE GOODS

DURING the early years of the civil war, Parliament had been particularly anxious to conciliate the navy. By a resolution of October 1642, sailors were given one-half the value of all prize goods captured after they had been duly declared before the court of admiralty. This resolution was embodied in the Acts of February 22, and April 17, 1649, the latter of which formulated in detail the procedure of the Prize Court. It also provided that half the remaining proceeds derived from the sale of prize goods was to go to the State and be used for the sick and wounded fund; the State, further, obtained one-third of the value of the prizes captured by merchant vessels.[1] At the same time another Act was passed appointing commissioners of prize and three paid collectors (who were increased in number to six during the Dutch war). After the reconstitution of the exchequer in 1654 the prize office paid the money into it instead of administering the fund itself.[2] The sums which the national exchequer gained from this source naturally varied very considerably in amount. The accounts of the commissioners who were in office during the Dutch war survive and show a net revenue of £208,658 3*s.* 11*d.*[3] Other figures are:

	£
Michaelmas, 1655–6 . . .	2,900
„ 1656–7 . . .	249,599
„ 1657–8 . . .	3,770
„ 1658–Easter, 1659 .	1,277

Cromwell himself believed prize taken by the navy might be made a highly important source of revenue. He could remember the capture of the silver fleet by Piet Hein in

[1] See E. S. Roscoe, *History of the Prize Court,* esp. 32–3; M. Oppenheimer, *History of Naval Administration,* esp. 309–10; Firth and Rait, ii. 9, 66. For a discussion of prize from another angle see below, p. 154.

[2] Firth and Rait, ii. 75. The Treasurers were at first paid 1*s.* in the pound. The six collectors in office during the Dutch war were superseded in March 1656, by three commissioners, a treasurer and a comptroller. These five were paid £100 a year and 2*d.* in the pound. *C.S.P.* (*Dom.*), *1655–6,* 224.

[3] Add. MSS. 5000 gives detailed accounts.

1628. During the war with Spain he wrote to his commanders at sea strongly urging the intercepting of the treasure fleets and he steadily refused to accede to the Dutch demands for a modification of a prize code that permitted the confiscation of enemy goods carried by neutrals.[1] But only on one occasion did this method of raising revenue near success. In September, 1656, Captain Stayner captured a ship from the Spanish plate fleet, and it was rumoured that the prize taken amounted in value to some million pieces of eight. In London it was thought for a moment that the financial embarrassments of the Government were ended. The disappointment was bitter when the treasure arrived at the Tower of London and was found, after deductions had been made for expenses and embezzlements, to be worth less than £250,000.[2]

PROBATE OF WILLS

Throughout the Middle Ages the management of testamentary affairs had belonged to the ecclesiastical courts. At the Reformation these courts continued to function in this respect and it was not until the abolition of episcopacy by the Long Parliament that the administration of testamentary justice was organized by the Government. By an Act dated April 8, 1653 (regularly renewed throughout the Protectorate), twenty judges were appointed for the probate of wills and ordered to divide the country into administrative units, to establish registers, to issue commissions and to hear and determine all matters concerning wills;[3] and the Protector was specially begged to place the jurisdiction entirely in the hands of civilian judges.[4] All profits arising out of the probate fees were to be paid, after the costs had been deducted, to three treasury commissioners (later into the exchequer) for the use of the navy. Treasury officials generally calculated on

1 See e.g. his letter to Blake and Montague in *Letters and Speeches*, ii. 488, and Thurloe's account of Anglo-Dutch relations in *English Historical Review*, xviii.

2 Cf. Thurloe, v. 557, and Bordeaux to Brienne, Oct. 12, 1656. Record Office Transcripts. The net value of the treasure to the exchequer given in the text is taken from Add. MSS. 32471, f. 15.

3 Firth and Rait, ii. 702, and the index for renewals.

4 Add. MSS. 32093, f. 389.

obtaining some £8,000 a year from this source. The actual yield during the Protectorate was as follows:[1]

		£
Michaelmas,	1654–5	5,746
"	1655–6	5,434
"	1656–7	5,748
"	1657–8	8,875
"	1658–Easter, 1659	5,448

Some complaints were heard during the Protectorate about this system, especially of the excessive sums exacted by the probate officers. It was also said in 1656 that the revenue then worth £8,000 or £9,000 a year would yield one-third more if the coercive power of sequestration for defaults in payment were substituted for that of excommunication.[2] At the Restoration the Court of Probate returned to the control of the Church and remained there until 1857.

THE POST OFFICE

The post office is the only instance to be found during the interregnum of a state-owned industry yielding a monopoly profit. Originally there had been more than one postal service, but Thomas Witherings (1633), who first charged fees for the King's post, had united the inland and foreign posts, and Edmund Prideaux, who was master of the posts as well as attorney-general in the Long Parliament, secured the suppression of the postal service of the London City Council as conflicting with a monopoly for which he paid £5,000 a year.[3] On June 1, 1653, the office having been put up to auction by the Government it was sold to Captain John Manley for £10,000, and an Act of Parliament passed in September, 1654, confirmed the grant and regulated the postal services.[4] At the expiration of Manley's two-year contract the office was sold to John Thurloe at the same figure and in August of that year the Protector gave orders for the regulation of the service, which were confirmed and extended

[1] See Appendix A.

[2] In Burton, i. 226 there is a short account of a debate on an Act of 1656; from this it appears that the salaries of the judges were first £300 and then £200 a year. See also *C.S.P. (Dom.)*, *1655–6*, 107–8.

[3] See H. Joyce, *History of the Post Office*; J. C. Hemmeon, *History of the British Post Office*; R. R. Sharpe, *London and the Kingdom*, ii. 322–3.

[4] *C.S.P. (Dom.)*, *1653–4*, 67. Firth and Rait, ii. 1007.

in an Act of June 9, 1657.[1] It was well known that Thurloe was entrusted with the control of the post offices for the purpose of spying on royalist and republican conspirators by opening and examining their correspondence. Thurloe did not, however, manage the financial side of the post office himself and appears to have employed Martin Noell as his agent. The postmaster paid £2,500 a quarter in advance into the exchequer, and the sum paid by Thurloe more than covered the costs of his secret service intelligence.[2] The organization of the post office on these lines continued throughout the century.

WINE LICENCES

Although the granting of licences to taverns to sell ale had from the beginning of the seventeenth century come to rest in the hands of the justices of the peace, the Stuart kings had used their prerogative to issue licences for the sale of wines.[3] This right had been farmed out to various individuals and efforts to bring in the arrears were made during the Protectorate.[4] The sub-committee of 1654 reported that in their opinion these licences could be made to raise £10,000 a year 'without exacting upon the Commonwealth'.[5] On June 20, 1655, Cromwell asked the treasury commissioners to examine the matter further and when the latter reported that the establishment of a wine licensing office was feasible, the Council of State appointed a committee to arrange the details. Ultimately, however, the customs commissioners were constituted the agents for regulating or farming these licences.[6]

[1] Firth and Rait, ii. 1110–13; *C.S.P.* (*Dom.*), *1655*, 285.

[2] See Firth, 'Thurloe and the Post Office', *English Historical Review*, 1898. Manley complained of having to pay in advance and said that his monopoly was not properly enforced. *C.S.P. 1653–4*, 327–8, 365; ibid., *1654*, 22–7, &c. On April 27, 1654, 'the money due from Mr. Manley, postmaster,' was ordered 'to be paid to G. Frost on account of the Council's contingencies', the fund out of which Thurloe was paid (ibid., 123, 240). In the exchequer rolls (pells), 1656–7 (E. 403/1757) Thurloe recorded three sums amounting to £3,852 received from Martin Noell 'for rent of postage of letters'. After Thurloe took over the post office, the figures recorded in the exchequer accounts vary in amount, being sometimes more and sometimes less than £10,000 a year; see Appendix A.

[3] Cf. S. and B. Webb, *History of Liquor Licensing in England* (1903).

[4] *C.S.P.* (*Dom.*), *1654*, 338, &c.

[5] The report of the sub-committee of the revenue of Dec. 4, 1654, is to be found in Add. MSS. 28854, Stowe MSS. 322, and Carte MSS. (Bodleian) 103.

[6] See *C.S.P.* (*Dom.*), *1655*, 342, 403–5, summarizing the recommendations of the

The Protector was optimistically allotted £5,000 a year out of the profits.

The licences in fact raised:[1]

		£
Michaelmas,	1654–5 . . .	370
„	1655–6 . . .	631
„	1656–7 . . .	2,700
„	1657–8 . . .	3,400
„	1658–Easter, 1659 .	1,200

THE TAX ON NEW BUILDINGS

The rate at which London and Westminster were expanding was long a cause of anxiety to seventeenth-century governments. Petty estimated in 1665 that there were 65,000 houses in London and thought so powerful a capital city a menace to the monarchy.[2] James I had introduced an Act to prevent further London building in 1611 and had levied fines by proclamation, an action which was much resented and only raised £4,000; further fines of this sort had been exacted under Charles I; the famous Puritan leather-seller Barbone or 'Barebones' is said to have proposed the renewal of this tax in 1653; and, finally, it had occurred to the advisers of Cromwell in 1657 to try again to make fines on new buildings a source of revenue.[3] A committee was appointed to draw up the details of the Bill and after some debate it passed the Commons and received the Protector's assent on June 26, 1657.[4] The Act was entitled 'for preventing the multiplicity of Buildings in and about the Suburbs of London and within ten miles of the same'. All houses built since March 24, 1620, without four acres of land attached to them, were to pay the value of a year's rent. The occupier was to pay the fine, half of which was due in

Committee of Council. *Clarke Papers*, iii. 123, notes that on June 17, 1656, the customs commissioners were appointed under the Great Seal commissioners for granting wine licences.

[1] See Appendix A.

[2] The estimate is in *Verbum Sapienti*, the remark about monarchy in *The Treatise of Taxes*: 'We might sometimes adde hereunto that housing is sometimes disproportionately taxed to discourage building, especially upon new Foundations, thereby to prevent the growth of a City; suppose London, such excessive and overgrown cities being dangerous to Monarchy, though the more secure when the supremacy is in Citizens of such places themselves, as in Venice'. *Works* (ed. Hull), i. 40.

[3] Gardiner, *History of England*, ii. 305–6, viii. 288.

[4] Burton, ii. 25 n.; Firth and Rait, ii. 1223.

the Michaelmas term, 1657, and half in the Easter term, 1658. The incidence of this tax was therefore that of a kind of capital levy on a limited class. The collectors of the tax were to receive 6*d.* in the pound. After September 29, 1657, a fine of £100 was to be imposed for any new building and £20 a month for each month it remained standing. Various exceptions were included in the Bill, the most important being that all houses built on lands sold by the Government were exempt. These exceptions involved a good deal of agitation in Parliament, and the committee which framed the Bill was so harassed by petitions that at least one member resigned.[1]

The clause about new buildings after the date of the Act was apparently intended to prohibit them altogether, but as the aim of the Act was fiscal, it was probably not enforced by the commissioners; for example, there is a note in the City of London Journals on February 19, 1658, that it was fined £234 for 'building contrary to the Act'.[2] A pamphlet, *Exceptions against the late Act for Preventing Multiplicity of Buildings* stated the case against the Act.[3] It claimed that the growth of London was entirely desirable, that the commissioners set up under the Act were both judges and jury in their cases, and that the Act was unjustly favourable to the City whose buildings within its own walls were exempted from fines whereas those in Westminster had to pay.

The tax yielded:[4]

	£
Michaelmas term, 1657 . .	11,798
Easter term, 1658 . . .	18,431
Michaelmas term, 1658 . .	10,718
	£40,947

The money was mostly borrowed and spent by the Government long before it had reached the exchequer,[5] and although the result of the Act was immediately to put a sum of money at its disposal, this fell far short of what had been hoped for, £400,000. On January 25, 1658, Cromwell informed the

1 Firth and Rait, ii. 159, &c.

2 Journal 41, f. 168.

3 There is a copy dated 1657 in the Goldsmiths' Library, South Kensington.

4 See Appendix A. Dr. Shaw made the total figure £41,377. Firth, ii. 212, n. 3.

5 See below, p. 101.

Speaker that 'some supplies designed by you for the public service, that of the buildings, hath not come in as was expected'.[1] It was, in fact, another instance of the enormous gap between estimated and actual revenue, and the numerous exceptions probably spoilt the rule. Nevertheless, Petty thought it a good tax when population was increasing, and it would have been re-enacted under Charles II had it not been for the Great Fire.[2]

SCOTTISH REVENUES

During the war between England and Scotland in 1651 the Scottish counties occupied by English troops were assessed towards the upkeep of the army instead of providing free quarter, while at the end of the war the estates of those who had fought against the English were confiscated and used towards the costs of the war and for maintaining fortresses along the border.[3] General Monk, who was left by Cromwell in command of the English army of occupation, was ordered to levy a monthly assessment of £10,000, but he soon wrote home to say that he found it very difficult to raise £8,000 a month and in fact the assessments seem only to have produced £7,500.[4] In accordance with the terms of the Act of Union (April 12, 1654), while customs duties between the two countries were abolished, the English systems of customs and excise were extended to Scotland. Hitherto excise had been unknown to the Scots. An ordinance of May 1655, ordered the levying of customs and excise at the same rates as those in force in England, and in August of the same year a commissioner was dispatched from London to regulate and farm out these taxes.[5] According to his report he succeeded

[1] *Letters and Speeches*, iii. 502.

[2] *Treatise of Taxes*, chap. iv. On June 3, 1663, some builders asked to be heard before 'the Act for New Building passes'. In the same year Sir John Denham, the Surveyor-General, was commissioned to inquire into the offences against the Act imposed by the late Parliament and to recover the fines due under it. These were granted to Col. Robert Lindsay. *C.S.P., 1663–4*, 164, 401–2.

[3] Gardiner, ii. 65, 67.

[4] Monk to Cromwell, July 23, 1654, in C. H. Firth, *Scotland and the Protectorate*, 146–8.

[5] See the introduction to the *Miscellany of Scottish Records* (1834), x–xxv and the Report of Thomas Tucker in ibid., 33–46, for the amounts of the farms. My calculation is only a rough one.

in letting the farms for about £48,820 a year, although in an audited account sent to Cromwell by General Monk in August 1657, these sources of revenue were given as worth £51,278, of which the excise on beer contributed some £35,000.[1] A manuscript estimate of all the sources of Scottish revenue except assessments dated June 11, 1657, made the total annual revenue £68,920,[2] so that together with the assessments, which were reduced by this date to £6,000 a month, the annual income from Scotland should have reached £140,000 a year. To receive these sources of revenue during the Protectorate, Lord Broghill, the president of the Scottish Council, established an exchequer court, modelled upon that of England and subordinated to it.[3] The annual charges in Scotland during the Protectorate were estimated at £25,943 for civil government and, after considerable reductions, £249,816 a year for the army.[4] It is therefore clear that the net cost of the union to England was at least £130,000 a year.

IRISH REVENUES

After the conquest of Ireland by Cromwell the country was settled by an English colony of 'Adventurers' who bought from the Government lands confiscated during the rebellion and contracted in return to pay assessments, customs, and excise towards the costs entailed by the army of occupation and the administration of the Lord Lieutenant and his council. According to an ordinance of June 23, 1654, the Adventurers were to pay £10,000 a month assessments for two years and then £12,000 a month for one year, the tax increasing thenceforward annually at the rate of £1,000 a month.[5] But actually this scheme proved unworkable and in fact the assessments were levied at £10,000 a month for three years from the date of the Act and then at £9,000 a

1 Thurloe, vi. 444.

2 Carte MSS. 73, f. 72, a paper compiled for Broghill. For assessments see above, p. 77. I have omitted from my calculation the special contribution of £45,000 towards the Spanish war.

3 *C.S.P.* (*Dom.*), *1655*, 322, 326. Thurloe, iv. 57, 326–30, &c.

4 Thurloe, vi. 444. Firth, *Scotland and the Commonwealth*, 114–19.

5 An Ordinance for the Further Encouragement of the Adventurers for Land in Ireland, Firth and Rait, ii. 924. The whole question of Irish finance is admirably dealt with in Firth, ii. 164–9.

month, while on March 25, 1657, a special levy of £20,000 a month for three months only was paid towards the expenses of the Spanish war.[1] Of the other Irish sources of revenue some idea can be gained from the figures for 1655 which survive and show a yield from the customs and excise of £37,258 in that year and from confiscated lands of £35,020;[2] so that the total Irish revenue (assuming that the assessments were worth their full amount) came to about £180,000 a year. As the army in Ireland alone cost £288,000 even after it had been largely reduced in size, there was a great gap between the revenue and expenditure. To fill this gap the English Government had to contribute to the revenues of the Irish out of its own assessments, and so far from Ireland being, as the Earl of Clarendon wrote, 'the great capital out of which all debts were paid',[3] the expenditure on that country cost England a minimum of first £32,000, then £17,000 and finally £8,000 a month.[4] This fact did not go uncriticized in the English Parliament and it was there argued that Ireland ought to pay high land taxes since the smallness of her population meant that her contribution from indirect taxes was much lower than that of England and Scotland. Moreover it was maintained that the Adventurers had had their lands so cheaply that they might reasonably be called upon to pay high taxes on them. Henry Cromwell, who was the effective head of the Irish government during his father's Protectorate, admitted that the lands there had been disposed of remarkably cheaply.[5]

In connexion with the indirect taxes, it is worth noticing that Thurloe strongly advised Henry Cromwell to meet the deficits, of which he constantly complained from 1655 onwards, by farming the customs and excise in the same way as was being done in England. This advice was reluctantly followed with the result that the customs alone trebled their yield.[6]

[1] See above, p. 77. [2] Thurloe, vi. 340. [3] *Life* (ed. 1888), ii. 218.

[4] Thurloe, ii. 631; vi. 538; *C.S.P.* (*Ireland*), *1647–60*, 817.

[5] Burton, ii. 211; Thurloe, iv. 509.

[6] This is stated by Petty, *Political Anatomy of Ireland*, *Works*, i. 197. Petty, as Henry Cromwell's secretary, should have been in a position to know. In a letter from Henry Cromwell to Thurloe, Oct. 6, 1657 (Lansdowne MSS. 822, f. 100), he says that only £25,000 a year net was obtained from the customs and excise, and in

CASUAL REVENUES

Among the papers of one of the treasury commissioners is a list of 'casual revenues' belonging, apparently, to June 1657.[1] The first three items in this list are sequestrations, prize goods, and 'Portugal money'. Sequestrations were revenues derived from royalist estates administered by parliamentary commissioners, a punishment inflicted on the owners for various reasons, generally for failure to pay taxes; in cases of treason the lands were entirely confiscated.[2] Estimates of the amounts likely to be raised annually from this source varied from £60,000 to £80,000; actually together with recusants' estates they appear to have produced £30,000 to £40,000.[3] Prize money has already been discussed. Neither of these two items were casual revenues in the sense that the yield from them was likely to disappear entirely, but merely in the sense that they might be expected to vary in amount considerably from year to year. The 'Portugal money' on the other hand was only one payment, made by the King of Portugal under the terms of the Treaty concluded in July 1654, as compensation for damage done to English ships; nominally the amount due was £50,000; actually £48,058 was paid.[4] The other items in this list consist of certain arrears and of money collected by the various special committees which had been set up by the Long Parliament for the purpose of selling capital resources which belonged to the State. Under the Act of September 2, 1654, these committees were instructed to pay their receipts into the exchequer, but they were not all wound up and continued to function in a small way throughout the Protectorate. The

a letter from Thurloe to Cromwell of Sept. 29, 1657, he says that £70,000 a year had been offered in England for the farm. This offer was accepted and the farm began in Apr. 1658. *C.S.P. (Dom.), 1657–8*, 287.

1 Among Edward Montague's papers, Carte MSS. 73, f. 15.

2 For a discussion of the character of sequestrations, see *inter alia*, Mrs. Green's introduction to the *Calendar of the Committee for Compounding*. Under the Excise Act of March 17, 1654, sequestration was one of the penalties imposed for non-payment. Generally those whose property was sequestered were allowed one-sixth of the revenues from their estates and the rest was paid into the exchequer.

3 Cf. Carte MSS. 74, f. 65; Add. MSS. 28854, f. 1; Lansdowne MSS. 232, f. 56 and Carte MSS. 73, f. 65; Add. MSS. 32471, f. 1.

4 Gardiner, ii. 477, n. 2. The money was paid into the exchequer on July 15, 1656. *Cromwelliana*, 157.

papers of these committees constitute the bulk of what are known as the 'Commonwealth Exchequer Papers'.[1] The value of the casual revenues is a matter of special interest because of the apparently contradictory assertions made by Cromwell and his opponents about them. According to Cromwell in his speech opening the first Protectorate Parliament:[2]

.... all your treasure was exhausted and spent, when this Government was undertaken: all *accidental* ways of bringing in treasure to a very inconsiderable sum, consumed; That is to say, the lands were sold, the sums on hand spent; rents, fee-farms, King's, Queen's, Prince's, Dean-and-Chapter's, delinquents' lands sold. These were *spent* when this Government was undertaken.... And that 's the reason why the taxes do yet lie so heavy upon the people....

On the other hand, Colonel Birch and his fellow republicans maintained that a large number of resources had been left by the Long Parliament available for Cromwell's use.[3] But the following figures indicate the truth of Cromwell's assertion:

1. Value of bishops' lands sold:[4]
   1647–53: £675,603; 1654–8: £784.
2. Value of deans-and-chapters' lands sold:[5]
   1647–53: £428,621; 1654–8: £27,000.
3. Value of fee-farm rents sold:[6]
   1647–53: £509,712; 1654–8: £16,822.

Judging by the warrants for payments out of the sale of the king's goods, which survive in the Record Office, the same story could be told in an even more marked way if we possessed the complete accounts of the commissioners responsible for this.[7]

Only one more source of casual revenue, which is not included in this list, but may be placed in the same category, need be mentioned, namely the 'decimation'.[8] This was a

[1] These form category S.P. 28 in the Record Office and vary greatly in quality; they are more important for military than for economic history.

[2] *Letters and Speeches*, ii. 357–8.

[3] Burton, iii. 58 and 60 n., but see this debate *passim* for the accusations that Cromwell wasted the national treasure, and for more detailed discussion above, p. 38 seq.

[4] Rawlinson MSS. B. 239.

[5] W. A. Shaw, *A History of the English Church*, Appendix vii.

[6] S.P. 28/286, account book headed 'sale of Fee Farm Rents by Sir John Wollaston', &c.

[7] These warrants are in S.P. 28/285 but seem incomplete.

[8] The fullest discussion, based on printed sources, of the decimations, remains

10 per cent. property tax imposed upon all royalists and levied by the eleven Major-Generals who were established in the counties in 1655. Naturally, owing to the varied distribution of the royalists in the counties, the decimation yielded a great deal less in some of the eleven Major-Generals' districts than in others. Hence, although they were originally instructed to pay the money they raised directly to the militia of their own counties, Major-General Goffe soon 'took the humble boldness to offer that all the money raised upon this account may be brought to the common treasury, and that we may all be paid alike out of the said treasury; or else I fear those associations that raise least money will have such a pitiful militia that the Major-Generals will have little honour or comfort in commanding them'. In due course this was done, the distribution of the decimation being put under the control of the army treasurers and the Army Committee.[1] But although no excessive difficulty was found in collecting the tax which, like the building fines, was a capital levy on a limited class of the community, the amounts realized did not suffice to pay for the militias which were commanded by the Major-Generals, and as soon as Parliament met, it refused to re-impose this tax which had been levied without its consent.

TOTAL REVENUE

We conclude this examination of the taxes of the Protectorate with the total *net* yields for each financial year. These totals exclude the Scottish and Irish revenues[2] and one or two casual items are also omitted. In comparing these figures with the figures of expenditure, it must be remembered that the latter are only approximate, *include* most administrative costs and in most cases contain the arrears owing from the previous year. Therefore each difference between the two sets of figures is equivalent to the total debt of the

D. W. Rannie's article on 'Cromwell's Major-Generals' in the *English Historical Review*, x. 471.

[1] *C.S.P.* (*Dom.*), *1655–6*, 140, 367–8; Thurloe, iv. 497–8. Mr. Rannie wrote 'the council appointed what it called an army committee', etc. He was apparently unaware that this committee had been in existence since the beginning of the civil war.

[2] See above, pp. 90, 91.

Government at that point of time and not merely the debt for that particular year:[1]

	Revenues paid into the Exchequer	*Assessments*	*Total Revenues*	*Expenditure*
	£	£	£	£
1654	800,596	785,579	1,586,175	2,877,079
1655	871,873	697,732	1,579,605	2,327,512
1656	1,018,803	796,745	1,815,548	2,067,357
1657	953,438	380,976	1,334,414	2,878,174
1658	832,498	333,036	1,165,534	2,197,985

[1] The revenues paid into the exchequer are from E. 401/1402–6, 1930–2, the assessments from E. 351/305. For the character and value of the figures of expenditure, see above, p. 46 seq.

X

THE PUBLIC DEBT AND ITS INFLUENCE ON THE FALL OF THE PROTECTORATE

A STUDY of Government expenditure and the yield of the taxes during the Protectorate has made it amply clear, despite the absence of annual budgets, that there was a regular deficit in the national accounts. Besides being faced with the necessity of meeting these deficits the Government had as far as possible to anticipate its revenue year by year and hence experienced a twofold pressure to borrow.

At this period the English Government was relatively backward in its methods of public borrowing.[1] In the United Provinces a number of modern practices including annuities already existed. In France a complicated but nevertheless effective system of *rentes* was to be found, not only in Paris, but also in provincial cities; and various schemes for floating the public debt had long been tried in the north Italian States. Students of public finance have found in England during the interregnum and the years immediately preceding and succeeding it certain methods of loaning money to the Government which seem to them to have foreshadowed the scientific funding of the national debt and the foundation of the Bank of England. Nevertheless, it is well to admit frankly that these methods are mainly of antiquarian interest; that they were often expedients little prized by their authors; and that it is very difficult to show any real continuity between them and the significant financial achievements of the eighteenth century. Necessity was of course the mother of invention, and similar difficulties bred similar expedients until by a process of trial and error a satisfactory system of Government borrowing was evolved. But it is not easy to point with confidence to any steps taken by Cromwell's advisers that were steps in the right direction.

The place where lenders had primarily to be sought was the City of London, but the question for Cromwell was how they were to be approached, as individuals, as groups, or

[1] While acknowledging my indebtedness to Mr. W. Harper's 'Public Borrowing, 1640–60', I must state that I am unable to agree with some of his conclusions.

through the agency of the City government. To consider the last method first. London had been a Roundhead stronghold, the very heart of the Puritan movement, and during the stress of the English civil war had contributed generously to the parliamentary war chest. Up to the year 1647 Parliament had regular recourse to the City Chamber (the Corporation treasury) which not only lent money on the security of the assessed and other taxes, but also acted as intermediary between the Government and the livery companies for this purpose.[1] But whereas John Pym and other parliamentarians were trusted by the City, the army leaders, largely because of their religious views, were not. Cromwell was by no means *persona grata* with the City government and it did not once agree during the Protectorate to lend him money in its corporate capacity. Indeed, it went further and protested regularly and vehemently against the share which it had to pay of the national taxes. In a petition of November 1656, showing 'why the arrears of assessments are not paid',[2] which has already been quoted, the first reason advanced was

> The vast sum they and not the rest of the Nation have lent and paid to the State in the late troubles One Hundred Thousand Pounds at one time, fifty Subsidies at another time Ten Thousand Pounds a week:— pounds a month for the weekly meal tax when the Army was under the conduct of the Earl of Essex and £80,000 at the new modelling thereof. . . .

The second reason given was that

> When the rest of the Nation hath bene plundered they have borne a deeper share thereof by reason of the debts oweing to them in those parts.

It seems in fact certain that a large part of the money owed to the City by the Long Parliament was never repaid.

On January 9, 1655, the City Council received a petition begging it to approach Parliament on the subject of the debt owing to the general public;[3] on January 16 it drew up a petition on this subject;[4] and on April 10 it appointed a committee to consider how to get back money borrowed from the City Chamber which had been heavily involved in debt as a result of its loans to the Government.[5] On December 3,

[1] See *inter alia* C. M. Clode, *London during the Great Rebellion* (1892).
[2] Journal 41, f. 142. [3] Ibid., f. 113v. [4] Ibid., f. 115. [5] Ibid., f. 116v.

1656, the City Council drafted another petition to the same effect,[1] but there is no indication either in the records of the City or of the Government that these petitions had more than minor successes. It is therefore not surprising, apart from any political considerations, that the City refused to lend to the Protector; but their refusal was not due to any lack of importunity on his part. In October 1655 he vainly approached the City magnates for £80,000 with which to pay off Blake's fleet, and in March 1658 he turned to them again, but 'they openly refused'.[2]

It does not appear that the City companies lent any more willingly to the Protector than did the City Chamber. The difficulty that they had experienced in getting back the sums they had advanced in 1642–3 made them very shy; and when the chartered trading companies lent to the Government it was less a loan than a payment for the confirmation of their privileges. One company we know to have made a loan to Cromwell which it could hardly refuse. The East India Company was awarded £85,000 damages to be paid by its Dutch rivals at the end of the Anglo-Dutch war.[3] Fifty thousand pounds of this was retained by the Government, and, although the loan was acknowledged among the debts of the State, it was never repaid.[4]

One of the commonest and crudest systems of anticipating revenue used under the Tudors and Stuarts was tax farming. The farmer paid a lump sum in advance and collected as much as he could at a fixed rate. Under the Protectorate the two biggest taxes, the customs and excise, were not farmed but put out on commission and the commissioners were paid so much in the pound for their trouble. They also had to advance a large part of the anticipated revenue as part of the regular duty of their office. Towards the end of the Protectorate the Government conceived that it could obtain more ready money by reverting to the old practice of farming. Some of the smaller taxes, e.g. the coal customs, the issues

[1] Ibid., f. 144.

[2] Thurloe, iv. 79; *Clarke Papers*, iii. 60; cf. *C.S.P.* (*Venetian*), *1655–6*, 239; ibid., *1657–9*, 173.

[3] See below, p. 113.

[4] Sir William Hunter said it was 'punctually repaid', but this has been conclusively refuted by Sir William Foster, intro. to *Court Minutes of the East India Company, 1655–9*, vi–vii.

of jurors, and the wine licences, were already let on farm. But the proposal was by no means popular even with the commissioners, who were after all the very City financiers whose tenders would be solicited for the farms. In the end only a portion of the excise was let in farms and the remainder of the customs and excise was collected by sub-commissioners. From the point of view of the Government it is possibly true, as Thurloe asserted, that farming was more profitable, more especially as the commissioners were able promptly to reimburse themselves for their advances plus the current rate of interest out of the taxes they were collecting. But under Cromwell advances from the commissioners was undoubtedly the commonest way of anticipating the revenue.

Another smaller and older method of anticipating the revenue was by means of exchequer tallies, the equivalent of the modern treasury bill. These were issued to certain classes of government creditors and made payable upon a particular fund. During the Protectorate they were practically confined to the excise.

Cromwell also made some use of individual lenders, especially Noell and Vyner, who were given the current rates of interest on all money paid out by them on behalf of the exchequer, while they obtained additional profits by carrying out various contracts for the Government. The student of the Cromwellian treasury records should bear in mind the variety of work that Cromwell called upon these men to do as his financial agents. They had to act as remittance agents for forwarding sums of money to British envoys and garrisons abroad, to arrange for the disposal of prizes captured at sea and for the marketing and minting of imported bullion. Most of the large sums of money paid by the Government to individual financiers which figure among the Record Office papers can be connected with work of this kind. Noell appears occasionally to have advanced money without specific security,[1] but as a rule taxes had to be hypothecated to meet all Government loans. The Venetian envoy in London related how when in 1658 the Protector was short of money and had

[1] e.g. on Jan. 26, 1655, he was repaid £400 lent 'att the speciall instance of his Highness' E. 403/1546. But in Nov. 1654, he had lent £16,000 on the security of the excise. *C.S.P.* (*Dom.*), *1654*, 393.

turned to the City of London for a loan which had been refused,

> Being unable in the present crisis to have recourse to severe measures and compel them to contribute, and to avoid further cause of offence, he applied to a particular merchant, who is a supporter of his, to supply him with money, assigning to him for payment the revenue of the excise or new impost and further pledging the £90,000 which is kept apart, being the amount collected for the Protestants of Piedmont. In this way he has obtained from the merchants an advance of £200,000 [sufficient to satisfy the soldiers].[1]

We need not place full confidence in the details of this story. One other outstanding example of hypothecating taxes to individual City financiers is to be found in the case of the tax on new buildings. Sir Thomas Vyner (£4,000), Sir Christopher Packe (£4,000), Sir Thomas Andrews (£3,000), Sir John Dethicke, Sir Thomas Foote and Sir John Ireton (£2,500 each) all lent money on the security of the Act, which was duly repaid in the course of 1658.[2]

The position of the individual lender to the Government was by no means a sinecure. This path to great wealth, as a few examples will show, was beset with many pitfalls. Samuel Vassal, one of the London M.P.s in the Long Parliament and a big merchant in the Portugal and African trades, who had staked his future in the Roundhead cause, lived to regret it. In June 1655, he was petitioning the Council of State for the repayment of £20,000 owing to him, alleging that without it he and his six children would starve. Although in the following May Parliament advised that he should be given £2,591 on account, bankruptcy was not staved off, for in the next year we read of him again petitioning, but this time as a prisoner of the Upper Bench.[3]

Customs commissioners were no more fortunate than Vassal. Samuel Avery, the principal commissioner from 1654–9, although M.P. for London in the first Protectorate Parliament and Governor of the Merchant Adventurers, found himself in the Fleet prison in 1656, and attributed his plight to his inability to recover part of the sum of money

1 *C.S.P.* (*Venetian*), *1657–9*, 174–5.

2 E. 403/2818, *passim*; cf. *C.S.P.* (*Dom.*), *1659–60*, 290.

3 *C.S.P.*(*Dom.*), *1654*, 81; ibid., *1655*, 214; ibid., *1656–7*, 384; ibid., *1658–9*, 48.

advanced by him to the Government when he was commissioner.[1] Edmund Harvey, who had acted as chief customs commissioner in succession to Avery and also sat in the first Protectorate Parliament, spent most of the succeeding years as a prisoner in the Tower, while the Government tried to obtain from him and his partners sums which were due from them out of the customs.[2]

Finally, the sad end of the great Martin Noell is not perhaps generally known. He had, as we have seen, involved himself in every conceivable kind of governmental financial venture. In England, Scotland, Ireland, and the West Indies he seemed dependent on the stability of the Cromwellian régime. The fall of Richard Cromwell and the depression of 1659–60 left him in a critical situation.[3] However, by some means or other (about which we can only speculate) he insinuated himself into the good graces of Charles II. He and his eldest son were in turn knighted by the restored monarch; although in 1661–2 Noell's debts 'grew big, and his Creditors cloudy brow'd. However, falling afterwards upon some branches of the Public Revenue, both in England and Ireland, he stopt his greatest Leaks, and bore fairly away before the wind'. But evidently he never really recovered from his financial enterprises on behalf of Thurloe and the Cromwells. When he and his wife were carried off by the Plague of London in 1665, his seven children were left unprovided for and his executors still optimistically but hopelessly included in his assets a miscellany of debts owed to him by the Government of the Protectorate.[4]

In addition to borrowing in the City the Long Parliament had made use of a critical situation to institute a forcible system of borrowing from the general public on a large scale. While forced loans were exacted from defeated royalists by the Committee for the Advance of Money, the supporters of Parliament were given 'public faith' bonds bearing interest at 8 per cent.[5] The holders of these bonds were often soldiers and quite poor people, but in many cases their loans

[1] *C.S.P.* (*Dom.*), *1656–7*, 84.
[2] Ibid., *1655–6*, 219, 273, &c.
[3] See below, p. 178.
[4] G. Robinson, *The Accompt of the Estate of Sir Martin Noell* (1677).
[5] *C.S.P.* (Committee for the Advance of Money), intro.

were never fully repaid. But the richer bond-holders were offered the option of 'doubling' on them; that is to say, if they advanced a further sum equivalent to that which they were already owed they would be given a first charge upon a fund to be derived from some form of State property or income, e.g. the State forests or the excise. This expedient of doubling was apparently invented by the City Council as a means of obtaining some definite mortgage for its early loans.[1] But the undoubled public faith bill was worth very little, although spasmodic efforts were made by the Protectorate Government to marshal its liabilities. On the other hand, the fact that Abraham Granger, who had already lost his ears for forgery, was arrested in 1655 for a widely spread and successful conspiracy to forge public faith bills[2] is in itself a sufficient refutation of the idea that they were entirely without value. In one of Granger's confessions he asserted that four-fifths of the public faith bills in existence were counterfeited and two-thirds of the claims for their repayment were false.[3] This assertion gave the Government a justification (or an excuse?) for further postponing debt settlement.

Together with these bills and suffering in the same way from forgery and rapid depreciation there were the debentures, which were issued to the soldiers as security for their arrears of pay. These were treasury orders payable as and when funds were available to meet them. They were theoretically not assignable instruments of credit, but in fact they became so, and army officers did a considerable trade by making advances on them to their men. Samuel Chidsley, a solicitor, native of Hitchin, was engaged in the course of 1653 in an agitation to obtain the repayment of debentures and public faith bills.[4] He complained that a committee set up by the Long Parliament on April 27, 1652, to examine the subject had done nothing but produce a doubling bill, and announced his intention of appealing at once to the Nominated Parliament. His importunities had evidently some effect, for on October 7, the Council of State gave

[1] City Journal, 40, f. 191. Some authors attribute the invention of doubling to a certain Dr. Barger.

[2] *C.S.P.* (*Dom.*), *1653–4*, *passim*; Whitelocke, 433.

[3] Ibid., *1654*, 397.

[4] S. Chidsley, *A Remonstrance* (1653); *A Further Remonstrance* (1654).

orders that lists of all persons who had received public faith bills or had paid money on them or had paid soldiers' accounts should be sent in to it by the following March.[1] In May a sum of money was assigned as the balance of £600 due to the very small debtors of the State who were owed amounts under £10.[2] On November 22 an Act was passed for 'disafforestation', the proceeds of which were to be subject in part to a charge for the repayment of public faith bills held by those who had exercised the option of doubling.[3] The first Protectorate Parliament seems to have done little beyond receiving petitions on the subject[4] and investigating the extent of Granger's fraud, but the second set up a committee to 'state and ascertain' the debt.[5] The committee reported that the public faith had been engaged to all who had lent money on security of Act of Parliament, that the county commissioners for assessments should be empowered to receive all claims, should distinguish between money lent willingly or unwillingly and with or without interest, and should draw up lists of claimants by counties. Finally, Parliament resolved that no further Irish or forest lands should be disposed of until the public faith debts had been satisfied.[6] It was in the course of this debate that Sir William Strickland offered the gloomy remark that, 'The Public Faith of the Nation is now become a public despair', but he added, 'rather than that faith should be violated I would give a great part of what I have'.[7] The votes of Parliament were duly reported to the committee and lists ordered to be compiled, but as far as can be ascertained the matter went no further.[8]

From the date of the dissolution of the second Protectorate Parliament the financial situation of Cromwell's Government grew daily more difficult. The supplies voted for the Spanish war had not come up to expectations; the City had been vainly approached for succour; the army and navy petitioned with menacing regularity for the payment of their supplies and arrears. 'The great want is money', wrote Thurloe in

[1] *C.S.P.* (*Dom.*), *1653–4*, 190.
[2] Ibid., *1654*, 38, 159–60.
[3] Ibid., *1653–4*, 264–5.
[4] Cf. e.g. Whitelocke, *Memorials*, 591; *C.S.P.* (*Dom.*), *1655*, 167.
[5] *C.J.* vii. 466; Burton, i. 93.
[6] *C.J.* vii. 556–7.
[7] Burton, ii. 238.
[8] *C.S.P.* (*Dom.*), *1657–8*, 43, 75–6.

March,[1] 'which puts us to the wall in all our business'. How was money to be raised? It could not be borrowed on a large scale. The perpetuation of the decimation had been decisively rejected both by Parliament and by Cromwell. The only solution left was to recall Parliament. 'Parliaments are so casual', wrote Henry Cromwell to Thurloe on March 31, 1658,[2] 'that one would not profane them by overfrequency; and yet, on the other side, to raise money without them is a condition from which I pray God to keep us'. Throughout the summer the dispatches of the French ambassador from London were full of rumours that Parliament was to be summoned, but political reasons made this almost impossible. Every public treasury was searched for money 'though not with all that success as was desired'.[3] In July Cromwell approached the City aldermen individually, but only succeeded in raising a few thousands to send out to Dunkirk.[4] Thus on his father's death Richard entered into a barren heritage.[5]

The first step Richard took to meet this situation was to ask Cardinal Mazarin for a loan of £50,000.[6] This was refused except in return for the surrender of Dunkirk, to which Richard was not prepared to agree. It would be interesting to know who prompted this request. Oliver never begged the French for money, but it was a habit which was to become characteristic of English ministers for the next thirty years. The well-known story that Richard was unable to pay for his father's funeral seems true, for it cost twenty or thirty thousand pounds;[7] and the attempt to borrow fifty thousand from the French occurred before the funeral took place.

At length, however, Richard found the money to pay

1 Thurloe, vii. 4. 2 Ibid., 39. 3 Ibid., 99.

4 Ibid., 295. The banker to whom Cromwell applied was Edward Backwell, who advanced £65,260 towards the upkeep of Dunkirk between Aug. 1, 1658, and Mar. 7, 1659. (See Richards, *Early History of Banking*, 31–3.)

5 Cf. Bordeaux to Brienne, Sept. 23, 1658 (Record Office transcripts).

6 The first of the letters on this subject dated Sept. 5, 1654, is in Guizot, and others are among the Record Office transcripts.

7 Twenty-eight thousand pounds is the figure given in the *Clarke Papers*, iii. 168 which is probably more correct than that of Heath (*Flagellum*), who says £60,000. According to the *C.S.P.* (*Dom.*), *1658–9*, xi, in Aug. 1659 £19,303 was still owing for the funeral.

three months' wages to the army, to which £1,200,000 was said to be owing, and on November 5 the Venetian envoy reported from England that Parliament would be summoned directly after the funeral as the exchequer was bare.[1] Parliament met on January 27, 1659, but owing to the obstructionist tactics of the republicans two months passed before it had time to turn its full attention to the subject of the public finance. Meanwhile, a committee under the chairmanship of Mr. Scawen had been set up to investigate the whole financial position of the Commonwealth, and on April 7 it reported that the governmental debt amounted to £1,888,352.[2] Thurloe contended that the report by overstating the expenditure in Ireland and Scotland, omitting the revenues of Dunkirk and the debt owed by the excise farmers, had exaggerated the amount of the whole debt which was really only £1,384,000.[3] Modern historians have, however, accepted the accuracy of Scawen's report[4] and £2,000,000 may be taken as a roughly accurate figure of the Government's liabilities at the end of the Protectorate. The bulk of this amount was of course due to the army and navy. According to the report they were owed respectively £801,055 and £541,465. The navy commissioners complained that their credit was so bad that even candles could be bought by them only for ready money.[5] The army demanded not only a settlement of arrears but a rise in pay. While Parliament was sitting the officers of the army began to cabal, using the debt owed to them by the Government as a powerful instrument of agitation. On April 9[6] Scawen propounded to Parliament a scheme for providing three months' pay for the soldiers, but the conspiracy of General Fleetwood and Desborough had gone too far to be checked by such palliatives. Richard was no soldier and was unpopular with the army and could rely only on the Scottish and Irish forces. 'It is clear', wrote the French ambassador on April 21,[7] 'that the majority of the Parliament is well disposed towards the Protector, but since his power

[1] *C.S.P.* (*Venetian*), *1657–9*, 261.

[2] *C.J.* vii. 627–31 has a copy of the report which makes the debt £2,247,290 minus £358,938 (643).

[3] Burton, iv. 365–7.

[4] Notably Prof. Scott and Dr. Shaw.

[5] *C.S.P.* (*Dom.*), *1658–9*, 87.

[6] *C.J.* vii. 633–4.

[7] Bordeaux to Brienne, Record Office transcripts.

depends on the army, if that should turn against him Parliament could not support him.' This in effect is what happened. The council of officers overthrew Cromwell and with the acquiescence of the City established a council of ten which issued three months' pay out of funds available in the exchequer, presumably those that had been accumulated in accordance with the proposals of Scawen's committee. It is therefore quite clear that it was Richard's weakness not Oliver's debts that overthrew the Cromwellian Protectorate.

An eminent modern historian has written that Cromwell's failure as a financier paved the way for the Restoration.[1] In doing so he was accepting the view not only of Cromwell's republican opponents, but also to a certain extent that of the contemporary French ambassador. But financial history must be in the main a question of figures and of the correct interpretation of figures rather than of *obiter dicta*. It is therefore necessary to examine carefully the reason for and the significance of the two million pounds debt inherited by Richard Cromwell from his father.

In this chapter it has been demonstrated that the debt was not the product of personal extravagance on Cromwell's part, that he did his best to cut down his expenditure on his accession to the Protectorate, and that this debt was accumulated essentially because of his inability to borrow except on very definite security and at short term rates, as was instanced in the case of the building tax. In February 1658, a royalist news-letter stated that the City would only lend money to the Government 'on the security of county estates'.[2] But some years before this Cromwell had no county estates left to offer.

A more justifiable condemnation of Cromwell's policy is in connexion with his erroneous belief that the Spanish war would pay its way. As Roger Coke wrote, 'Cromwell's expedition to Hispaniola from which he expected Mountains of Gold, proved not only dishonourable, but thereby he contracted so great a Debt, as he could never live to outgrow.'[3]

[1] Prof. Andrews in the *Cambridge History of the British Empire*, i. 315; cf. Prof. Tanner in the *Cambridge Modern History*, iv. 477.

[2] *C.S.P.* (*Clarendon*), *1657–60*, 15.

[3] *A Detection of the Court and State of England*, 397.

The £400,000 which Parliament promised him to pay for the war was inadequate and was not realized by the taxes allocated. Charles II was treated in the same way by an equally subservient Parliament over the second Dutch war. Yet the assertion of many writers that the Spanish war caused a shrinkage in the indirect taxes cannot be sustained with any certainty. If the Venetian envoy told his Government that the customs yielded little,[1] 'as owing to the war with the Catholic king the trade which brought the largest amount of gold to the exchequer is interrupted', the French ambassador told his Government (and there was no reason for him to deceive it) in this same year, 1658,[2] that the war had not materially damaged the customs receipts.

Apart from the problem of the reason for this debt, it is important to remember that the debt itself would by no means have been insurmountable in ordinary circumstances of political security. It was roughly equivalent to a year's revenue. In France during the same period the Government was not merely one but three years in debt.[3] In the United Netherlands, as in England, heavy taxes had to be paid to meet military expenditure, and in 1650 its debt was 120,000,000 gulden (or about £11,000,000). Indeed, Sir George Downing, ambassador at The Hague at this date, and himself an able financier, wrote to say that if England wished to maintain its powerful position among nations it must raise and not lower its taxes.[4] The Cromwells' basic difficulty was that for political reasons they were unable to create a funded debt in England.

The real interest of the financial policy of Oliver Cromwell is not that its extravagance and incompetence 'explains' the Restoration, but that it stereotyped the fiscal expedients produced under the stress of civil war. The excise and the land tax were to become a permanent part of the national sources of revenue. Henceforward squire, shop-keeper, manufacturer, and the poorest beer drinker had to contribute in a visible

[1] Report of March 15, 1658, cited above, p. 101, n. 1.

[2] Report of Sept. 18, 1658, Record Office transcripts. The report is quoted in full below, p. 143.

[3] Cf. G. Martin, *Histoire du Crédit Publique en France sous . . . Louis XIV* (1913).

[4] Cf. Blok, *History of the People of the Netherlands*, chap. vii; *Clarke Papers*, iii. 177–8.

manner to the State expenditure. No poll tax was exacted during the interregnum and before many years it was to fall into disuse. By its institution of a convoy tax the Government recognized the fiscal importance of foreign trade. By the final break-down of the system of allocating specific taxes to specific services, a sectional system of finance gave way to a general system over which Parliament exercised control through the appropriation of supplies, the germ of which can perhaps be seen in the grant of £400,000 voted especially for the Spanish war. Moreover, although Cromwell's Government did not succeed in dispensing altogether with the services of tax farmers, the full control exercised both over them and over the tax commissioners by the treasury and the Council of State pointed the way to better things.

Finally, the constitutional aspect of Cromwell's financial policy is a striking illustration of the continuity of history. We have seen how on his accession to the protectoral throne Oliver took it for granted that the twenty-seventh article of the 'Instrument of Government' empowered him to collect an ordinary revenue from customs, excise, assessments, and other sources. But public protests were made against his doing so, the Instrument being interpreted to mean a full parliamentary control of all taxation; and when Parliament met in the autumn of 1654 it claimed to control not merely Cromwell's extraordinary revenue, but his ordinary revenue as well. Cromwell was forced to accept the position. All revenues except a few casual incomings and the monthly assessments went through the exchequer course, and both his Parliaments tried to get control over or even abolish the monthly assessment. The reduction in assessments towards the end of the Protectorate and Cromwell's 'modest denial of assuming the legislature of the nation' in imposing them were in fact surrenders to the landed interest in Parliament. With the substitution of the excise for the feudal dues it was no longer possible for the head of the executive to 'live of his own'. Cromwell made a few unavailing efforts to tax without Parliament's consent, but both he and his son were driven by sheer want of money to summon Parliaments. From the Protectorate onwards parliamentary control over taxation became a reality. To rule without Parliament was to rule without money. And thus Charles II was driven into the arms of Louis XIV.

In some respects, therefore, so far as financial history is concerned, the Protectorate, both from its fiscal and constitutional aspects, marks the waning of the Middle Ages.

XI

THE GOVERNMENT AND THE CHARTERED TRADING COMPANIES

DURING the first half of the seventeenth century English foreign trade was largely in the hands of commercial companies. Each company was allotted by royal grant a market in which to trade and all merchants interested in that market had to be members of the appropriate company. Only one of the bigger companies, the East India, was a joint-stock company, and that not altogether in the modern sense of the term. The principle of limited liability had not yet been legally recognized, nor was the capital of the company of a permanent character but was subscribed only for one voyage or a group of voyages. From their very inception the trading companies had a chequered career. They suffered violent public criticism as monopolies, were forced to pay considerable sums of money to the Crown for the maintenance of their privileges, and even then were liable to find themselves suddenly faced with rivals set up almost at the mere caprice of the Stuart kings. For example, both the bigger companies, the East India and the Merchant Adventurers, had under the early Stuarts to engage in a difficult and long-drawn-out contest with rival groups trading actively in their markets with full royal approval. Moreover, the promoters of agitation against company monopolies were most often themselves would-be monopolists who were anxious to obtain a foothold in the distant fields of profitable enterprise discovered by the pioneers and fortified by the military posts of the original adventurers.[1]

Public agitation against the monopolies of corporate companies received considerable and much more disinterested support as a result of the Puritan revolution, firstly, because the wasteful and expensive method of indirect taxation through the agency of companies was generally regarded as not the least of the royal misdemeanours, and secondly, because Puritan thought, especially among the Independents

[1] This fact has been established with many illustrations in W. R. Scott, *Joint Stock Companies*, vol. i.

and the Quakers, genuinely regarded the limitation of trade to members of companies as contrary to natural justice and the Christian law.[1] During the civil wars existing strongholds of industrial monopolies fell with local government oligarchies and lay broken, unregretted by the rulers of the State;[2] but since commerce involved issues of naval and foreign policy and was necessarily more dependent upon a system of centralized organization, its problems were less easily decided by the simple conceptions of Puritan economic theory.

The history of commerce in the mid-seventeenth century is therefore essentially the history of trading companies—not even the chill blast of the Puritan revolution could do more than shake them—and to arrive at a clear understanding of Cromwell's commercial policy it is necessary to study briefly the history of the English companies and their rivals after the interruption of trade consequent upon the civil war.

The East India Company[3] was long 'alleged to lie out of the common rules of trade',[4] and the attacks made upon it came from merchants who were actually engaged in the trade rather than from outside opinion. The East India merchants had, it is true, to defend themselves as exporters of bullion and importers of luxuries against the cruder criticisms of ignorant nationalists, but intelligent men knew that they traded predominantly in re-exports and that their privileges had a basis of justice in the diplomatic and military expenses incurred by them in dealing with native traders in far-off lands. The Government had little reason to grumble at a company which made ample use of English shipping and brought home a regular supply of the raw materials of gunpowder. Furthermore, the criticisms of the Company put forward by merchants were by no means on account of its being a monopoly, but because it was maintained that the joint-stock principle was inelastic and precluded that maximization of profit obtainable by a number of individuals each engaging

[1] See above, pp. 34–6.

[2] Cf. M. James, *Social Policy during the Puritan Revolution* (1931), chaps. iv and v.

[3] J. Bruce, *Annals of the Hon. East India Company* (1818); W. W. Hunter, *A History of British India* (1900); W. Foster, Introductions to the calendars of *Court Minutes of the East India Company, 1640–59* (1907).

[4] Cf. 'Britannia Languens' (1680) in MacCulloch, *Early English Tracts*, 335.

separately in the business and benefiting from the fixed capital as well as the monopoly of the company. This latter method of commercial organization was known as 'regulation' as distinct from joint stock.

That the Long Parliament was not hostile to the East India Company is shown by the approval it bestowed upon an agreement concluded between all the competing groups of East India merchants, who formed a United Joint Stock at the beginning of 1650. Throughout the next two years the rivalry of the Dutch was the chief concern of the Company, but when war actually broke out between the two countries it was injurious to Dutch and English traders alike, especially as the native Indian rulers feared to do business with either, lest they should offend the other. The effects of the war on the fortunes of the United Joint Stock were important and significant. It does not seem in the long run to have damaged the Company seriously, as a dividend of 205 per cent. was paid on the stock stretching over a period of six years. The Dutch Company was forced to pay £85,000 in damages to the English Company in settlement of a variety of past claims. Moreover, the treaty awarded to the English Company the valuable island of Pulo Run in the Bandas. But whether because they were dissatisfied with the profits of the stock or because they believed the trade was so rich that it could be more profitably managed by 'a company under good regulation with freedom and liberty to supply their own factors, stock and ships',[1] the groups which had coalesced to form the United Joint Stock broke up into their original elements at the end of the war, and the old supporters of the method of regulation, headed by Maurice Thompson and including no less personages than Andrew Riccard, Martin Noell, Richard Hutchinson, and John Blackwell, besought the Protector to leave the trade alone and not renew Government approval for a joint stock. For the next three years the trade was thrown open to all comers. The Protector and Council of State were besieged with petitions and counter-petitions from the rival groups, but found themselves too busy to attend to the matter. Nevertheless, it is important to appreciate that both sides expected the State to take action in

[1] Petition of Sept. 21, 1654, *Court Minutes, 1650–4*, 340.

the matter, and the Government fully acknowledged that it was of political significance. In 1654 the Treasury borrowed £60,000 out of the £85,000 paid over by the Dutch;[1] in 1656 Cromwell requested the Company to colonize Pulo Run; and in both these ways the corporate existence of the Company was recognized.

From 1654 to 1657 trade continued actively between England and India. Maurice Thompson dispatched eleven ships on his own account and the United Joint Stock sent out three ships in 1656, while a syndicate was formed by members of the Company and merchants outside it to compete with the numerous private adventurers who now interested themselves in the trade.

The enemies of chartered companies were to look back upon these years as a golden age:

> whilst the Trade was open, viz. in the years, 54 to 55 and 56, our Merchants sold the Indian Commodities so low, that they furnished more parts of Europe than since we have done, nay, Holland and Amsterdam itself; and this very much sunk the actions of the Dutch East India Company: a thing which stands with reason; and which therefore recommends an open Trade to India. . . .[2]

The Company continued throughout these years to press Cromwell for a new charter authorizing the formation of a joint stock. But it was rumoured that the Protector favoured the Maurice Thompson group;[3] and considering his intimate relations with Noell, a member of this group, the rumour would appear to have been well founded. A committee of the Council of State, however, reported in favour of a joint stock with certain qualifications; and the official group had powerful means of enforcing this recommendation. The Government still owed £46,000 to the Company, which was willing not to insist upon repayment if it were granted a new charter. Moreover, all the establishments in India, forts, houses, guns, ports, were the property of the original Company and it gave notice in January 1657 of its intention to sell them by auction. This threat sufficed. In the course of the year the Government and the Thompson group fell into

[1] The Government had already borrowed and repaid £4,000 to the company and was to borrow and repay a further £15,000 before the end of the interregnum.

[2] 'Britannia Languens', loc. cit.

[3] Thurloe, iii. 80.

line with the wishes of the Company, and on October 17 a new charter was issued by Cromwell. No copy has survived, but it cannot have differed much in detail from earlier charters. The Company was now reformed on the basis of a New General Stock which was to be for seven years and to consist of a capital ten times the amount of the original foundation.[1] Thompson himself was elected the new governor.

In the previous year the King of Portugal, under the menace of Blake's guns, had finally ratified an Anglo-Portuguese treaty signed in 1654, which permitted Englishmen to trade throughout the Portuguese colonies.[2] This was especially beneficial to the East India merchants. But during the remaining years of the interregnum the East India Company had several disputes with the Dutch and the average dividend of 13 per cent. over the seven years mentioned in the charter seems to indicate that it would have been more profitable to the nation if the trade had been left open. It must, however, be borne in mind that the political disturbances in 1659 and the Restoration itself proved a heavy drain on the resources of the Company, which was compelled to lend money to needy governments, a fact very possibly contributing to the fall in its profits.

A small joint-stock company, *The Guinea Company*, led a very precarious existence during the interregnum. It had obtained a charter from Charles I and traded mainly in slaves. In 1649 its monopoly was referred to the consideration of the Council of Trade by the Council of State, which confirmed its charters and laid it down that 'that part of the trade by the two chief factories near Sierra Leone be granted to the Adventurers for 14 years, the rest of the coast southward to be free to all traders'.[3] Actually the Company had to face throughout the Protectorate competition from interlopers as well as from the Swedes, Danes, and Dutch.

In 1662, when the original grant to the Company expired, Charles II gave a charter to the Royal Adventurers in Africa, who in turn ten years later gave place to the highly successful Royal African Company. During this prosperous epoch, writers on the African trade looked back upon the

[1] Cf. Thorold Rogers, *History of Agriculture and Prices*, v. 146.

[2] See below, p. 147.

[3] *C.S.P.* (*Colonial*), *1574–1660*, 355. April 9, 1651.

interregnum as a period during which interlopers 'assumed unrestrained liberty of trading as they pleased without any regard to the rights of the Company',[1] when foreign merchants effectively competed with the English, and when trade was altogether in a feeble condition. It is at least certain that the Company was then unable to keep up its establishments, but let them fall into the hands of the East India Company in 1657, and from that date until the Restoration both trades were carried on by the same merchants.

The Levant Company,[2] like the East India Company, began as a joint-stock organization, but after a few years became a regulated company dispatching an annual fleet of ships in which all its members could send goods on individual account. Its trade was chiefly with the Turkish empire and Persia, to which it sold cloth and tin, getting in return silks, spices, and other valuable re-exports. The trade with the Morea, which was mainly in currants, was gradually cut off from the rest, and in 1657 was organized by a separate company.[3]

The principal difficulties met by the Company, especially during the early part of the interregnum, were the attacks of French privateers and the competition of the Dutch. It perpetually petitioned the Government about these matters and suggested various remedies. It claimed that it had lost twenty large ships taken by the French between 1642 and 1650 and was among the foremost agitators for convoys to protect its merchandise against pirates and privateers.[4] It pleaded for the establishment of a Council of Trade to investigate its grievances and, after complaining of the way in which Levant goods were being carried over to England by the Dutch from the Netherlands, agitated for a Navigation Act.[5]

Both its proposals were accepted. A Navigation Act was passed, and although the convoy system was not strictly adhered to throughout the Protectorate, yet the presence of an English squadron in the Mediterranean during the years

[1] Charles Davenant, *Reflections on the African Trade* (*Works*, v. 85); *Certain Considerations on the African Trade* (1680), 3.

[2] My acknowledgements are due to Mr. G. P. Ambrose for allowing me to read in manuscript his valuable essay on 'The Levant Company, 1640–1753'.

[3] *C.S.P. (Dom.)*, *1657–8*, 314.

[4] S.P. 105/144, ff. 21–2, 55, 368, &c.

[5] See below, p. 160.

1655 to 1659 proved an adequate protection for its commerce; on September 24, 1658, the Venetian envoy in England reported home that English vessels no longer had anything to fear from the Mediterranean pirates.[1]

Like the East India Company, the Levant Company had to bear heavy overhead charges of a diplomatic and military character, for it supported an ambassador and two consuls (at an annual cost of £3,500), forts, factories, and armed ships (some of which it hired out to the Venetian navy). But it was not on account of these burdens that the parliamentary renewal of its charter in 1644 was authorized. It had to pay for its privileges with a loan of £8,000.[2] Despite this confirmation of its monopoly the Company was attacked, together with other trading corporations, both by theoretical opponents of monopoly and by interlopers in the trade, and thought it worth while to expend much paper and ink in replying to the accusations formulated against it.[3] Its apologists maintained that the Company exported annually 20,000 dyed cloths and paid £10,000 in taxes, while the French and Dutch were said to have lost trade when they had made it free. On the other hand, the establishment of a Dutch factory at Smyrna was attributed to the uncertain position of the English trade due to the increase of interlopers.[4] The Council of State and the Committee of Trade investigated the matter, and although they did not recommend any abrogation of the Company's privileges, so vast were the Company's difficulties from foreign competition and unruly factors that at one time it contemplated recalling its ambassador and voluntarily surrendering its charter.[5] Nevertheless, the Company struggled on, and was especially grateful for Blake's campaign in the Mediterranean in 1655, which exemplified the beneficial effects of Cromwell's forceful foreign policy.[6] At the Restoration it strongly emphasized its right to exact oaths from its members as the assertion of an authority which had been impaired during the Protectorate.

Statistics relating to this trade suggest an interesting

[1] *C.S.P.* (*Venetian*), *1657–9*, 249.

[2] Firth and Rait, i. 395–6.

[3] Cf. S.P. 105/144, ff. 64 seq.

[4] *C.S.P.* (*Dom.*), *1650*, 71; ibid., *1651*, 290.

[5] Ibid., *1653–4*, 148. *Historical Manuscripts Commission, Report on the Finch Papers*, i. 357.

[6] *C.S.P.* (*Dom.*), *1655*, 356–8.

possibility. The 'profits' of the Company[1] fell from an average of £52,587 in 1642–6 to £14,865 in 1655–8, yet the yield from impositions paid by members to the Company show that the volume of trade cannot have materially decreased during these later years. We have no reason to suppose that the Dutch share of the Levant trade had increased enormously during this period, but rather the contrary, while the French trade under Mazarin was negligible. It is therefore probable in view of its complaints against its factors and the difficulty it experienced in controlling its members, together with the growth of criticisms of the Company's monopoly, that there was a marked invasion of interlopers into the trade which depressed prices and possibly individual profits during the Protectorate.

The 'Muscovy' Company—its original title was the company 'for the discovery of places unknown'—was the earliest English joint-stock company, having been founded in 1553. By the middle of the seventeenth century it included two distinct trades, the whale fisheries off Greenland and commerce with Czarist Russia. In Russia[2] the Company had enjoyed extraordinary privileges, exemption from taxation and a practical monopoly of foreign trade. But by this date the Dutch, who offered goods at much lower prices, had completely undermined the English factors. A Russian ambassador had arrived in England in 1645 to propose a political and commercial alliance, but his terms implied the full liberation of Charles I and were rejected.[3] The semi-barbaric Czar, partly because he was disgusted by the English rebellion against their king, but chiefly because he preferred the Dutch merchants to the English, thereupon took the opportunity to deprive the English of their privileges, and drove them from the country. In the summer of 1654 Cromwell dispatched William Pridaux as his ambassador (paid for by the Company) to try to persuade the Czar to restore the English merchants to their previous position.[4] But Pridaux could gain nothing except permission for the English merchants

[1] i.e., the balance between their expenses and receipts.

[2] For a detailed discussion see two papers by I. Lubimenko in *Transactions of the Royal Historical Society*, 4th series, i, xi.

[3] Whitelocke, *Memorials*, 214; *C.S.P.* (*Dom.*), *1653–4*, 340.

[4] See Thurloe, *passim*.

to go as far as Archangel (and no further) for their mart; and having suffered the indignity of seeing his cooks put in chains, Pridaux returned home the next summer empty-handed. Whitelocke wrote in his *Memorials* in 1656 that in future English commerce with Russia was to be carried on from the Swedish town of Narva.[1] But this statement can have had little foundation, for in the same year the Council of Trade proposed to allocate Narva to the sphere of interest of the Eastland Company.[2] In 1657 Cromwell dragged an unwilling Richard Bradshaw away from his quarrels with the Merchant Adventurers and sent him off on a mission to Moscow which proved an even greater fiasco than that of Pridaux.[3] The Muscovy Company, that is to say, the body of merchants trading in joint stock to Russia, was thus moribund during the Protectorate; but it had failed, even before the civil wars had begun, to maintain its originally unique position, and the loss of its trade cannot be laid to the charge of Cromwell, who made every possible effort to secure its re-establishment.

From 1620 *The Greenland Company* had become a separate joint-stock company and was confirmed in its exclusive privileges in 1636 and 1645. Nevertheless, there were a number of other firms engaged in whaling which could muster between them almost as large a tonnage of shipping as the Company. Whale oil was used for the manufacture of soap and also in the cloth trade and was therefore essential to industry. In 1654 the Company failed to produce sufficient oil for the country's needs and the Navigation Act had to be suspended in order to allow the Dutch to supply the deficiency.[4]

In the course of 1654 an interesting attempt was made by the Government to reconcile the claims of the Company and their rivals. It was proposed that a committee should be set up composed equally of representatives of the Company and of the various other interests concerned in the fisheries, which was to receive subscriptions, allot a fishing station for each ship, and distribute the profits to the adventurers in proportion to the tonnage and men they had employed and the risks they

[1] Whitelocke, 623.
[2] S.P. 18/128, f. 74; cf. below, p. 127.
[3] Thurloe, vi. 216 and *passim*.
[4] Burton, i. xlix.

had run. This scheme met with much criticism from the groups outside the Company who were dissatisfied with their proposed representation on the commission, which they thought would allocate the available harbours unfairly. The whole plan therefore broke down, and the Company was given permission to fish as before.[1]

Throughout 1655–6 Francis Ashe, the governor of the Company, and his fellows protested at the difficulties under which they worked. Their harpooners were taken and pressed into the navy and the Navigation Act continued to be suspended in favour of their Dutch rivals.[2] When these grievances had been remedied, the Company concentrated their attention upon ousting the interlopers. It proposed to Cromwell that it should be given the exclusive right to fish in the Bell Sound and Horn Sound, asserting that it was impossible for two interests to fish in the same harbour; two boats had been known to harpoon the same whale, and the presence of more than one tended to disturb the fish 'who are settling down to gender, feed, and rub themselves'. The interlopers contested these facts and maintained that the two harbours named were the only valuable ones and large enough for all interests, while the other harbours 'were many times inaccessible by reason of the ice'.[3]

The question of the differences between the Greenland Company and the interlopers was referred to a committee of Council which reported on January 7, 1658, to the Protector in favour of the Company, which was said to be 'beneficial to navigation' and to be an importer of necessities, whereas the interlopers were declared to have damaged the trade and 'given the advantage of it' to foreigners.[4] On March 9 Cromwell published a proclamation 'declaring the right of the Fellowship and Company of English Merchants for Discovery of New Trades (commonly called the Muscovia Company) to the sole fishing for Whales'; by it only members were permitted to fish in the harbours of Bell Sound and Horn Sound while other traders were to be granted free licences to fish elsewhere.[5]

[1] *C.S.P.* (*Dom.*), *1654*, 1, 8, 50, 57.
[2] Ibid., *1656–7*, 280, 355.
[3] S.P. 18/65, ff. 139, 140.
[4] *C.S.P.* (*Dom.*), *1657–8*, 257.
[5] The proclamation is in the British Museum, 669, f. 20 (78).

The Merchant Adventurers,[1] the oldest established trading corporation, met with the most persistent criticism as a monopoly.

They had the exclusive right to export undressed cloths to the Continent and consequently met with regular attacks from the cloth manufacturers in England, who maintained that this right was a menace to the prosperity of English industry. Under James I, Alderman Cockayne had the ingenious idea of obtaining a royal charter for a company which would supersede the Merchant Adventurers in their European markets by exporting only dyed and dressed cloth, but the experiment proved a complete failure and the Adventurers were re-established in 1617. They operated in accordance with the staple system of the Middle Ages from two mart towns: one of these had been Hamburg from the time of Queen Elizabeth, the other was always a town in the Netherlands. The Adventurers were given special rights and even exemption from national customs duties in the United Provinces by means of an agreement with the Dutch Merchants of the Intercourse, who were given similar privileges in London.

After their experiences under James I, the Merchant Adventurers were anxious to keep in the good graces of governments, for fear lest their privileges should again be suspended. They advanced £40,000 to Charles I, but were, nevertheless, well-known supporters of the parliamentary opposition to him; they protested against the seizure of pepper by the King and refused to pay tonnage and poundage. In revenge directly after the outbreak of the civil war the King threw their trade open. The House of Commons immediately turned to the Merchant Adventurers for financial assistance. Thirty thousand pounds was at once advanced by them for the supply of the navy and during the years 1642–9 the Company appears to have lent a total of at least £60,000 to the Government. 'I was in the Chair', wrote Whitelocke, in September, 1643, 'of a committee to treat with the Merchant Adventurers (with whose business I was well acquainted) about confirming some of their Patents and

[1] For this section see especially W. E. Lingelbach, *The lawes . . . of the Merchant Adventurers* (1902).

their loan of £60,000 to the Parliament.'[1] In October the charter of the Company was confirmed by parliamentary ordinance.[2]

The Company's trade with the Netherlands was of far less importance than that through Hamburg. Indeed in the seventeenth century the Company was often known as the Hamburg Company. There it was able to sell the new draperies and bays with especial ease. The trouble in the German trade under Cromwell was of a political rather than an economic kind. Richard Bradshaw,[3] sometime Mayor of Chester and a relative of the John Bradshaw who presided over the trial of Charles I, had in 1650 been appointed Resident and Deputy of the Company at Hamburg. The factors there maintained that it was not desirable that the two offices, one a government post, the other a commercial post, should be in the same hands. In 1654 they succeeded for a time in ousting Bradshaw from the deputyship and elected one Francis Townley in his stead. According to Bradshaw, Townley's faction, which had a majority in the Merchant Adventurers' court, were royalists. Cromwell intervened. He used his influence with the London court (actually the head office of the Company although nominally subordinate to the one at Hamburg) and sent letters to the Hamburg court ordering it to reinstate Bradshaw, while Townley was to be shipped back to England to defend himself. The Company obeyed, but throughout the rest of the Protectorate there was an unremitting conflict between the Bradshaw and Townley groups. The post of Resident at Hamburg was a key position during the interregnum. Thurloe obtained thence all his reports of North German and Scandinavian political and economic conditions. Bradshaw, who thoroughly approved of the Navigation Act of 1651, was also able to keep his Government informed as to how far the Adventurers were adhering to it by employing English shipping, and he was able to arrange for the Government the transport of naval materials, notably masts, from the Baltic.

The trade with the Netherlands involved the Company

[1] *Memorials*, 73. Of this £10,000 went to the pay of the Scots army; the legal rate of interest, 8 per cent., was paid. Add. MSS. 5501, f. 23.

[2] Firth and Rait, i. 310. [3] For Bradshaw see *D.N.B.* and Thurloe, *passim*.

more directly than any other commercial interest in questions of foreign policy. If it were to have its mart town in the Dutch Netherlands, England must be at peace with the United Provinces. If it were to have it in the Spanish Netherlands, England must be at peace with Spain. In any case the Company's trade was with both parts of the Netherlands and war with either Spain or Holland was bound to affect it adversely. Actually the period of Cromwellian supremacy was filled with wars with both countries. In 1651 the Merchant Adventurers had been engaged in negotiations to move their staple to Bruges. In the same year they proposed to the Council of State the formation of a joint-stock company for the trade if the tariff war between England and the Spanish Netherlands could be brought to an end.[1] When the Dutch war began they moved into Flanders and Brabant, but the negotiations with Bruges broke down. Thereupon they urged upon the Government an alliance with Spain to secure for them the same privileges they had enjoyed in the Dutch Netherlands.[2] But even before the war was over the Dutch were trying to persuade the Company to return to a mart town in Holland.[3] Rotterdam was the first to invite their return, and the Company petitioned the Protector to send letters to the States-General and Provincial States to obtain full permission for them to settle wherever they chose,[4] the point being that the Dutch would not invite them back until their privileges were confirmed.[5] Cromwell acceded to their request and the States-General were informed of the 'no small advantage that hath accrued to that trade and to the common good of all therein concerned by their seeking the seat of their state and residence in one place'.[6] In 1655, after lengthy negotiations, the Company decided to settle at Dordrecht and they remained there for the rest of their existence. On May 13, 1656, the Protector published a proclamation confirming the Merchant Adventurers in their ancient privileges, but a few days later the proclamation was suspended, upon the representations of interlopers; on May 29, however, it was redrafted by a committee of the Council, and the regulations of

[1] Thurloe, i. 199–201. [2] Ibid. 217–19. [3] S.P. 84/160, f. 66.
[4] *C.S.P.* (*Dom.*), *1654*, 345, 392. [5] S.P. 18/127, f. 110.
[6] S.P. 84/160, f. 76.

the Company and the settlement of outstanding disputes were referred to the Council of Trade.[1] The clothiers then proceeded to attack the Company before the parliamentary standing committee on trade, of which William Burton the diarist was a member. Burton thought that the clothiers' case was unanswerable, but noted that 'the merchants by their influence and power at court have always mastered them'. So it was now. The result of the committee's vote was heavily in favour of the Merchant Adventurers, for whom, among others, Martin Noell voted. With Noell voted Sir Christopher Packe, M.P., the Master of the Merchant Adventurers, who was thus a judge in his own case.[2] But the question was not yet finished. The Company had only been attacked by one section of their opponents. On January 6, 1657, the same committee debated a petition of the free merchants against the Company which 'set forth the great prejudice to the commonwealth that the trade of the woollen manufacturers should be engrossed in the hands of one company'. Despite the fact that Packe charged into the debate 'like a horse', answered all his opponents and spoke thirty times, the vote went overwhelmingly against the Company, and the committee resolved to allow all native merchants to trade freely to Germany and the Netherlands.[3] A sub-committee, of which Whitelocke was a member, was then appointed to draw up a bill to settle the matter. In March, Whitelocke was 'furthering' it.[4] But no bill saw the light. A few weeks later Sir Christopher Packe appeared upon the stage of political history to offer Oliver Cromwell a crown.

In 1658 the position of the Company still appears to have been unsettled. On May 13, 1658, we read of a council order 'on the petition of the Merchant Adventurers to advise a like proclamation on their behalf as was issued on May 30 [*sic*], 1656, with the addition of a clause like that for the Muscovy Company'.[5] The presumption is therefore that the Company were to allow other merchants to dispose of their goods in its allotted area outside the mart towns. When two months later the merchants of Exeter complained of the

[1] *C.S.P. (Dom.), 1655–6*, 318, 329, 335, 340; British Museum, 669, (f.) 20, no. 26.
[2] Burton, i. 115–17, 221.
[3] Ibid. 308–10.
[4] Ibid. 345; Whitelocke, 655.
[5] *C.S.P. (Dom.), 1658–9*, 23.

incorporation of the merchants trading to Germany and the Netherlands, the petitioners were informed by the Council of State that the matter had been finally settled.[1]

We have discovered no statistics of the Company's trade under the Protectorate. Undoubtedly it was injured by the Navigation Act policy which had long been a nightmare of the Merchant Adventurers. Yet the extent of the injury should not be exaggerated. It is curious that the Newcastle Merchant Adventurers, who after the introduction of the Act had violently protested against its provisions, were in 1659 asking that it should be enforced against the ubiquitous Martin Noell who was said to be contravening it in the coal trade.[2] Bradshaw in 1656 sent a report from Hamburg on 'the decay of trade' there, which he attributed partly to the heavy taxes imposed on the export of cloth from England and partly to the lack of standardization in the new types of manufacture.[3] As in the case of other companies there were universal and justifiable complaints of the increase of interlopers and the inability of the Company to control its factors, so that it is not unlikely that such a fall as there was in the Company's business was closely related to the competition of unauthorized English traders.

The Eastland Company, another regulated company, which made claim to have discovered the Baltic trade in the fourteenth century and had received a charter from Queen Elizabeth in 1579, exported cloth and skins and imported mainly timber and other naval materials. It stated in 1656 that it had employed as many as 200 ships a year, costing £60,000, and was 'a singular nursery of seamen'.[4] The figures of the Sound toll registers (if an accurate test) show that this assertion of the Eastland Company was no exaggeration. In 1647, 265 English ships had passed into the Baltic sea.[5]

Just as the civil war had caused disturbances between the Royalist and Roundhead Merchant Adventurers at Hamburg, so a similar contest took place among the Eastland merchants

[1] Ibid. 100.

[2] *The Newcastle Merchant Adventurers*, i. 195–6.

[3] Thurloe, v. 127.

[4] S.P. 18/123, ff. 69 seq.

[5] Cf. N. Bang, *Tables de la navigation et du transport des marchandises, 1497–1660* (1906).

at their principal outport of Danzig.[1] Later the Dutch war had a disastrous effect on the fortunes of the Company, for although the Eastland merchants had helped to persuade Parliament to pass a Navigation Act which would have enabled them to obtain control of the Baltic trade,[2] except for the rivalry of the Scandinavian carriers, the vital need of Baltic products to provision the Commonwealth navy in 1652 caused Cromwell totally to suspend the privileges of the Company.[3] Moreover, in the course of 1653 the King of Denmark, who was the ally of the Dutch, shut the Sound and seized twenty-two ships belonging to the Company and valued by it at £157,000.[4]

Although the Navigation Act, theoretically at least, prevented Dutch participation in the trade, when the war was ended the trade remained for a time open to all English ships. The complaints of the Company were bitter: 'a most licentious and confused kind of commerce' was being permitted, they said, 'which caused the trade to be reduced' to 'a very low condition'. In the course of 1654–5 Cromwell gratified the Company by forcing the King of Denmark to sign a treaty with him which put an end to exclusive Dutch privileges in the Sound, promised freedom of trade between England, Denmark, and Norway, subject to the laws of the respective countries (e.g. the Navigation Act), and obtained the restoration of the Eastland Company's ships and cargoes.

Earlier, Whitelocke had concluded a commercial treaty with the Swedes which, besides general expressions of good will, included a clause (xi) allowing each of the contracting parties to trade with the enemy of the other in war-time except in contraband, while by clause xii ships were to be provided with safe-conducts signifying the neutral ownership of goods carried.

[1] M. Sellers, *Acts and Ordinances of the Eastland Company* (1906), xlvi.

[2] During the closing years of the sixteenth and the opening years of the seventeenth century by far the largest part of European trade with the Baltic States had been in the hands of the Dutch, but by the middle of the latter century the number of vessels employed in this trade fell, and it is therefore likely that the Swedes and Danes were carrying more of their own trade. If this was the case, it may have been to some extent true, as English pamphleteers often asserted, e.g. 'Britannia Languens', § vi, that the Navigation Acts benefited Swedish and Danish shipping.

[3] See below, p. 164.

[4] See the petition of the Company for restitution. Add. MSS. 22546, f. 165.

Cromwell was very pleased with these treaties; in his speech of September 1654, to Parliament, he said:

> You have the Sound open; which was obstructed. That which was and is the strength of this nation, the shipping, will now be supplied thence. And, whereas you were glad to have anything of that kind at the second hand, you have now all manner of commerce and as much freedom as the Dutch themselves there and at the same rates and toll....[1]

The Eastlanders took advantage of this favourable situation to petition the Protector and the Council of State that the trade should again be closed and their charter renewed.[2] They asserted that the only remedy for the evil condition into which their trade had fallen was for all merchants engaged in it to be incorporated into one company since, they said, it was far easier to obtain national commercial privileges from the Danes and the Swedes 'if they looked upon them as one society'. Cromwell and his Council were urged to take large shares in such a company and to use their influence to obtain fixed customs duties and selling prices from the Baltic Powers. Among other grievances of which they informed the Government was that the open trade had caused a fall in prices which did not affect the interlopers, since they were mainly retailers as well as importers and made their profits out of their shopkeeping. Finally, the merchants of the Company maintained that an open trade had helped the Poles and the Prussians to set up cloth manufactures of their own by procuring English workmen (presumably on account of the lack of employment in England), 'and they boldly affirmed' that 'nothing hath more hindered the Cloth-making beyond the Seas [in the past], then the Government of Companies'.[3]

All these arguments apparently impressed the Council of State, and the Committee of Trade to whom the matter was referred by Cromwell drew up a draft charter which only differed in two points from the Elizabethan charter; these

[1] *Letters and Speeches*, ii. 355.

[2] S.P. 18/123, ff. 69 seq. This petition, dated Jan. 4, 1656, is endorsed by Thurloe, 'His highnesse is pleased to referre this petition & Representation to the Committee of trade, conceiving it a business very fitt for & worthy of their confidence'.

[3] S.P. 18/123, ff. 16–64; cf. S.P. 95/5*a*, f. 139. 'Considerations and Propositions to be represented to His Highness the Ld Protector for the managing the Trade of Sweden and the King of Denmark.'

were: a reduction of the admittance fines by 50 per cent. and permission to be given to the Company to trade at Narva, previously the preserve of the Muscovy Company. The matter went no further, and we may reasonably assume that the reason for this was the intensification of the war with Spain which once more caused the Government to demand an unrestrained supply of naval materials. No doubt Cromwell felt that, although an open trade might lower prices, at least its concomitant was an ample supply.[1]

Despite its failure to obtain a new charter the Company continued to trade, not without some measure of success. They seem in the course of the interregnum to have come to a kind of understanding with the Merchant Adventurers, and to a great extent the two companies worked in harmony. The Eastland Company prided itself, however, on being unlike the Merchant Adventurers, in that its members were not dominated by its London court. This union of the two companies is said to have been brought about by their common misfortunes. The Eastlanders explained what these misfortunes were in petitioning Charles II for the renewal of their charter at the Restoration. The Company asserted that the countenance given them by the monarchy made them

remain the more sensible of the discouragements we have for these last twenty years lain under for want of countenance and support in the sure observance of our charter which hath produced sad effects, and almost a total loss of this important trade by the intrusion and . . . . irregular and unrestrained trade of foreigners and interlopers, and by their debasing our English manufacture, and consequently diminishing its vent abroad and augmenting the price of foreign commodities both there and here, losing sundry privileges obtained and settled by us with great trouble and charge and exposing us to scorn and infamy in the places of our trade.[2]

It is quite clear from this brief study of the history of Cromwell's relations with the trading companies of his time that he was by no means opposed to their existence. He and his Council of State were opposed on principle to monopolies, but the difficulty they found was how to define a monopoly.

[1] There is no doubt that Cromwell's chief concern was naval materials. His attitude to Sweden during the Protectorate was determined by the consideration not to allow it a monopoly of supply. See, especially, P. Meadowe, *A Narrative* (1677), 55–6.

[2] Add. MSS. 25115, ff. 23 seq. Petition of Nov. 13, 1660.

Was the post office a monopoly, for example? Surely not; it was rather a patent. 'You seem to think', wrote Henry Robinson to Anthony Ashley Cooper, 'patents might be blasted as monopolies, but this could not be, for the trust and power of laying post stages could not be prostituted to the generality'.[1] But was not the same argument applicable *mutatis mutandis* to all trading societies, and especially those engaged in foreign commerce? If the Eastland Company or the Levant Company could show that the fact of their being a corporation trading with the approval of the Government enabled English merchants to obtain special privileges from kings or pashas, while unrestrained competition in these markets forced down prices to an uneconomic level, it was at least arguable that there was an analogy between a chartered company and a post office—in both cases free competition involved confusion, waste, and, incidentally, loss of revenue to the State.

There are few indications of Oliver Cromwell's own views on these matters. But on February 27, 1655, in the second year of the Protectorate, one George Sanderson petitioned Cromwell for letters patent to have the exclusive right of exporting coal from Newcastle to France. The Protector referred this petition to his Council, writing the following words in his own hand:[2]

> Wee desire the Councell to consider of this Peticion and whether the same bee not a monopolie, and soe prejuditiall to the libertys of ye people, or whether it may not lawfullye bee granted, to the advancement of the publicke revenus upon the reasons and groundes annexed.

This distinction between a desirable patent and an unlawful monopoly was a puzzle that had long agitated the official mind. It is to be remembered, however, that the Statute against Monopolies, passed under James I, expressly excluded all the London companies from its scope.

In practice, as we have seen, the Protectorate made a compromise with regard to the foreign trading companies. The companies were, in effect, confirmed in their privileges, but interlopers, notably in the whale fishing trade, the Guinea

[1] *C.S.P. (Dom.), 1653–4*, 21.

[2] S.P. 18/94, f. 103.

trade, and in the markets of the Merchant Adventurers, were not suppressed. The East India Company was given a charter; the Eastland Company was promised one; the Levant Company was confirmed in its privileges. In a sense, in assenting to the companies' privileges, Cromwell was following in the footsteps of the Long Parliament, which either by its own enactments or through the agency of the Council of State had actually confirmed the charters which they had received under the monarchy. But whereas the Long Parliament's approval of the Companies was in most cases in return for a monetary contribution to the expenses of the war, Cromwell, so far as we know, only borrowed from the East India Company, and that in very exceptional circumstances. In other words, it is practically certain that Cromwell and his advisers genuinely believed that foreign commerce was most effectively managed by companies.

Yet despite the approval bestowed upon them by the Cromwellian Government, it cannot be doubted that the effective monopoly of the companies was seriously impaired during the interregnum. We do not have to rely solely upon contemporary petitions of companies for this conclusion, for these petitions are reinforced by the evidence of the Government's own committees set up to investigate trade questions, as well as by the writings of pamphleteers much later in the century. The movement against monopolies, semi-political and puritanical in character, could not logically stop at monopolies in industry and manufactures; and so when Charles II entered upon his inheritance, his Council of Trade had to listen not only to the complaints of sugar refiners, framework knitters, and coal merchants as to the injuries they had suffered amid the general confusion of the interregnum, but also to equally accurate stories of the irregular and unrestrained interloping that had taken place in foreign trade.[1]

Thus, although it may well be questioned whether British foreign trade was ever completely in the control of monopolist companies in the seventeenth century, yet in view of the facts that Restoration trade committees had to sit listening to lengthy complaints of the sufferings of merchants under

[1] Cf. Add. MSS. 25115, *passim*.

the Commonwealth, and that Royalist merchants instructed the Government that the only way to end the depression was to restore companies and corporations to their old supremacy,[1] there is considerable reason for supposing that there had in effect been under Cromwell a period of freer trade than at any other time during the century.

[1] Cf. Bland, *Trade Revived*, 3.

XII

FOREIGN TRADE OUTSIDE THE COMPANIES

ENGLISH commerce with the colonies was never confined to a single trading corporation. As the Indian and African trades have already been discussed, there remains only the question of English commercial relations with North America and the West Indies during the period now under examination.[1] So far as these two areas are concerned, colonial historians have of recent years drawn especial attention to the significance of the Long Parliament's Act of October 3, 1650, which totally forbade not only European but even English commercial intercourse with the colonies of Antigua, Barbados, Bermuda, and Virginia, the four colonies which had openly declared themselves Royalist in sympathies. Now it may be true that this Act is of fundamental constitutional significance in British colonial history, but nevertheless, it can hardly be doubted that its economic importance was small.[2] It was a war measure, the retaliation of the victorious party in the civil war upon the vanquished. It was obviously not intended as a permanent measure, and when the Barbados were subdued by a fleet sent out under the command of Sir George Ayscue from England, the articles of settlement arranged between Ayscue and the colonists specifically stated that they were to be free to trade 'with all nations that do trade and are in amity with England'. Similar agreements were made with the other Royalist colonies whose submission followed in due course.[3] A year later the Navigation Act was passed which confined the import trade to the plantations and the export trade thence to England entirely to British vessels. Although historians have been able to quote one or two references during the Protectorate to trading in the colonies being carried on in

1 Cf. G. L. Beer, 'Cromwell's Policy in its Economic Aspects', in *The Political Science Quarterly* (1901–2) and *The Origins of the Old Colonial System* (1926); J. A. Williamson, *The English in Guiana* (1923) and *The Caribbee Islands* (1926); V. T. Harlow, *The Barbados* (1925); A. P. Watts, *Les Colonies Anglaises aux Antilles* (1924).

2 For the opposite view see G. Beer, *Origins of the British Colonial System*, chap. xii; J. A. Williamson, *The Caribbee Islands under the Proprietary Patents*, 172–3.

3 Add. MSS. 11411, f. 95; cf. N. D. Davies, *Cavaliers and Roundheads in the Barbados*, 208–9.

defiance of the Act of 1650, the majority of cases of illicit trading were clearly violations of the Navigation Act.[1] The Act of 1650 was never repealed, but it is certain that so far as economic affairs were concerned the Act of 1651, which Cromwell himself evidently regarded as the most important Statute governing the relations between England and her dominions,[2] was intended to supersede it. Contemporary pamphleteers and observers even suggested that the Navigation Act was put on the Statute book largely through the efforts of English monopolists interested in the colonial trade.[3] This Act governed, or was intended to govern, the trading relations between England and her colonies until the Restoration.

During the civil wars the Dutch obtained a command of the trade of carrying provisions from Europe to the English colonies and taking back such local products as sugar and tobacco. When Ayscue's fleet arrived in the West Indies, several Dutch ships were found trading against the law, and on other occasions foreign ships were seized by the fleet for violating the English monopoly.[4] But Cromwell and his Council of State rapidly realized that the English colonies could not be provisioned without Dutch aid, and a piecemeal system of licensing foreign ships grew up, especially towards the end of the Protectorate.[5] So far as the colonies on the mainland were concerned, both in North and South America, and including Guiana and the newly acquired territory of Surinam, Cromwell's policy was to leave them alone except in regard to one matter. The tobacco industry received definite encouragement from the State. An Act passed on April 2, 1652, forbade tobacco-planting in England (there were not inconsiderable plantations in Gloucestershire and Worcestershire) and various attempts were made throughout

1 Various instances are quoted by Miss H. Crump, *Colonial Admiralty Jurisdiction in the Seventeenth Century* (1930).

2 Add. MSS. 11611, f. 13.

3 Bland, *The Humble Remonstrance . . . on behalf of the Inhabitants and Planters in Virginia and Maryland* (1661 ?); Dutch report of June 12, 1654, in *Verbael van Beverning* (1725), 459.

4 Besides Ayscue (1652), Penn (1655) seized fifteen ships, and Myngs (1658) seized six ships from Holland and Hamburg for trading illegally in the West Indies. *C.S.P. (Colonial), 1675–6*, 91–2, 126.

5 See the list of licences printed in Harlow, p. 92.

the Protectorate to enforce the Act.[1] Actually, however, it was found impossible to administer and was suspended altogether in the years 1655 and 1656. The object that Cromwell had in view in trying to enforce a policy of suppressing home-grown tobacco must have been mainly fiscal, and in this sense the policy was not his own, but had been initiated by James I. On the other hand, the theory expressed in Stuart proclamations that tobacco was an 'unprofitable' industry which it was not really desirable to stimulate in preference to more necessary commodities was abandoned during the interregnum.[2] Whereas James I compiled a book against tobacco smoking, Cromwell liked to puff his pipe at Hampton Court or Whitehall.

During the Protectorate the principal product of the West Indies was sugar. Sugar plantations had been established in Barbados and Nevis between 1640 and 1650, and speedily became so profitable that during the early part of the interregnum English sugar was underselling Portuguese in the European markets.[3] The biggest planters were Colonels Modiford and Drax; the latter was knighted by Cromwell at the beginning of 1658[4] for his services to the colony. Tobacco was also grown extensively in the West Indies, and the values of other commodities were measured in terms of a double standard of tobacco and sugar.[5]

Undoubtedly, despite all complaints of the planters, the Protectorate was a flourishing epoch in West Indian history, and the relative value placed by Cromwell upon the two areas of the North American coast and the West Indies is clearly indicated by his approval of the proposal to transplant the entire population of New England to the Jamaicas.[6]

The expedition which Cromwell organized against the Spanish West Indies in 1654 and which resulted in the capture of Jamaica is extremely interesting to the student of Crom-

[1] Firth and Rait, ii. 580, 870, 1137; C. M. MacInnes, *The Early English Tobacco Trade* (1926), chap. iv.

[2] For the reduction of tobacco duties, see above, pp. 66–7.

[3] Egerton MSS. 2395, f. 632.

[4] Thomas Povey to Daniel Searle, Jan. 9, 1658, describes how Martin Noell and James Drax waited on Cromwell, and how the latter was knighted, 'Mr. Noell escaped the title'. Add. MSS. 11411, f. 55.

[5] Cf. Egerton MSS. 2395, ff. 69–83.

[6] See F. Strong, *A Forgotten Danger to the New England Colonies* (American Historical Association Report, 1898).

well's policy. To Professor Gardiner it marked the rise of a mundane spirit, and the latest historian of the expedition holds that 'de toute évidence les raisons prédominantes étaient purement économiques qui inspirèrent à Cromwell de s'engager dans une voie si radicalement différente de tout ce qui était fait jusqu'à ce jour dans les annales coloniales anglaises'.[1] It is clear that there were powerful mercantile interests that favoured this attack upon the wealthiest and most populous of the Spanish islands, San Domingo, then called Hispaniola. When Ayscue had set out in 1652 to subdue the Barbados, a group of merchants had begged to be allowed to send ships along with him, the captains of which should urge the islanders to submit and then bring back £200,000 worth of their goods for sale.[2] The contractor for the anti-Spanish fleet, commanded by General Venables, was Martin Noell, while his brother, Thomas Noell, was secretary for the affairs of the island of Barbados. The fact that the latter made himself unpopular in Barbados as promoter and supporter of the expedition is the clearest proof we have of the Noell interest in this venture.[3] After the ignominious failure of this venture and the establishment of a colony at Jamaica, it was Noell and his partners who pleaded with the Government for the formation of a West India Company as a joint-stock on similar lines to those of the East India Company.[4] Nevertheless, it would be wrong to assert that Cromwell's motives were entirely economic.[5]

[1] Watts, p. 101. [2] *S.P.* (*Colonial*), i. 11, Nos. 29, 30, cit. Watts.

[3] Thurloe, iii. 157–9.

[4] Attention to this fact was first drawn by Prof. C. M. Andrews. The evidence is ample among the Povey Papers, e.g. Add. MSS. 11411, f. 116, 'Proposals for a West Indian Council' (1656) and Egerton MSS. 2395, f. 202, 'Draft of an Act incorporating a West Indian Company' (1659).

[5] If one tries to read Thomas Gage's *New Survey of the West Indies* in the kind of spirit in which one imagines Cromwell read it, one realizes that it appealed with tremendous force to his Protestant and nationalist outlook. The first three chapters of this remarkable work are devoted to an attack on the Pope as 'a man of sin', whose agents, the Jesuits and the Friars, were hand in glove with the Spaniards. Roger Williams, one of the earliest writers in favour of liberty of conscience, is said to have urged an enterprise against the Spanish empire as a means of spreading that liberty. It was thought, too, by more than one letter-writer of the day, that it was Cromwell's intention to use Hispaniola as a stepping-stone to higher things, such as the religious duty of absorbing all the South American possessions of Spain. The authorities are collected in F. Strong, 'Causes of Cromwell's West Indian Expedition', *American Historical Review* (1898–9), 235.

During the latter part of the Protectorate interested merchants begged permission to form a company to carry out attacks upon the Spaniards from the islands, and they were so far successful that the Governor of the Barbados learnt of the great encouragement to be given to those willing to develop this privateering trade with their own resources. As to Jamaica a special advisory committee was set up to look after its interests, and Cromwell took a deep personal concern in dispatching provisions and colonists to the island. Among other things he was anxious to send a host of Irish boys and girls to people his conquest. Yet in his heart, his intimates confessed, 'the old Protector' did not think Jamaica worth keeping.[1] We know that Cromwell believed that the failure of the expedition had been a punishment from God, and it is possibly for this reason that he allowed further conquests in the neighbourhood to fall into the hands of private enterprise. He did everything in his power to develop Jamaica, but the evangelizing impulse which had initially actuated him seemed in some measure to die.

There seems to have been a very real conflict over commercial policy in the West Indies between the English merchants and the colonists. An unpublished manuscript bearing the heading,[2] 'The state of the difference between the merchants and the planters in relation to free trade about the Caribee islands and the means of reconciliation and general satisfaction proposed', summarizes the attitude of each side. The planters demanded an uninterrupted freedom of trade because they had established themselves without any support from the State, because 'when in the greatest straits they had found help and relief among foreigners', because a restraint on trade would, they were assured, enable the English merchant to set his own price on what he brought and took away, and because they were entirely dependent on foreign trade for the import of their provisions. They also pointed to the articles granted to them on their surrender to Ayscue as promising 'as great a free trade as ever'. The merchants argued that the French and Dutch imported goods were calculated to debauch the planters, that their

[1] Thomas Povey to Searle, Add. MSS. 11411, f. 21.
[2] Add. MSS. 11411, f. 4.

competition was ruinous, and that no other country allowed its colonists free trade. The extremely one-sided 'compromise' offered as a solution was that the Governors should enforce the Navigation Act and appoint a committee to see that the islands were adequately victualled. From other evidence it seems that although trading companies were unable to establish monopolies in the colonies, the exclusive joint-stock principle was encouraged there by the Protector because of the risks that necessarily had to be run in the trade. Moreover, some of the companies were of that piratical character which was so attractive to Cromwell's mind. A document of 1655[1] of 'Reasons propounded by the Adventurers of America why they desire to be incorporated by Act of Parliament and not by Letters Patent, under the Privy Seal', stated that by this means they would be able to arm and lead forces from England and 'in a warlike manner' to land them in foreign countries, and with them to invade and conquer in the name of the Commonwealth the lands and dominions of others, and to hold the same and fortify them by force. That this policy of private piratical enterprise was approved by Cromwell as a substitute for another official expedition to the West Indies, we learn from a letter written to the Governor of the Barbados a year or so later, in which the writer says:

> I may not omit giving you an account of greater encouragement given by the State to certain persons here, merchants and others, who as adventurers do raise among themselves a considerable stock for the setting out twenty frigates to proceed into the West Indies to make what advantages they can against the Spaniard by sea and land.[2]

This policy cannot be said to have been directly imitated from the Dutch, because it was clearly the kind of colonial policy which the circumstances of the time would dictate. Nevertheless, it is significant that when the original Dutch West India Company was formed in 1624 proposals for the formation of a similar company were suggested to the English Government,[3] while the Dutch West India Company, long subsidized and supported by the State, was of an almost

[1] Egerton MSS. 2395, f. 103.
[2] Ibid., f. 178.
[3] Harleian MSS. 1583, f. 196. This early proposition for a West India Company clearly belongs to about 1624.

identical character with that envisaged by Cromwell's colonial advisers.

The economic relations of England and France during the interregnum do not seem to have been so important as they were to become after the Restoration. In 1662–3 our imports from France amounted in value to over £643,000 and exceeded in value our imports from any other country.[1] Economic pamphleteers then turned part of the vituperation at their disposal, hitherto concentrated on the Dutch, upon the French, who were said to be 'usurping' English trade, because of the unfavourable balance against England.[2] No doubt the wars between France and Spain, the French civil wars and the lack of interest displayed by Mazarin in commerce account for the smaller Anglo-French trade under Cromwell. It is at any rate certain that at this time English trade with Spain was bigger than that with France, for we have the statement of the contemporary French ambassador in London to this effect,[3] and he had every reason to exaggerate rather than minimize the relative amounts. During the early part of the interregnum trade between the two countries almost ceased altogether, largely for political reasons. In 1649 a tariff war began between them, the French forbidding the importation of English manufactured cloth, the English the importation of French wines and silks, 'luxuries' in the eyes of the Puritan, and competitive products to the East India merchants. But French wines still came in, either smuggled or under licence.[4] Spanish and Portuguese wines are no substitutes for those from Bordeaux.

Besides the tariff war there was a fierce and unremitting naval conflict.[5] The French not only gave shelter to Royalist privateers, but from Brest, St. Malo, and elsewhere corsairs preyed upon our Channel and Mediterranean trade. The French fleet is even said to have joined in the attacks upon English commerce, and in 1652 Blake fell upon seven

[1] Add. MSS. 36785.

[2] Cf. S. Fortrey, *England's Interest and Improvement* (1663); J. B., *An Account of the French Usurpation upon the Trade of England* (1679).

[3] Bordeaux to Brienne, Aug. 23, 1655. Record Office transcripts.

[4] See above, p. 61.

[5] This account is based on the standard works of Gardiner and Guizot.

French men-of-war as they approached Dunkirk and carried them into Dover as a reprisal. This war had by no means ceased with the Protectorate. It continued, despite the recognition by Mazarin of the English Republic in December 1653, with renewed vigour. The Spaniards, who were pressing for an English alliance, pointed to the encouragement given by the French to Royalist privateers as an argument for their proposals, and in February 1654, Cromwell, hoping to assist the French Protestants by doing so, opened negotiations for an 'inexpensive' alliance with Spain. But the French also held out attractive baits for his friendship, and Cromwell suggested to the Spaniards an 'underhand' war in Elizabethan style in support of the Huguenots. Angered by this, the French laid an embargo upon English ships and goods in France,[1] which was followed by a general seizure of English property. Meanwhile piracy and privateering continued unabated.[2] At length Cromwell decided on an agreement with France in preference to one with Spain. It was to take the form of a commercial treaty. Thurloe relates that the dangers English commerce met from the French in the Mediterranean, and Cromwell's anxiety that there should be no Franco-Dutch commercial treaty prejudicial to English interests were the economic considerations underlying the alliance of 1655.[3] The treaty defined contraband and contained a number of precautions against the recurrence of a general war of commerce-destroying. Finally, the treaty renewed full commercial intercourse between the two countries, and in the taxes on French imports a new source of revenue was open to a straitened exchequer.

For the remainder of the Protectorate the relations of the two countries remained friendly, and it is reasonable—to account for the outcries of the Restoration pamphleteers[4]—to assume that during Cromwell's last years there came an increase in trade.

The relations between England and Spain during the interregnum were of exactly opposite character to those

[1] *Clarke Papers*, iii. 35.
[2] Whitelocke, *Memorials*, 588–9; S.P. 78/113 *passim*; Thurloe, iii *passim*.
[3] Stowe MSS. 185, f. 187; S.P. 78/115, f. 161.
[4] The view about the French 'overbalance' was also expressed by R. Baker in 1659.

between England and France; for whereas Spain had promptly recognized the Republic and had given no encouragement to Royalist privateers, yet during the Protectorate, while England was at peace with France, she was at war with Spain.

Although the tendency of Cromwell's foreign policy during the later months of 1654 and the beginning of 1655 was hostile to Spain, he had not supposed that his piratic expedition against the Spanish West Indies would lead directly to a breach in Europe. As late as September 21, 1655, the Venetian envoy, Sagredo, reported that Cromwell was 'certainly no enemy of the Spaniards'.[1] But the following month the King of Spain laid an embargo on English trade; English factors were confined to their houses; and it was reported that the Spaniards 'were in disorder for loss of their trade with the English'.[2] The importance of English commerce with Spain at this period was great. The merchants engaged in it said that it was equivalent to the rest of our foreign commerce put together. They asserted further that three-quarters of the fish caught in English waters were sent to Spain, besides large quantities of manufactured cloth. Our imports thence included two essentials, wool and bullion.[3] There were at least twenty-three merchants specially interested in the trade, and it is notable that a petition in favour of the trade drawn up in 1659 was signed by the Lord Mayor and most of the aldermen of the City of London.[4]

Apart from the trade with Spain itself, which was indirectly a trade with the Spanish colonies, there was considerable commercial intercourse between England and Spanish Flanders, chiefly in cloth. This trade was in the hands of the Merchant Adventurers, who had in 1651 and 1652 urged on Cromwell an alliance with Spain so as to obtain favourable tariffs for their exports there.[5]

[1] *C.S.P.* (*Venetian*), *1655–6*, 117. [2] Cf. Whitelocke, *Memorials*, 617.

[3] Cf. 'the humble remonstrance of the merchants trading to Spayne and its Territories' (Add. MSS. 4107, f. 10). This paper is undated, but is probably the petition first referred to in R. Baker's *The Merchant's Humble Petition* (1659). It may be dated Oct. 1655.

[4] Cf. the signatures to a petition dated Sept. 20, 1655, in Thurloe, iv. 44. The principal merchants were N. Manton and R. Baker. The other petition referred to is quoted in Baker.

[5] See above, p. 123.

The embargo of September, 1655, was a prelude to war. The Spanish ambassador in London was recalled, but before he departed he urged the merchants whose property was affected by the embargo to petition against war.[1] The merchants duly petitioned the Protector. They urged upon him that the embargo was probably imposed by the Spaniards 'in design to' a treaty, but, as they afterwards explained, 'it was far from our intentions to give the least motive that might incense you, or foment a breach between the two nations on our behalf'. Cromwell regarded this embargo, however, as did the French, as tantamount to a declaration of war, and from this month till his death the two States were in conflict.

The resultant interruption of trade was not only widely held to be damaging to England through the loss of customs, but the trade itself was considered to be specially advantageous to national industry and therefore a fatal loss. It was also alleged that if our cloth were long kept out of Spain, the Spaniards would set up their own manufactures or sell their merino wool to our rivals the Dutch.[2] It is indeed generally maintained by modern writers that this war was most damaging to the commerce of the country. There is no statistical evidence available on the subject, but the unanimity of petitions and pamphlets referring to a general decay of trade due to the war make it impossible to doubt that much injury was inflicted by it upon our commerce. It is of course evident that the existence of hostilities between two countries which habitually had important commercial relations, even in days when hostilities did not put a complete stop to economic intercourse, must have had an adverse effect. But while there is no need to question the injury inflicted by the war on English industry, there is possibly a tendency to exaggerate its extent. The pamphlets and petitions which describe the trade losses caused by the war nearly all belong to the year 1659. If the trade between the countries had stopped completely or even largely during the whole of the last years of Cromwell's life, and if commercial opinion had been as united and influential against the war as some writers have implied, it would indeed be astonishing that the Government

[1] *C.S.P.* (*Venetian*), *1655–6*, 137 *sub* Nov. 2, 1655.

[2] Authorities cit. n. 4, p. 140 above.

was not induced to conclude peace earlier than it did. The contrary happened. The war was extended by the alliance made with France on March 23, 1657, which placed six thousand 'Ironsides' at the disposal of the French for their attack on Spanish Flanders. By the terms of this alliance the English were promised the possession of Dunkirk.

An interesting State Paper exists, written apparently in 1652, which relates the reasons why English officials wanted this port.[1] It states that the town could be used as a staple for the cloth trade and as a trading centre for Germany; it describes it as a place coveted for its herring fisheries; and suggests that a little encouragement would induce the Portuguese Jews to desert Amsterdam in its favour. We cannot tell how far these considerations influenced Cromwell's policy, but it is certain that even as early as 1652 the acquisition of Dunkirk for England was taking shape in his mind as a desirable project. It is more than likely that one very definite object he had in view was the suppression of the Dunkirk pirates, who were perhaps more troublesome to England than any others. Early in 1656 they released some of their prisoners with instructions to tell Cromwell 'that while he was fetching gold from the West Indies, they will fetch his coals from Newcastle',[2] and on June 1, 1656, a Venetian report stated:

> The Dunkirkers have captured two more very rich ships of this mart. The merchants clamour and their cry has reached the Protector; but he does not seem inclined to afford them much help as the loss is personal and does not touch the interests of the State. He seems the more reluctant because when he formerly asked money of the City, it was refused.[3]

The Venetians misread the mind of the English ruler; two years later Dunkirk fell into his hands. At the head of the paper written in 1652, in favour of the English acquisition of Dunkirk, it was stated that 'the places that at present give contribution will be able to pay the soldiers that shall be necessary for the keeping of that garrison', but the facts of 1658–9 did not bear out this belief. Dunkirk proved an

[1] Add. MSS. 32093, f. 29; *English Historical Review*, xi. 484–6.
[2] S.P.Dom. Feb. 26, 1656, cit. Oppenheimer, 346.
[3] *C.S.P.* (*Venetian*), *1655–6*, 232.

expensive prize; it cost £60,000 a year to garrison and its revenues only came to £15,000.

When Richard Cromwell at his accession to the Protectorate tried to borrow £50,000 of the French Government, Mazarin offered to let him have the money in exchange for the surrender of Dunkirk.[1] The offer was refused. The sale of Dunkirk was left for Charles II.

What evidence is there that English trade with Spain was continued during the years 1657 and 1658? In a remarkable letter, written a few days after Cromwell's death, the French ambassador in London reported to Mazarin that

> There is also talk of peace with Spain to satisfy the mercantile community which desires it. I do not think, however, that this point has been under consideration. And moreover the war has not up to now been so burdensome to England that she does not find more advantage in continuing the war than in making peace: it being proved by the customs registers that since the rupture as much merchandise has come in and gone out as before the war.[2]

There is no reason to suppose that the ambassador was not telling the truth about this matter. His letters were always well informed, and he frankly admitted that the English merchants were opposed to the Spanish war. Although no detailed figures of individual foreign trades have yet been made available to the historian, the total customs figures, as has already been shown, indicate an upward and not a downward trend during this period.[3]

It therefore seems probable that trade with Spain was carried on to a large extent despite the hostilities between the two countries. It may originally have been connived at by the authorities in Spain. Later it was openly permitted. On January 1, 1657, the French ambassador in England reported that in hopes of peace the Spaniards were permitting the entry of English goods which hitherto had been prohibited.[4] Moreover, it is to be noticed that the essence of the grievances of the English merchants who petitioned for peace was not

[1] The discussion can be followed in Bordeaux's reports in the Record Office transcripts.

[2] Bordeaux to Mazarin, Sept. 16, 1658. Record Office transcripts.

[3] See above, p. 57.

[4] Bordeaux to Brienne, Jan. 1, 1657. Record Office transcripts.

so much that trade was totally stopped as that it was mainly in the hands of Dutch carriers:

The whole trade of the exports and imports of goods, to and from Spain, was necessarily to be done in Dutch bottoms which they were necessitated to buy, and cause to be sailed by Dutchmen; and the most part of the goods exported carried first into Holland, for the better disguise both of the goods and property of them, and procuring convoy. . . .

So ran a parliamentary petition of 1659. Thurloe tells the same story. Another petition states 'to carry on trade we have been forced to employ Hollanders and Spaniards who are thus taught to be merchants [*sic*]'.[1] Judging by these petitions there seem to have been two streams of intercourse. There were, firstly, the foreign carriers employed by English merchants so as to protect their goods against seizure, and secondly, independent trading between the two countries carried on by Dutch and Hamburg merchants. Apart from this there was a roundabout trade through Portugal and possibly through Italy. On June 16, 1656, Philip Meadows, the English envoy at Lisbon, wrote to Thurloe to suggest that 'If this Spanish war continues, it may possibly be worthy of consideration, how to drive a secret trade with Spain by the way of Portugal from Pharo, paying the king some little customs'. He adds significantly, 'Surely nothing will more discontent the people in England than the not sending of their manufactures'.[2] On April 21, 1657, our envoy at Leghorn discussed the situation of the Spanish trade and mentioned his own purchase of Saragossa wines to be sent home for him.[3]

From the time of Cromwell's death, however, the Government was increasingly urged to end the war, and it was even rumoured that the merchants trading to Spain had offered to pay off the arrears owing to the army and navy if the Government would make peace.[4] On February 15, 1659, this group of merchants drew up a petition which they presented to Parliament and published as a broadsheet.[5] In this, after describing the losses they had suffered, especially to the Dutch carriers, and their inability to call their agents to

[1] See Baker, loc. cit., *A Letter from York* (1659), *The Humble Petition* of Feb. 15, 1659.

[2] Thurloe, v. 124.

[3] Longland to Thurloe, Apr. 15, 1657. Thurloe, vi. 201.

[4] T. Clarges to H. Cromwell, Oct. 5, 1659. Thurloe, vii. 424.

[5] See n. 3, p. 140 above.

account, they proposed that Parliament should totally prohibit the importation into England of Spanish goods and thus force the Spanish merchants to work for peace. Spanish imports had never been totally prohibited during the war, but an Act of June 26, 1657, had increased the duties upon Spanish wines and raisins, thus benefiting the French, who paid lower rates. On March 25, 1659, the Venetian envoy stated that the exchequer was losing the customs duties paid on Spanish merchandise, and a week later he referred to the petition of the English merchants for a retaliation on the Spaniards by a total prohibition of their goods in England.[1] The republican minority in Parliament seized on this prohibition as a weapon with which to attack Richard Cromwell's Government. Henry Nevile, the friend and disciple of James Harrington, said in a debate on foreign policy 'there is a general decay of trade.... I could tell you of one thousand particular decays of trade by want of the Spanish trade'. It is remarkable that in these debates there was a tendency amongst the speakers to use the trading losses in the Spanish war as a means of rousing anti-Dutch feeling.[2]

One other question arises in connexion with the Spanish war: how great was the loss of English shipping to the Spaniards? Cromwell is alleged to have encouraged privateering among the English merchants trading with Spain; but outside their commerce in the New World the Spanish merchant vessels were very few. The complaint was made in Parliament that there were no prizes to be had as there were during the Dutch war. No exact figures are available. Slingsby Bethel stated in 1668 that a loss of 1,500 ships had been 'reported' to Richard Cromwell's Parliament, but this was actually an assertion in debate, which was later denied by Thurloe.[3] On the other hand, there is the statement of Richard Baker, a leading merchant dealing with Spain, who said 'we have lost 1,800 ships'.[4] The merchants were, however, naturally disposed to exaggerate their losses. It cannot be doubted that the English losses were considerable, but it

[1] *C.S.P.* (*Venetian*), *1659–1661*, 4–5. [2] Burton, iii. 314 *et passim*.

[3] *The World's Mistake*, Burton, iii. 348; iv. 366. The statement was made in debate by Bampfield, who later became Speaker.

[4] *C.S.P.* (*Dom.*), *1657–8*, 245. The editor dates it 1657 (?) but it was more probably of later date.

is probable that only research in the Spanish archives will reveal their exact extent.

Cromwell's break with Spain drew him into closer relations with her traditional enemy, Portugal.[1] From 1580 to 1640 Portugal had formed part of the Spanish empire and during that period had lost many of her colonial possessions, especially a large part of Brazil, to the Dutch. In 1640 the yoke of Spain had been thrown off as the result of a revolution headed by a university professor and a Spanish princess, and the first steps of the new Government had been to seek for foreign allies. The recognition of the new Portuguese king was bought from Charles I by a commercial treaty, favourable to England, signed in 1642. As certain much disputed points were left unsettled by the treaty and as its conclusion was followed by the English civil war, it was never really put into effect. During the civil war the Portuguese showed themselves thoroughly royalist; one of their envoys intrigued against Parliament, a course of conduct for which he afterwards acquired merit in the eyes of Charles II; and Royalist privateers under Rupert found their most hospitable shelter in the harbour of Lisbon. Between 1649 and 1654 there was a desultory war of commerce-destroying between the two States. Blake captured nine ships arriving from Brazil,[2] while the English factors resident in Portugal (who had been numerous before the Portuguese revolution) suffered severe losses at the hands of Prince Rupert. In 1653 negotiations began for a commercial treaty between the two countries. These were guided on the English side very largely by political and religious objects, the freedom of English merchants from the Inquisition and the expulsion of Stuart sympathizers from Portugal; but economic questions were also not neglected. On the Portuguese side there was anxiety to convert a powerful enemy into a friend.

[1] For this section generally see S.P. 89/4; Shillington and Chapman, *Commercial Relations of England and Portugal*; J. L. de Azevédo, *Epocas de Portugal Económico*; F. d'Almeida, *Historia de Portugal*, iv; E. Prestage, *Diplomatic Relations of England and Portugal* (1925).

[2] S.P. 89/4, ff. 92–116. It is interesting to notice that these ships were English, hired by the Portuguese, and their condemnation caused the prize court no little difficulty.

It had long been the object of English merchants to obtain a firm foothold in Brazil, with which the Dutch had established a profitable trade; the treaty of 1642 had allowed only two English ships a year to go there. Moreover, Richard Wylde, a prominent East India merchant and sometime president of Surat, had addressed a petition to Cromwell during the course of the Anglo-Dutch war in which he pointed out that the Portuguese power in India had decayed before the rivalry of the Dutch and begged him to conclude a treaty with Portugal in order to obtain new ports and strongholds for the English trade there.[1] Other East India merchants advocated a Portuguese treaty for similar reasons. The trade with the Portuguese colonies was much more important than that with the kingdom itself, which was said (inaccurately) to consist solely in the re-export of sugar.[2] Another source of profit available to the English was the employment by Portugal of their shipping. There had been difficulty in negotiating the treaty of 1642 because the Portuguese were apparently promising simultaneously to the English and Dutch the exclusive monopoly of supplying them with ships. The English victory over the Dutch and the prolonged quarrels between the Dutch and the Portuguese settled the matter in 1654 decisively in the English favour. By the new treaty[3] the English were allowed to trade freely with all the Portuguese colonies in Asia, Africa, and South America, and were to have the monopoly of hiring out ships to the Portuguese if their own did not suffice, while the goods of English merchants were never to be charged with import duties in excess of 23 per cent. The two nations agreed to recognize the principle of 'free ships, free goods', and finally, English merchants were completely exempted from any interference by the Inquisition either with their persons or their property. One exception only was made to the English freedom to trade with the Portuguese dominions, namely, that the carriage of certain commodities, of which the most important was dried cod, was to be confined to the ships of the Portuguese Brazil Company; but that exception was

[1] 'The Humble Remonstrance of R. Wylde Merchant' (Sloane MSS. 3271), undated, but clearly belonging to 1653. Thurloe, iv. 30.

[2] S.P. 89/4, f. 76.

[3] An English translation of the treaty is in *Collection of Treaties* (1732), vol. iii.

a 'platonic' one, as the bulk of this fish came from England and it was natural to employ English ships for its transportation.[1]

This was the most advantageous of all the commercial treaties concluded by Cromwell. English historians rightly regard it as marking the zenith of our influence in Portugal. Portuguese historians look back upon it as a nightmare.[2] It is therefore not surprising that the Portuguese king was reluctant to ratify it. Moreover diplomatic relations continued to be unfriendly between the two countries. The brother of the Portuguese ambassador at London was put to death by Cromwell's order for participation in a murderous affray, and in revenge an attempt was made to murder our envoy at Lisbon. Recourse had to be made to the threat of Blake's guns before the ratification came in May, 1656.[3]

Beyond all doubt the treaty gained for us a 'favourable balance of trade'. Throughout the seventeenth and eighteenth centuries English trade with Portugal was regarded by our politicians as very advantageous. Indeed the customs figures of 1662–3 (which omit all reference to re-exports) show that our trade with that country was the only one in which the value of our exports exceeded that of our imports.[4]

From the period of Cromwell, too, may be dated the steady development of the English consumption of port wine. There had been a consul at Lisbon before 1642, but the position of consuls was first defined in the treaty of that year, confirmed in the treaty of 1654, and the first consul was appointed at Oporto in 1659. This latter fact and others have led the historian of the port wine trade to affirm that

> It was decidedly during the Protectorate of Oliver Cromwell that the English in Oporto and Vianna were most successful. . . . He seems to have fathomed Portuguese commercial genius deeper than the present generation can.[5]

1 Azevédo, 403. The Portuguese lost the trade of cod-curing to the English at the beginning of the seventeenth century.

2 Ibid. 476. This was the opinion of the great Pombal, cf. Azevédo, *Pombal*, chap. i.

3 Thurloe, v. 79; Gardiner, iii. 476.

4 Add. MSS. 36785. Charles Davenant, to whom this document belonged, makes the statement about re-exports, *Works*, v. 351 seq.

5 C. Sellers, *Oporto, New and Old*, 18 and 24. Thomas Maynard was the first consul at Oporto. For Cromwell's personal interest in the trade with Portugal, cf. also *Letters and Papers*, ii. 505.

In 1660 there were many complaints by the English factors in Portugal of violations of the treaty of 1654 by the Portuguese.[1] No doubt the recently established Government at Lisbon did find difficulty in enforcing it. Yet we read few complaints during the Protectorate as to the conditions of the Portuguese trade in which at least fifty merchants were engaged. In return the English Government in conjunction with the French supported Portugal against her enemies in the trying period preceding her decisive victory over the Spaniards at Elvas (1659). There is therefore every reason to believe that British trade flourished from the ratification in 1656 of that treaty which a nineteenth-century statesman described as the Magna Carta of the English in Portugal.[2]

By way of concluding this survey of the Cromwellian attitude to trade outside the companies, we shall examine briefly the governmental applications of the entrepôt policy described in Chapter III. Although the Protectorate favoured the militaristic advocates of self-sufficiency to a great extent, especially with regard to export licences and the Navigation Act, it also recognized the desirability of creating an entrepôt trade, and attempted to do so in various ways.

Thus in the first place, whenever the domestic supply was sufficient, permission was given for the exportation and re-exportation of essential commodities. Parliament allowed wheat to be exported when the market price was less than 36*s*. a quarter,[3] and there was a regular export of saltpetre. In 1656 an Act was put on the statute book for 'the transportation of several commodities of the breed, growth, and manufacture of the Commonwealth'.[4] These included meat, corn, and horses when the price did not reach certain levels. The French ambassador in London said that the main design of the Act was to increase the customs revenue,[5] but although the fiscal consideration was undoubtedly in the Government's mind, it is hardly likely that the Act made a vast difference to the customs, as most of these commodities had previously

1 Cf. S.P. 89/4, ff. 70 seq.; Add. MSS. 25115, no. 10.

2 Hansard, cit. Schorer, 'Der Methuenvertrag' in *Zeitschrift für die gesamte Staatswissenschaft* (1903) p. 597.

3 Whitelocke, 589; Burton, i. xlix.

4 Firth and Rait, ii. 1043.

5 Bordeaux to Brienne, Apr. 7, 1656. Record Office transcripts.

been exported under special licence. The preamble to the Act lays stress upon the national importance of foreign trade.

On March 17, 1654, an excise Act suspended the rebate on re-exports. This threat to the entrepôt system caused an immediate outcry from the London merchants. A sub-committee was appointed under General Lambert to investigate the matter, and reported at once in favour of the reinstatement of the allowance of a rebate of 50 per cent. of the customs and all the excise upon goods brought in for re-export.[1] The figure of rebates of customs give some indication of the volume of re-exports during the Protectorate:[2]

	£
June 24, 1653—June 24, 1654 . .	6,970
June 24, 1654—Sept. 29, 1655 . .	17,729
Sept. 29, 1655—Mar. 25, 1656 . .	5,260
Mar. 25, 1656—Mar. 25, 1657 . .	18,515
Mar. 25, 1657—Mar. 25, 1658 . .	?
Mar. 25, 1658—Sept. 29, 1659 . .	33,291

In the summer of 1651 the City of London began an agitation for permission to become a free port, and the question of free ports generally was referred by the Council of State to the Committee of Trade, and by the Committee of Trade to the Committee of Trinity House. This last Committee recommended that London, Newcastle, Hull, Berwick, Dover, Southampton, Plymouth, and Bristol should be made free ports, as they had been assured that all these places possessed the necessary accommodation for warehousing and storage of goods destined for re-export.[3] They asserted that the establishment of this system would be most beneficial to the general trade of the country in employing the cellars, warehouses, and boats of the inhabitants of the ports chosen, besides conferring 'the great advantage to those places of strangers expending'.[4] But the matter went no further. We have no evidence as to the reasons for the rejection of the recommendation, but we can guess what they were. It was probably felt that in view of the position of the national budget the customs rebate of 50 per cent. was all the Govern-

[1] Firth and Rait, ii. 834, 889; *C.S.P.* (*Dom.*), *1654*, 117–19.

[2] These are taken from the Declared Accounts, A.O. i. 603–4.

[3] On the other hand, the Restoration Council of Trade said that only Dover had the necessary accommodation.

[4] Trinity House Transactions, 1613–61, 66–7.

ment could afford to allow. It is also possible that the policy of free ports was thought incompatible with the Navigation Act which was enacted in the same year. These speculations are confirmed by the approach of the Restoration Council of Trade to the question. The Council reported that it could discover no argument for free ports in the sense of permitting the import of foreign goods and letting them go out again without payment of duty; the analogy of the Italian free ports (to which the supporters of this policy always appealed), it said, was not a valid one as Italy, unlike England, was divided into a number of small principalities, between which a large entrepôt trade was vital. Although this Council recommended the re-establishment of the 'composition' trade at Dover, which had existed before the civil war and was held to be slightly different from a free port, the mayor, commonalty, and jurats of Dover promptly petitioned for a suspension of the Navigation Act without which, they asserted, it could not be re-established. The matter was then referred to the customs commissioners who agreed that the Dover trade would involve an infringement of the literal sense of the Act; but thought it would make 'more than sufficient requital' by way of export shipping; the Government therefore agreed to the petition.[1]

The admission of foreigners to reside in England, another part of the entrepôt programme, was fully accepted by Cromwell as appealing to his views of religious toleration, besides his common sense. The Protectoral Council of State exerted its influence to obtain permission for French and Dutch Protestant colonies, both in London and Norwich, to trade freely despite the protest of the natives,[2] and over two hundred and fifty foreigners were granted letters of denization or naturalization between 1655 and 1658, figures much higher than the yearly average figures under James I and Charles I.[3]

[1] Report on Free Ports, Feb. 5, 1661 (Add. MSS. 25115, ff. 116–20); Petition of the Mayor, &c. of Dover (ibid., f. 225). This was refused by the Council of Trade, but granted by the Council of State, *C.S.P.* (*Dom.*), *1661–2*, 29; see also *Calendar of Treasury Books*, *1660–7*, 44, 117, 250.

[2] *C.S.P.* (*Dom.*), *1653–4*, 159, 356; ibid., *1654*, 354; ibid., *1655*, 366; ibid., *1655–6*, 390, &c.

[3] W. A. Shaw, *Letters of Denization and Acts of Naturalization for Aliens in England and Ireland*, *1603–1700*, 66–74.

Experts like Peter Blondeau, the inventor of milled coins, and Joachim Hane, who demonstrated his new siege gun with telling effect during the civil war, were also made welcome by Cromwell and his Council.[1] In 1657 sixty alien merchants settled in London and the complaints of the native merchants in 1660 at this intrusion were very bitter. The Restoration Government, however, disregarded these complaints and recognized the wisdom of Cromwell's policy by permitting the aliens to remain.[2]

Modern historians have laid it down that up to the Restoration England was generally believed to be over-populated and after it to be under-populated.[3] Interregnum pamphleteers appear to have been divided in their views. But so far as the Government was concerned, in view of the fact that only undesirables and political prisoners were sent out to the colonies, while there was this marked encouragement of foreigners to settle, it seems likely that it already believed in the theory of under-population.

[1] For Blondeau, see *C.S.P. (Dom.) 1656–7, passim*; or Hane, see C. H. Firth, *Journal of Joachim Hane* (1896).

[2] Add. MSS. 25115, ff. 171 seq., and see above, p. 22, n. 2.

[3] For a modification of the view about over-population see Professor Mildred Campbell's essay in *Conflict in Stuart England* (1960).

XIII

TRADE AND SHIPPING

WHILST the Government endeavoured to promote foreign trade by granting, or at least confirming, privileges to exclusive trading companies, and to encourage the colonies by tariff concessions on their exports, it sought to stimulate English commerce also by action directed towards the protection of merchant shipping. One of the most difficult problems with which the early English merchant was faced was how to ensure the safe arrival of his cargo at its destination when it had to encounter on the way not merely the usual risks of maritime enterprise, but also swarms of pirates, all animated by the desire for booty and some also by the passions of political antagonism.

During the interregnum the pirates from whom the English merchant might expect attack could be divided into three groups. There were the corsairs of Northern Africa, who centred on Algiers and the Barbary States and preyed chiefly on the Levant trade; there were the Royalist pinnaces led by Prince Rupert and operating under licences (worthless in international law) granted by Charles II, whose crews regarded their work of spoliation as a semi-patriotic duty; and thirdly, there were groups of marauders established along the western European coast at Ostend, Dunkirk, St. Malo, Brest, and elsewhere, for whom piracy was a livelihood, if not connived at, yet unchecked by the French and Spanish authorities.

Furthermore, the English merchant had to contend not merely with pirates, but also with privateers who did not differ in essentials from the former class except that their trade had behind it the authorization of their Government's approval. If a merchant was unable to recover a private debt due to him from a citizen of a foreign State his Government would give him 'letters of reprisal' or 'letters of marque', and he was then legally empowered and encouraged to take his vengeance at the expense of any ship of the nation at whose hands he had suffered loss. The regular issuing of letters of marque by one nation against another meant in effect a state of naval warfare between them. In the course of the years

1643–54 such a condition was in existence at various times between England on the one side and Scotland, Holland, France, and Portugal on the other.[1]

What protection did a merchant possess against these threats to his trade routes? His ships were always armed, but unless he was himself a professional privateer he was naturally far from anxious to engage them in battle every time he sent a cargo across the seas. He could insure, but in such circumstances the premiums were beyond the means of all except the wealthiest traders.[2] He therefore looked to the Government to safeguard his business.

Cromwell has been widely credited with success in making the seas safe for commerce, but it must be fully recognized that most of the lines of policy associated with his name had been evolved before the civil wars had begun, and effect had been given to them by the Long Parliament under the stress of circumstances. In the first place, in 1644 a fund was set aside for the redemption of captives taken by the Barbary corsairs: originally this amounted to 1 per cent. of the total customs revenue, but later it was reduced to $\frac{1}{4}$ per cent.[3] This continued to be levied and administered throughout the Protectorate. In the second place, an attempt was made to co-ordinate and codify the prize laws. At the beginning of the civil war Parliament issued an ordinance for guarding the seas which invited 'well intended subjects to man vessels against pirates and enemies of the Commonwealth', if approved of by the Lord High Admiral, and to enjoy prizes captured if properly declared before the court of admiralty; and Robert, Earl of Warwick, was appointed Lord High Admiral. In the following year it was made clear that foreigners were free to trade with England if their country was in amity with it, and thenceforward letters of marque were only to apply against nations which were friendly to the Royalist cause. On January 29, 1646, an ordinance concerning reprisals specified the precise form of a letter of marque and both the office of admiral and the functions of

[1] See above, Chap. XII.

[2] Cf. V. Barbour, 'Marine Risks and Insurance in the Seventeenth Century', *Journal of Business and Economic History*, vol. ii.

[3] Act of Oct. 24, 1644; Firth and Rait, i. 544.

the court of admiralty were put into the hands of a parliamentary committee. Finally, on April 17, 1649, an Act 'declaring the grounds and causes of making prizes' recited all the earlier ordinances, incited English privateers to seize enemy ships and ships carrying contraband, and authorized the Council of State to grant letters of reprisal. The Act specifically named Portugal and Scotland as enemies of the Commonwealth.[1]

Modern authorities on the history of the prize law stress the fact that this Act was the first to lay down a detailed procedure for the admiral's court as a prize court.[2] It may seem surprising that the court of admiralty should at this date have met with the approval of Parliament; for during the reign of James I, Edward Coke, the great legal opponent of royal prerogative rights, had attacked the court of admiralty as being a prerogative court and urged its supersession by the courts of common law. After Coke's fall, his warning received emphasis from two interferences by the executive with its jurisdiction. But the growth of work during the civil wars, and the experience of a parliamentary committee which was accused of mismanagement, may well have decided Parliament, once it had ejected all Royalist officials, to entrust the business of examining prize claims and the legality of letters of marque to a court with a procedure simpler and more expeditious than that of any courts of common law and with a tradition of admiralty law which was essentially 'civil' in character. When one is told that a new epoch in the history of the court began under Cromwell, however, it is necessary to remember that there is no reason to suppose that the Act was his work, and in fact Cromwell's later policy as Protector of suppressing privateering tended rather to reduce the activities of this court.[3]

In the early years of the republic the national fleet was greatly strengthened. One hundred and forty-seven warships were built between the years 1649 and 1654, whereas under Cromwell only sixty were built.[4] This diminution in the amount of naval construction was not due to any opposition

[1] Acts in Firth and Rait, i. 392, 500, 829; ii. 66–75.

[2] Cf. Roscoe, *History of the Prize Court* (1924).

[3] See below, p. 171.

[4] Lists in W. L. Clowes, *The Royal Navy* (1897), and Oppenheimer.

on Cromwell's part, but merely to a shortage of funds. Moreover, the special pressure upon ship-building during the war with the Dutch partly explains the size of the fleet during the earlier period. The navy was now employed as a regular instrument for the protection of commerce. On January 16, 1649, an Act regulating naval officers[1] set up a committee of merchants to arrange a system of naval convoy for the mercantile marine. On April 25, the Council of State, instigated by petitions complaining of the number of pirates, especially in the Mediterranean, implemented this Act by summoning 'the governors, deputies, assistants, of the companies trading to East India, Turkey, Muscovy, Eastlands, Merchant Adventurers, and some of the merchants trading to Italy, France, Spain, Portugal, Guinea, and Barbados, to confer and agree on means that may conduce to the future safety of trade, and satisfaction for past losses'.[2] The result of the deliberations of this committee was the Act of October 31, 1650, 'an Act for setled convoys', which ordered a sum amounting to about 15 per cent. of the total customs revenue to be devoted in future to the provision of convoys.[3] In the following year (March 28, 1651) another Act instituted a special imposition on coals for building and maintaining ships to guard the seas.

The policy of convoys now set in motion was a policy common to nearly all States at that time. It had long been practised in the United Provinces, and about this same date was established by Queen Christina of Sweden.[4] The chief difficulty of convoys was to arrange co-operation between the merchants who used them and the Government which supplied them. It was clearly easier for the Government to arrange convoys in the case of regulated or joint-stock companies than in the case of individual traders, for the former dispatched annual trading fleets and it was a simple matter to send war-ships to escort them; indeed the Government tried to induce merchants sailing to open markets to send their ships 'in companies'.[5]

[1] Firth and Rait, i. 1257.

[2] *C.S.P.* (*Dom.*), *1650*, 21.

[3] Firth and Rait, ii. 444; cf. a discussion by Sir W. Foster in intro. to *Court Minutes, 1651–4*.

[4] Thurloe, i. 425–6.

[5] Order of the admiralty to the Virginia merchants, *C.S.P.* (*Dom.*), *1650*, 280.

On the whole, there is no doubt that the convoy system worked well and with a minimum of friction.[1] Certain modern writers declare that this system, together with Cromwell's vigorous foreign policy, drove piracy from the seas during the Protectorate.[2] This opinion is confirmed so far as the Mediterranean is concerned by a statement of the Venetian envoy in England in 1658, which has already been quoted, and although this generalization needs some qualification with regard to the Channel pirates, one nest of these at least was destroyed when the English captured Dunkirk in the year of Cromwell's death.[3]

In 1659 there arose new complaints against piracy, backed by no less a person than Downing, but in January, 1660, there were some twenty-five vessels employed on convoy duty.[4] In March, 1661, the Council of Trade, following the precedent of ten years before, summoned a committee of merchants to lay before them a scheme for the distribution of the fleet and for the regular provision of convoys.[5] From the Restoration until the advance of civilization put an end to piracy a system of convoying became an accepted part of national commercial policy.

Side by side with its creation of a powerful navy, the Government of the English Commonwealth intensified the long-accepted policy of stimulating, partly for military and partly for commercial reasons, the employment by merchants of English shipping. The instrument and symbol alike of this policy was the Navigation Act of 1651.

The origin of the Navigation Act of 1651 has been the subject of considerable differences of opinion among historians.[6] Some have maintained that it was a purely military measure promoted by the Long Parliament to assist the expansion of the navy. Others have thought that its enactment at this date is an important proof of the powerful influence of commercial and shipping interests upon the

[1] There were of course many criticisms of the Government's convoy organization e.g. that the merchants had to wait so long for convoy that they lost their markets and that the convoyers themselves were guilty of trading and even smuggling.

[2] e.g. Clowes; P. Gosse, *History of Piracy* (1932).

[3] See above, p. 142.

[4] Thurloe, vii. 480; Tedder, chap. i.

[5] Add. MSS. 25115, ff. 133–40.

[6] For latest views, see introduction above.

Commonwealth Government. The question has long been so open and the information about it is so scattered that it is worth while to examine it somewhat closely.

To contend that the idea of a Navigation Act—the confining of the English carrying trade to English ships—was a product of 'seventeenth-century mercantilism' would of course be mistaken, for this plan had been advocated through the later Middle Ages and the first Navigation Act had been passed under Richard II. Nevertheless, a continuous history of efforts to enforce a Navigation Act policy can be traced most definitely from the accession of the Tudors and developed *pari passu* with Tudor enthusiasm for a royal navy, which could best be built up on the basis of a flourishing mercantile marine.[1] Likewise the chartered companies formed at the end of the sixteenth century to engage in world commerce were favoured by the Government of Queen Elizabeth because they were conducive to 'the increase of shipping'.[2] These companies were not unwilling to keep the carrying trade in their own hands so as to obtain the profits of that as well as of merchanting.

This impulse for the revival or enforcement of the old Navigation Acts grew even stronger under James I and Charles I. To give one example of this, we read in 1622 a petition to the Warden and Assistants of Trinity House from the masters and owners of ships of London, Ipswich, Aldborough, Yarmouth, and other coast towns, who

> have heretofore implored to your worships that our English merchants by whom the most part of the English bottoms and generally all sorts of seamen of this land are set on work to the maintenance of them .... have and do lade and return the most of their goods to and from France, Middleborough, Dansicke, Quinsborough [Königsberg], and Melvin [Memel] in strangers' bottoms, notwithstanding there are English ships in the same places instantly to be had.[3]

Trinity House made every effort to bring these claims of English seamen before the Stuart Governments.

When the civil war came, both impulses, military and

[1] Cf. J. A. Williamson, *English Maritime Enterprise, 1485–1558* (1913).

[2] Cf. the charter of the East India Company (1601).

[3] Petition of 112 shippers from London and the outports, Trinity House Transactions, 1609–25, 90.

commercial, were sharpened. The king had been almost completely deserted by the navy at the outbreak of the war, but unable to attack the parliamentary party by the usual methods, the Royalists used the way always open to the weaker side and opened a campaign of commerce-destroying with privateers. At the same time also a long-standing quarrel between English and Dutch merchants came to a head. One result of these troubles was the heavy increase in the national fleet. Disputes were fostered by English jealousy of the commercial success of the Dutch, who not only controlled the Baltic trade and the spice trade with the Indies, but also predominated in the herring fisheries and admittedly did the carrying trade of the world.[1] The English Navigation Act of October 9, 1651, which was first introduced into Parliament when Cromwell was away in Scotland,[2] was deliberately aimed at permanently taking the shipping of English goods from the Dutch.

The immediate effect of the civil wars was a temporary collapse of the system of monopolistic companies and the throwing open of the foreign trade of the country to all comers. The problem that faced the Government and the merchants alike was therefore how to maintain a profitable commerce while at the same time shutting out the foreigner from participation in it. For example, the East India trade had fallen into the control of a number of rival groups and individuals who were united only in not wanting foreigners, especially the Dutch, to share in it and in looking to the Government for assistance. The original chartered company had always employed and continued to employ English shipping. The natural consequence of the break-up of the Company was for all East India merchants to favour the limitation of the trade, essentially an import trade, to English ships. The petitions of the East India merchants to the Government during the years before 1651 are full of grievances against the Dutch; and although no petition has come to light actually in support of a Navigation Act we have

1 See especially John Thurloe on the 'Relations of England and Holland' (*English Historical Review*, xxi. 320) and *The Advocate* (1651). The latter is a propaganda pamphlet in favour of the Act.

2 Yet even a standard authority like Clowes refers to 'Cromwell's Navigation Act'.

the authority of leading experts on early Indian history for the belief that the Act had the fullest approval of all East India merchants and especially of the successful interlopers.[1]

In the case of the other great Eastern commerce of England, the Levant trade, we have much more definite evidence of proposals for a Navigation Act. Like the East India Company, the Levant Company always traded with English shipping, but during the interregnum the trade had become 'more open and free'. Consequently the Government was subjected to pressure to prohibit the Dutch carrying trade, from all Englishmen interested in the Levant, as well as from the official Company. As early as 1647 the Government was asked to confine the Greek currant trade to ships sent out from England or from 'places of their growth', and throughout the following years a succession of petitions in favour of a general Navigation Act was compiled and presented to the Council of State by the Company.[2] For example, on December 30, 1650, the Company presented a petition to the Council of Trade which stated that whereas for the last thirty years the importation of Levant goods had been confined to the Company, which had used only English ships, 'insomuch that the serviceable shipping of this land were within a few years increased three-fourth parts', now English and foreign merchants imported from the Netherlands and elsewhere in foreign ships or in small barks and thus exposed the trade 'into the hands of the Hollanders who [were] frequenting the Levant seas with store of great ships at cheap freight and easier charges, and buying also their commodities with ready money which we have by the proceeds of English manufacturers. . . .'

For remedying whereof your petitioners most humbly desire that some speedy means be used for hindering the employment of strangers' ships, and particularly that currants, galls, cottons, and all other goods of the growth and manufacture of the Levant, or of any other place,

[1] Cf. Sir William Hunter: 'Under the Commonwealth the desire for an open trade to India gained strength. The Navigation Act of 1651 gave it a decisive impulse', and again 'The East India Company, its charters and its rivals [were] merely instruments for carrying out the great design of the Navigation Act' (*History of British India*, ii. 105, 118).

[2] General Court Minute, Mar. 7, 1644; cf. S.P. 105/144, f. 22; ibid./143, f. 368.

may (as formerly) be prohibited to be imported from the Netherlands or elsewhere, but directly from the place of their growth upon English shipping.[1]

A third interest which supported a Navigation Act was the Eastland trade. It was abundantly clear that the Eastland merchants could hardly hope to hold their own against the Dutch without Government aid. In 1651, 2,437 Dutch ships passed through the Baltic Sound as compared with 51 English and Scottish ships.[2] In June of that year twelve 'well-affected' English merchants residing at Danzig were optimistically petitioning the Council of State to

consider the great obstructions of trade in that place and take care that no Eastland commodity be imported or exported but in English bottoms, so that the navigation of the Commonwealth which now, together with the trade, decays, may not only be maintained but increased.[3]

On February 3, 1652, the Eastland Company at London resolved to petition Parliament for the preservation of the Act and wrote to the merchants at York asking them to second them with another petition, while in October 1654, the merchants at Ouse Bridge in York, ordered a letter to be written to the Eastland Company at London that 'as there will be some things moved to the Parliament (and that by no mean ones) against the Act of Navigation. . . . we will join with them for the continuance thereof'.[4]

We have further evidence that these three companies, the East India, the Levant, and the Eastland, pressed for the passing of the Act. We know that in the course of 1650 these companies joined together to impress on the Council of State and Parliament the vital necessity for some speedy action for 'the recovery and establishment of their trades'. At their request the Long Parliament set up a Council of Trade; and this Council of Trade was at work when the Navigation Act was put on the Statute Book.[5]

A smaller company which supported the Act was the Greenland Company. In 1645 a separate Act had limited

[1] S.P. 105/144, f. 55.

[2] N. Bang, op. cit.

[3] *C.S.P. (Dom.), 1651*, 273–4.

[4] *Acts and Ordinances of the Eastland Company*, 76. The first of these two letters is there wrongly dated 1651.

[5] *C.S.P. (Dom.), 1649–50*, 462, 476–7.

the importation of whale oil to English ships, but this Act was superseded by the Navigation Act, and in 1657 the Company was begging the Government to enforce it against all who attempted to evade it.[1] On the other hand, we know that the interlopers in the trade employed Dutch shipping.[2]

The Act was passed by the Long Parliament on the eve of the Anglo-Dutch war and was a contributing factor to the causes that brought it about. A very similar situation had arisen in 1542, when Henry VIII's Parliament enacted a Navigation Act before the Anglo-French war.[3] The English victory in the Dutch war made the Act permanent and Government officials hastened to write congratulating Thurloe on its enforcement.[4]

Who then were the 'no mean ones', spoken of by the Eastland merchants who at the end of this war tried to obtain the suppression of the Act? At the beginning of the century it had been the Merchant Adventurers, who were intimately associated with the Dutch and extensively employed Dutch shipping, that successfully resisted the introduction of a Navigation Act policy. The Dutch war was greatly to damage the interests of the Company. It is certain that the principal mercantile opposition to the Act of 1651 came from the Merchant Adventurers and from the Dutch merchants resident in London.[5]

Apart from merchants and industrialists constant complaints came from Government officials in the colonies about the regulations of the Act, which confined the bringing over of their supplies to English ships, on the ground that these were too few in number and too infrequent in their calls to permit an adequate victualling of the plantations. The colonial trade was competed for by more than one group of English merchants, and although it is certain that Noell and his partners, who were closely in touch with the Government, favoured the Act, there were other exporters who regarded

[1] *C.S.P.* (*Dom.*), *1655–6*, 26, 280; Firth and Rait, i. 679.

[2] Petition of R. Ford, N. Manton, and T. Papillon to import whale oil from Holland. British Museum, 69 (f.) 19/54. Cf. *C.S.P. 1656–7*, 280.

[3] Cf. Williamson, *English Maritime Enterprise*, 213–14.

[4] Fleetwood to Thurloe, May 17, 1654; Bradshaw to Thurloe, Apr. 4, 1654 (Thurloe, ii. 209, 290).

[5] Cf. *The Newcastle Merchant Adventurers*, i. 164–79.

it as the instrument of their competitors to monopolize a very profitable trade.[1]

The Navigation Act is, therefore, a very interesting example of a matter on which divergent economic groups influenced the Government in different ways and on which there was a difference of opinion among the Government officials themselves. The Levant, East India, Eastland, and some of the Greenland merchants supported the Act; the Merchant Adventurers, some Greenland merchants, and all native colonial merchants were opposed to it. Thurloe promoted it, but it is probable that Cromwell with his Dutch sympathies was not fond of it. Indeed, in March, 1656, the exiled Royalists were informed that Cromwell was prepared to offer the repeal of the Act in return for a Dutch alliance against Spain.[2] In turning to the question of the enforcement of the Act, these differences must be borne in mind.

The opinions of historians about the enforcement of the Act of 1651 are even more at variance than their views as to its origin. Some maintain that it was effectively enforced; others that it was not. Some affirm that it injured the Dutch, others that it not only did not hurt the Dutch but that it actually damaged English shipping. Again the scattered character of the evidence accounts for these contradictions.

To begin with, one thing is certain. The Eastland merchants, who were among the foremost supporters of the Act, derived little or no benefit from it. It was well known to the Government that the Eastland merchants did not possess adequate shipping to deal with the requirements of the Scandinavian 'bulky' trades. In the draft of exemptions from the Navigation Act among the Trinity House records a scheme was proposed whereby an English and a foreign vessel should take it in turns to trade with Norway, Sweden, Denmark, Halland, and the places adjacent. This would imply that the English traders were believed to possess only half the shipping necessary. The Act itself contained no clause to this effect; it was obviously impracticable; but a year after its appearance on the Statute Book merchants under-

[1] Compare G. N. Clark, 'The Navigation Act of 1651' in *History*, vii, No. 28, with Bland's *Humble Remonstrance* (1661 ?). See also above, p. 133 and n. 3.

[2] Nicholas correspondence, March 21, 1656, in *C.S.P.* (*Dom.*), *1655–6*, 236.

taking to import Eastland commodities were promised by the Government full security against confiscation under the Act.[1] There can be no doubt that the Act was not enforced during the Dutch war, so far as the provision of naval materials was concerned.[2] After the war was over the Government had to deal with fresh complaints by naval officials against the prohibition of the Dutch carrying of timbers and boards, especially to Ireland—'the English merchants not trading thither in the commodity'.[3]

A pamphleteer of 1660 stated that the Act was a failure, because it was put into force too suddenly before we had sufficient shipping to deal with the Eastland trade,[4] and some modern writers have described how the price of Eastland commodities rose sharply because we had to depend on the producers to send them over, and thus conferred an effective monopoly on the Scandinavians. On the other hand, Roger Coke, writing during the reign of Charles II in very critical terms of the Navigation Act policy, commended 'Old Oliver' who

> permitted the English merchants to trade in foreign bottoms for timber whereby he was not only better and cheaper supplied than the nation hath since been, but he enforced the King of Denmark's subjects to sell their ships built for that trade, and wherewith they used to impose what terms they would upon the English, being better and cheaper supplied than they could.[5]

Apart from the Eastland trade the Act seems to have been enforced in Europe. The original reception of the news of the Act in the United Provinces was a mixed one, but it figured among the grievances mentioned in the Dutch declaration of war. During the war itself the Act was of little importance, as enemy ships or ships carrying enemy goods were in any case confiscated.

At the end of the war the Dutch pleaded for the withdrawal of the Act, to which Cromwell himself would probably have agreed if the Republic would have entered into

[1] *C.S.P. (Dom.), 1651–2*, 448; cf. *C.S.P. (Dom.), 1653–4*, 7.

[2] S.P. 95/5A, f. 124. The Council of State to the Commissioners of Customs. Permission to violate the Navigation Act in respect of Baltic commodities was renewed on June 27, 1653.

[3] Thurloe, ii. 404.

[4] Bland, *Trade Revived*, 17; cf. *Britannia Languens*.

[5] *A Discourse of Trade* (1670), 36.

some kind of Protestant union with him. But this scheme fell through and the Act continued. In the course of 1655 sixty Dutch ships, besides eighteen others, were seized for violating the Act. Many of them were released, some compounded for a small fine, and the Dutch ambassador made bitter complaints.[1] Every artifice known to merchant's or sailor's ingenuity was used to evade the Act. Foreign ships were entered under English names at the custom house, no doubt with the connivance of friendly associates.[2] Ships stopped at an English port to water and smuggled in a cargo; 'a great leak' was sprung in a Dutch ship homeward bound from Portugal and it had to land its goods in Sussex; *The Cat* laden with deal boards for France, 'being warned of a general embargo of Dutch goods in France', steered towards the Isle of Wight and there grounded.[3]

The second Protectorate Parliament appointed a committee to draw up a Bill to amend the Navigation Act. Unfortunately, we do not know its exact clauses. The Dutch ambassador was unable to learn whether its aim was to cause the Act to be more strictly enforced or to mitigate it. But there is good evidence that the former object was under consideration; for in 1658 a group of shippers in petitioning the Council of State to enforce the Act more strictly, made reference to a Bill which Parliament did not sit to complete in that sense.[4] Actually all Parliament did was to rescind the clause of the Act limiting the export of fish to English ships.[5]

There exist a number of other petitions both favouring and condemning the Act, beyond the ones which have been quoted, but their mere existence is sufficient proof not only that the policy was one of public concern, but that in some

[1] This information is supplied from the exchequer remembrancer rolls. It is probably an incomplete list of seizures, as foreign ships were also summoned before the court of admiralty and possibly before the court of chancery. I owe this information to my friend, Mr. F. Fisher. L. A. Harper, *The English Navigation Laws* (1939), p. 51, states that sixty foreign vessels were seized for trading with the colonies and forty seizures a year of merchandise illegally imported were recorded in the exchequer rolls. For criticisms of the compositions for violations of the Act, see *C.S.P.* (*Dom.*), *1656–7*, 280 and ibid., *1658–9*, 8–9. [2] S. Lambe, *Seasonable Observations* (1658).

[3] S.P. 84/160–2 (Holland) are full of these stories, some of which are also in Thurloe. These show also that cases sometimes went before the Admiralty court.

[4] *C.J.* vii. 530; Thurloe, v. 735; *C.S.P.*, *1658–9*, 8.

[5] Firth and Rait, ii. 1099.

measure it was being enforced. Ships were actually seized for violating it, and cases were heard before the highest courts of the realm. Even in the year of anarchy, 1659, fifty-seven seizures were brought to the notice of the exchequer court. In many cases the prosecution was dropped or the accused acquitted; in some cases the Government preferred to fine rather than to confiscate; but nevertheless, the knowledge that seizure and litigation lay ahead of all who tried to employ foreign shipping to import their goods must have discouraged Dutch and other shipowners from the English trade.

Some historians have rightly pointed out that the effectiveness of the Navigation Act was dependent upon the amount of English shipping available at the time of its enactment, and as an illustration of its limitation in this respect it has been stated that there were no ships available for the Baltic trade. But as to that particular case it has been shown that Trinity House was of opinion that English ships could carry half the freight in that trade and that the Eastland Company at one time employed some two hundred vessels in it.[1] And generally, the port books—unfortunately not available for London during all first half of the seventeenth century, but for Hull and Newcastle, the two next largest ports—indicate a steady increase in the number of English ships engaged in the carrying trade.[2] True, a pamphlet of Charles II's reign is quoted to show that the cost of freight rose as a result of the Act; but that might well be the result of the restriction of foreign competition, and does not necessarily imply a shortage of English shipping.

The Act was not put into force as regularly in the colonies

1 See above, pp. 125, 163.

2 The following figures from the port books have been given to me by Miss E. Hall, who has been writing a thesis on the Newcastle trade:

Ships sailing from Hull in	*Hull ships*	*Other English*	*Foreign*	*Total*
1609	36	6	20	62
1614	24	9	11	44
1634	45	15	9	69
1640	47	14	1	62

There was a similar tendency in Newcastle.

as it was in Europe.[1] During the civil wars and even after the Act of 1650, the Dutch, who supplied cheaper provisions than the English merchants, had obtained a firm hold on the trade between Europe and the English colonies. The colonial governors were, therefore, very reluctant to dispense with Dutch assistance. Native colonial merchants found the paucity of English ships bad for their trade which, they observed, was not like that of the Indies in commodities 'rich and rare', and if they could not dispose of their goods cheaply they could not sell them at all.[2] Although there was some enforcement of the Act in Virginia, in New England little attention was paid to it. Governor David Searle, in Barbados, encouraged the Dutch trade,[3] and brought upon himself the personal behest of Cromwell to put the Navigation Act into effective operation.[4] Moreover, there was no developed legal machinery for condemning ships and goods seized under the Act in the colonies. No admiralty courts had yet been established, and it was well known that juries in common law courts were certain to acquit offenders.[5] The only effective enforcement of the Act came when the English fleet made a sudden appearance and captured Dutch or Hamburg ships peacefully plying their illegal trade. Even then the colonial officials seem to have been willing to let the prizes go.[6]

The Navigation Act of 1660 is a commentary on the Act of 1651.[7] It defines exactly English shipping, makes clear that a seizure can be examined and condemned in any court of record as well as an admiralty court, strictly conjures all colonial officials to obey the law, and imposes oaths upon colonial governors. It takes measures to prevent smuggling frauds, places alien duties on the goods of many foreign importers (a suggestion of at least one Cromwellian pamphleteer),

[1] This was Lambe's opinion.

[2] Cf. Bland, *Humble Remonstrance* (Virginia and Maryland).

[3] Thurloe, iii. 249–52.

[4] Add. MSS. 11411, f. 13.

[5] See the interesting discussions in Beer and Crump.

[6] See above, p. 133; cf. Doyley to Thurloe, Feb. 27, 1658: 'Captain Mings coming hither took some ships trading with goods at Barbados contrary to the Act, and offered them to condemnation to me; who, perusing all the commissions and instructions sent hither did not find any authority to proceed. The authority sent under the great seal to General Brayne and others for erecting an admiralty court mentions only the Spaniard, with cautions and provisoes for our allies and confederates' (Thurloe, vi. 834).

[7] *Statutes of the Realm*, v. 246.

and restricts exports as well as imports to English shipping. This last was the most natural consequence of all; ships must carry and fetch, or not come at all.

This Act of 1660 was directly the result of an investigation into the advisability of renewing the earlier Act by the Restoration Government; as soon as it had settled down, the question was taken into consideration. Thurloe patiently explained to Clarendon, Charles II's leading minister, the commercial iniquities of the Dutch, especially during the Anglo-Spanish war.[1] The Dutch being at peace and the English at war, the English were invited to carry on their own trade in Dutch bottoms. The Dutch ambassadors in England gave as a reason for the repeal of the Navigation Act the possibility of this situation arising. 'The Committee for Encouraging and Regulating the Manufacture of Wool and Navigation' called into consultation the Masters of Trinity House on the question of renewing this Act. The latter put forward a scheme very similar to the Long Parliament Act, but forbidding the export of fish in foreign bottoms (the clause which their old enemies at Yarmouth had had suppressed) and laying it down that native owners of foreign-built ships should employ a crew at least two-thirds English. They were then directly asked if they favoured the re-enactment of the 'pretended' Act of 1651. The response was:

> As to the Act or pretended Act made in the year 1651 . . . whether it be fit to pass such an Act or what alterations are fit to be made, we humbly conceive that that Act was made when there was inclination to have wars with the Dutch, and as the same was afterwards put in execution we cannot find nor satisfy ourselves that it tended to the advantage of the English navigation, unless it had been more exactly performed.[2]

The masters of Trinity House were now of course expelled Royalists who were re-entering upon their heritage. But their judgement was just: the Act of 1651 was 'performed', but not 'exactly'.

The Navigation Act was a cause but not a major cause of the Anglo-Dutch war of 1652–4. This was brought about

[1] *English Historical Review*, xxi. 326.
[2] Trinity House Transactions, 1613–61, 167.

partly by political disputes, but immediately by quarrels over privateering, a tariff war, and a race in naval armaments. It was probably fomented by the East India Company and certain privateering organizations, but was disliked by Cromwell himself and by the army. Its economic effects were the injury of our Mediterranean trade, but the comparative Dutch and English customs figures seem to suggest that Dutch trade was hurt more severely by it than the English.[1] On the conclusion of peace Cromwell refused to rescind the Navigation Act, but some efforts were made to clear up disputed points of international maritime law. The problems of this period centred mainly on the right of neutral ships to carry enemy goods in war-time, and there were three principal contentions about it, Dutch, English, and French.[2] The Dutch view (which ultimately prevailed) was that neutral ships might carry enemy goods, but that neutral goods on enemy ships were liable to confiscation. The phrase that summed up this policy was 'free ships, free goods—enemy ships, enemy goods'. It is obvious that this point of view was appropriate to a country which had an effective monopoly of the carrying trade of Europe,[3] but it is important to notice that it obtained support from only one leading jurist in the seventeenth century. The goal of Dutch policy was the insertion of this clause in all their commercial treaties. The English contested the Dutch point of view. An interesting paper compiled by Dr. Walker, the judge advocate, and dated July 1, 1656, exists 'Touching that supposed maxime of Free Ship, Free Goods. That is to say, that it is so far from being a Maxime, that it is utterly erroneous.' Dr. Walker exemplifies the difficulties of the maxim when an enemy freights a friend's ship and fills it with his own goods (not contraband) or when a free ship is laden both with friend's goods and enemy's goods, and concludes by asserting the English position in its most naked form, 'the object of a country must always be to intercept trade with its enemies'.[4]

1 See above for figures, p. 58. De la Court, op. cit., 57, comments on the injury done to Dutch commerce by the war.

2 This discussion is based on the works of Wheaton and Reddie. The treaties are in Dumont, *Corps Diplomatique*, and translated in a *Collection of Treaties* (1732).

3 Thurloe in the *English Historical Review*, xviii. 320.

4 S.P. 18/129, ff. 14–19.

The English practice was that enemy goods on neutral ships could be seized, the ships being permitted to go free. The French, on the other hand, confiscated both the ships and the goods. The English and French policies involved the right to search suspected ships, a right which caused great interruption to trade. During the Dutch war the Danes and Swedes seem to have practised the English policy against its promoters.

A further problem was the question of contraband. It was generally agreed that neutral ships might not carry contraband of war to hostile States, but the difficulty lay in the definition of contraband. Clearly gunpowder and muskets were contraband, but what of corn, horses, money, and naval stores? This question arose especially in the course of the Anglo-Swedish negotiations of 1655–6. The English and Swedes, related Whitelocke, our representative,[1]

> had long debates touching contraband goods, in which list was inserted by the council [of state], corn, hemp, pitch, tar, money, and other things. The [Swedish] ambassador said, that if they would likewise add copper and tin it would take all the commodities of his master's dominions and he might insist upon cloth to be added as necessary for soldiers as corn and money. . . .

Eventually in the treaty signed in 1656 only horses, money, and munitions were defined as contraband. In the Anglo-French treaty of 1655 'arms, ammunition, horses, and military furniture' were labelled contraband, but corn was specifically excluded from the list. In the Anglo-Spanish war of 1655 only arms and instruments of war were considered as contraband.[2] It is said, however, to have been the constant aim of English policy to define corn as contraband.

Another disputed point during the interregnum was a question arising out of the convoy system which was now being universally adopted by trading nations. The Dutch maintained that since warships were plainly not liable to search, convoyed merchant ships were likewise exempt. This view never commended itself to Cromwell.

In the years 1654–5 the Protector concluded treaties with the United Provinces, Denmark, Sweden, Portugal, and

[1] Whitelocke, *Memorials*, 621.

[2] *C.S.P. (Dom.)*, *1655–6*, 40.

France, but in only one case, that of Portugal, was the principle of 'free ships, free goods' conceded by him. As the Portuguese were the enemies both of the Spaniards and of the Dutch, Cromwell may well have felt that this concession was unlikely to damage British interests, while the countervailing privileges conferred by this treaty on English merchants were enormous.[1]

These treaties were essential to English traders because in the earlier half of the century the distinction between peace and war was so shadowy that unless a definite agreement had been made between States, exporters and importers could never be certain of security in the pursuit of their callings. Moreover, although the practice of general reprisals between nations was no longer common, except in war-time, the uncontrolled issue of letters of marque was still a source of distress to commercial interests. These treaties put an end to unchecked privateering. Henceforward commercial grievances must be discussed between the Governments concerned before vengeance was committed to private hands.

But after the Anglo-Dutch peace treaty the Dutch remained dissatisfied. Their ambassador in England, Nieuport, complained in December, 1654, that the treaty was not being enforced, and begged that Cromwell and his Council would

> conceive it not only convenient but necessary that by a good Treaty of Marine all things may be so regulated, that in future no cause may be given for further complaints.

He alleged that some of the privateering captains had deserted the service of the Royalists and were endeavouring, 'like Simon, the Inventor of the Trojan Horse', by indirect means to serve them better than ever. Their aim, he said, was again to stir up the English against the Dutch and hinder true confidence between the two peoples. As late as June 21, 1655, Nieuport was complaining that privateering continued despite the treaty, and three weeks later (July 12) Cromwell issued a proclamation suspending all letters of marque.[2] Possessing a powerful fleet, Cromwell does not appear to have conceived of privateering in European wars as desirable,

[1] See above, pp. 147–9.

[2] S.P. 84/160, f. 95. Cf. ibid., ff. 154, 199, 213, 282, &c. The proclamation is in British Museum 669 (f) 20/7.

although he approved of and encouraged it in the Atlantic. There exists in the Record Office a list of prizes taken during the Protectorate which confirms the view generally held that privateering, like piracy, was effectively if not entirely suppressed by Cromwell. According to this:[1]

Year	*No. of ships seized*
1654 (to May)	159
1654 (June–Dec.)	109
1655	130
1656	46
1657	30
1658	26
1659	26

From the list (which only gives complete details in a certain number of cases) we learn that in 100 cases the goods were condemned, in 68 the ships, and in 358 both; and that (so far as recorded) 169 of the captures were by the fleet and 95 by English privateers. Of the ships whose nationality is given, 63 were French, 63 Dutch, and 43 Spanish (including the Spanish Netherlands).

Throughout the Protectorate the Dutch continued to press for 'a good treaty of marine', but to this the English authorities would never agree. The Dutch demanded, Thurloe told Clarendon, 'liberty of having free trade and commerce with all kingdoms in amity and neutrality with them, though the declared enemies of other states', that is to say, the clause 'free ships, free goods'. By this means 'they being in peace themselves, must necessarily have all the trade, because whoever employs and trades in their ships, his goods are in safety'.[2]

Although there was little English privateering against the Dutch after 1655, they still had a source of grievance in the frequent seizure of their vessels for violating the Navigation Act.[3] Moreover, towards the end of the Protectorate there arose a new antagonism between the two countries over the Baltic situation, since the Dutch were said to be encouraging the Danes to close the Sound against the English. Later in 1656 Nieuport had reported[4] an unfounded rumour that 'the French maxim that the goods of an enemy confiscate those

[1] Record Office Ind. 9009.
[2] *English Historical Review*, loc. cit.
[3] See above, p. 165.
[4] Thurloe, v. 698.

of a friend. . . . is likewise to be practised here in England against the inhabitants of the United Netherlands'. This is only one instance of the state of tension between the two nations. After Cromwell's death the tension increased and Thurloe related to Clarendon the dangers that English commerce still suffered from the Dutch:

> It being evident that no agreement could be made with them. . . . without condescending to some things very prejudicial to the kingdom in the great concernments of trade, the thoughts of such alliances were laid aside, and the considerations of preserving the commerce and navigation of the state, as well in Europe as India were applied to, lest the English should be wholly eaten out by the people of the United Netherlands.[1]

At the Restoration the Council of Trade had to listen to the grievances not only of the East India and Eastland Companies but also of the Merchant Adventurers against the Dutch. In due course these disputes led the way to the second Anglo-Dutch war.

[1] *English Historical Review*, loc. cit.

XIV

THE DEPRESSION OF 1659–60[1]

THERE has recently been published under the auspices of the London School of Economics a book by Dr. Margaret James on *Social Policy during the Puritan Revolution*. The reader of this book derives as his main impression of the economic life of the country during the interregnum that it was an epoch of almost unrelieved depression. We are not concerned here with Dr. James's conclusions about the effect of the civil wars on trade, but it is necessary, by way of ending this outline of Cromwellian economic policy, to examine her view of the Protectorate; for there is always in the public mind a close (but questionable) association between Government policy and the economic state of the country.

Dr. James derived the information for her study largely from the magnificent Thomason collection of pamphlets in the British Museum. She describes the years 1650–1 as a period of recuperation, and then, after briefly noticing the 'damaging effects' of the Navigation Act on trade, sketches the Protectorate as a period of deepening economic gloom. It is arguable, on the other hand, that if one takes a mass of material, of the sort which Dr. James quotes, at any period in modern times one would tend to gain an impression of widespread social distress. For example, the correspondence and representations addressed over the last thirty years by traders and manufacturers to a department like the Board of Trade would give a very one-sided impression of the commercial situation of the country as a whole; for men seldom put pen to paper (except when composing prospectuses) to record how well their business is doing. The nature of Dr. James's material would therefore tend to darken her picture. She has for her view, however, the support of no less an authority than Professor W. R. Scott, whose book on the English joint-stock companies up to 1720 is a standard work on economic

[1] For this section generally I must acknowledge the kindness of Lord Beveridge in permitting me to inquire into the results of the work of his international price statistics research committee on my period. The index numbers I quote are provisional numbers made out by this committee; the wheat prices, however, are final.

history in the seventeenth century. Here again it is necessary to appreciate that Professor Scott's approach to his subject must have tended to a certain extent to exaggerate the general position. He has described the period of the Protectorate as one of 'depression'. Such it was, in the main, for the joint-stock companies. Was it for the country as a whole?

When the civil war was over there was a great increase in confidence and business. The increase in confidence is seen especially in the fall in the rate of interest from 8 to 6 per cent. in 1651. The Dutch are said to have withdrawn their investments during the civil wars[1] but may well have re-invested upon the resumption of diplomatic relations between the two countries. The price of wheat had fallen from an index figure of 57·66 in 1649 to 48·87 in 1651, 43·1 in 1652, and 32·69 in 1653. Thus the burden of wages upon employers grew less; money wages fell from 8*s.* 5¾*d.* a week in 1650 to 7*s.* 11¼*d.* in 1651 and 7*s.* 5*d.* in 1652, while there was a slight rise in real wages to the benefit of the employee. This fall in wages contributed to an outburst of business activity especially exemplified in the United Joint Stock of the East India Company.[2] Sir Josiah Child, himself an active merchant during the interregnum, asserted that England's wealth greatly increased from 1650 to 1670, due undoubtedly to the strengthening of England's position among nations under Cromwell.[3] Customs duties were expanding.[4] Thorold Rogers speaks of the rates of wages prevailing during the Protectorate as higher than at any previous period in the century.[5] There is no evidence for any increase in unemployment.[6]

Uncertainty about the privileges of the chartered companies had led during the years following the execution of the king to an extension of interloping in foreign markets, and competition in commerce grew keener. The Dutch war,

[1] *C.S.P. (Dom.), 1650–1*, 23. [2] See above, p. 113.

[3] Cit. Rogers, *Agriculture and Prices*, v. 146; cf. Petty's observations on the 'prodigious' growth of wealth since 1636 in Hull, ii. 271.

[4] See above, p. 57. [5] Rogers, v. 14.

[6] Dr. James in chap. vi of her book gives the impression that there was considerable unemployment throughout the interregnum. On the other hand, Dr. Cunningham (*Growth of English Industry and Commerce* (ed. 1892), ii. 203) thought that pauperism declined between 1650 and 1660. In fact, the local records do not enable us to arrive at a conclusion either way.

although it led to trade losses in certain directions, seems to have brought with it the capture of some Dutch markets. Wheat prices continued to fall, reaching bottom with an index number of 21·0 in 1654.

While competition in foreign trade was increasing, the general level of prices appears to have fallen, but in a manner not sufficiently marked to indicate a depression. Yet all the factors making for a depression, shortage of money, falling prices, and, no doubt, over production of certain commodities, were already present during the first years of the Protectorate. (A similar situation but on a vaster scale occurred in 1929.)

In 1659 the depression actually began. The capture of Spanish bullion in 1656 and the minting of Cromwellian coins in the same year checked the fall in prices in 1657–8, but this tended to make the fall sharper in the following years.

The evidence for the fall in prices in 1659–60 consists firstly, in the general comments of the time,[1] especially in the widespread complaints of the fall in the price of cloth;[2] secondly, in the fall in coal prices,[3] the only prices at present available to us which, unlike wheat, were not affected by such special factors as the weather; thirdly, in the continued under-valuation of English gold in the mint ratio.[4]

The price of foodstuffs, having at first stimulated industry by falling, rose again in a very marked manner in 1658–61. Thorold Rogers speaks of 'the great dearth' of wheat in those

[1] Cf. James, 75–6.

[2] e.g. *A Letter from York.* Unfortunately such cloth prices as we possess come from institutions where the nature of the contracts for supply caused the price to vary little over long periods. The fall in price came in the export trade especially, and was attributed to the Spanish war.

[3] 1657, 80·0; 1658, 78·5; 1659, 71·2. See the Eton and Cambridge prices in Rogers.

[4] Sir Ralph Maddison in his *Great Britain's Remembrancer* (1654) stated that our gold was being attracted into France and that our mint would have been at a standstill if it had not been for the capture of Dutch prizes. According to figures given in Ruding's *History of the Coinage*, only £154,000 in gold was coined during the interregnum as compared with £3,000,000 during the reign of Charles II. The proportion of gold to silver coined during these three periods was as 3 : 20, 3 : 8, and 4 : 3 respectively. It appears from 'A Brief Discourse' (Add. MSS. 10402, f. 18), written not earlier than 1657, that the undervaluing of gold in terms of silver at the English mint continued to the end of the Protectorate.

years. The figures that he prints are probably too high,[1] and the latest index numbers we have for the Protectorate give us:

1654 . . .	21·04	1657 . . .	44·43
1655 . . .	35·13	1658 . . .	50·13
1656 . . .	36·77	1659 . . .	47·42

The price of beef also rose:

1654 . . .	81·9	1657 . . .	90·7
1655 . . .	79·0	1658 . . .	103·5
1656 . . .	89·7	1659 . . .	102·5

This rise in food prices meant increased labour costs, especially as there was no fall in money wages, which always lag behind a fall in prices. It thus follows that in 1659–60 producers found their profits squeezed between rising costs and falling selling prices. Finally, the depression was due to monetary factors and a swamping of the available markets. This latter phenomenon generally accompanies any change in methods of commercial organization, such as occurred in this period with the expansion of individual trading.

The general shortage of money during the Protectorate and the improvement in Dutch trading figures during the years 1658–61[2] gives cause to believe that the principal factor in the depression of these years was a political one. The death of Cromwell and the weakness of his son undermined confidence, and the Republican Government speedily found itself in conflict with the City,[3] and unable to borrow money even at short-term rates. Furthermore, political uncertainty injured all merchants who had built up prosperous business undertakings under Oliver Cromwell. Thomas Povey, writing to his brother Richard on October 29, 1659, told him how 'this last year of violence and mutation' had

[1] The annual prices per quarter at Cambridge (Rogers) were:

	s.	d.		s.	d.
1654 . . .	21	8	1657 . . .	46	3¾
1655 . . .	33	2¼	1658 . . .	57	6¾
1656 . . .	37	1½	1659 . . .	52	1

[2] The figures of Amsterdam customs were:

1658 . .	828,870 gulden. The total figures	1,665,282
1659 . .	886,135 " " "	1,757,182
1660 . .	1,122,390 " " "	2,048,254
1661 . .	989,064 (Pringsheim).	1,800,882 (Becht.)

[3] Cf. Sharpe, *London and the Kingdom*, ii. 352–78.

ruined his business plans and 'hath blasted and crushed some considerable attempts which would have yielded me some fruit'.[1] In another letter written about the same date, he noticed how his famous business associate, Martin Noell, had also been badly hit by the change of Government[2] and had withdrawn himself both from Whitehall and the Exchange.

On the whole, then, we may suppose that if there was not exactly a boom, at least there was a very marked improvement of trade during the Protectorate of Oliver Cromwell, and that the depression of 1659–60, which helped to pave the way to the Restoration, was due less to the economic policy practised during his lifetime than to the political anarchy which followed his death.[3]

[1] Add. MSS. 11411, f. 25.

[2] To the Governor of the Barbados, Oct. 20, 1659. Ibid., f. 90.

[3] This is the view of Dr. Shaw, who lays more emphasis on pure monetary factors: intro. to *C.S.P.* (*Treasury Books*), *1672–5*.

XV
CONCLUSION

THE genius of Adam Smith still influences, and is allowed to distort, the economic history of the seventeenth century. His description of the 'Commercial or Mercantile System' in the fourth book of *The Wealth of Nations*, although not inexact in itself, has unhappily provided writers with a title to cover a number of essentially different economic policies. Moreover, 'the mercantile system', not a seventeenth-century word but Smith's own invention, is often employed as a term of disparagement to dismiss economic ideas as silly or ignorant. But the real value of the academic theory of *Mercantilismus*, as expounded by List, Schmoller, and others, is to be found in the stress upon the fact that the principal policies which Smith grouped together, namely, the creation of national monopolies and national restrictions on commerce, were mainly political and not economic in character and aim. In so far as their analysis applied to the Cromwellian era, there is no doubt that they were right. This does not mean, however, that the pressure of economic interests upon the Government was insignificant.

The seventeenth-century merchant understood his trade probably as well as his successor of to-day. His basic principles were both up-to-date and understandable:

> To buy at the first or best hand or there, where they may have the commodities cheapest.
> To fetch commodities from the immediate places of production or growth.
> To sell commodities to the utmost market at the highest price.[1]

He knew what measures would benefit him and he did everything in his power to persuade the Government to introduce those measures. Yet he could not induce the Government to do what he wanted unless there was already in existence a type of political outlook that was favourable to him. In this monograph it has been shown how many of the schemes for a governmental economic policy were not put forward by

[1] *The Advocate* (1651).

merchants at all but by semi-official propagandists like Thomas Violet and Henry Robinson.

There were in fact two strains of thought that predominated in the mid-seventeenth century, the merchant's, and the politician's or soldier's. The former was interested primarily in 'opulence', his personal opulence, the latter in 'defence', the national defence. Hence, as Adam Smith pointed out, the merchant tried to persuade the Government to pursue the policy which he desired by advancing arguments derived from the Government's own point of view, the point of view of defence:

> Those arguments . . . were addressed by merchants to parliaments and to the councils of princes, to nobles, and to country gentlemen; by those who were supposed to understand trade, to those who were conscious of themselves that they knew nothing about the matter. That foreign trade enriched the country, experience demonstrated to the noble and the country gentleman, as well as to the merchants; but how, or in what manner, none of them well knew. The merchants knew perfectly in what manner it enriched themselves. It was their business to know it. But to know in what manner it enriched the country was no part of their business.[1]

The economic conceptions of the merchants themselves give a modern impression. They called upon the Government to control the banks, to force down the rate of interest, to pass an Alien Act, and to protect maritime trade by keeping the seas free of pirates and thus reduce the cost of insurance. At the same time, despite all their specious arguments in favour of one tax rather than another, they agitated persistently against the payment of any taxes at all, alleging they crippled their commerce and weakened their competitive power.

But while the merchants aimed at low taxes on the ground that these raised unduly the prices of their goods, they readily asserted that their main object was to sell abroad as dearly as they possibly could.[2] Whatever the true reason,

[1] *The Wealth of Nations*, Bk. IV, chap. i.

[2] If one compares the mercantile policies of Cromwellian England with the theories flourishing in the North American colonies, backward, primitive, and badly lacking both capital and labour, one is conscious almost of crossing a bridge between the new and old world of economic ideas. To the men of Massachusetts riches were 'mutable things of this unstable world'; John Cotton sought to refute the false

the English Puritan merchant was no less prepared than his brother Anglican to seek profitable business wherever it might be found and to drive out his Dutch Protestant competitor by hook or by crook from his markets. The attitude of the merchant exporters to the monetary question was likewise extremely modern. They all deplored the world shortage of the precious metals, but they understood from experience that trade could best be increased by means of a free flow of gold and silver from South America to Spain and Portugal and thence outward to Turkey, Norway, or the East Indies. If it was desirable for bullion to come to London, let banks be built, they said, and let the mint price of gold be raised, and the City would replace Amsterdam as the financial centre of the world.

Under pressure from various mercantile and religious groups the policy of the Government was naturally to some extent confused and uncertain. In times of wars and revolution governments have to practise a definitely opportunist policy. The Protectorate was at least a period of greater stability than that of the Long Parliament, and it is possible to see during it a clearer and more consistent governmental policy than might be expected on *a priori* grounds. The general conclusion drawn from a survey of Cromwell's economic policy is the acceptance in the main by the Government of the doctrine of 'self-sufficiency'. The country, it was felt, must be economically self-supporting and ever ready for war. The Navigation Act was enacted and enforced in order to give the nation the ships and sailors of which it stood in need; and in every way and in many directions the Government encouraged the production of all munitions and stores necessary to fill the magazines of an island State in time of war. Many of the arrangements preached or practised with this aim are curiously suggestive of the war of 1914–18.

It will be remembered that immediately upon the outbreak of war in 1914 there was brought into operation a scheme of State marine insurance which had been prepared in advance; it was only at a much later stage and under pressure

doctrine 'that a man might sell as dear as he can, and buy as cheap as he can'; and the years 1630–41 were looked back upon as 'the golden age of New England, when vice was crushed. . . . especially oppression and extortion in prices and wages'. Cf. E. Johnson, *American Economic Thought in the XVIIth Century* (1932), 86, 125, 128.

from the submarine campaign that a convoy system was established and proved very successful. During the interregnum convoys were promptly established and marine insurance only thought about. From the outset of the Great War also there was a Government-encouraged campaign to oust enemy trade from neutral markets, and during the latter part of the war a maritime blockade of Germany was so effective that her trade was almost wholly reduced to that with her overland allies. Had English energies not been diverted to the manufacture of munitions, we should, as during the Anglo-Dutch war of 1652–4, have enjoyed a marked expansion in our export trade at the expense of the enemy. The sole value of this analogy is to show how military in character were the economic achievements of the Protectorate.

As a broad generalization it may be said that in questions of commerce and public finance the period was more prolific in new facts than in ideas. There was of course the triple assault on the trading companies, from the cloth manufacturers, from the interlopers, and from the Puritans, but the arguments used were old and not peculiar to England. It is, however, to be observed that although the Puritan criticism of monopolies in foreign trade was partly based upon religious convictions, it was not dependent upon them but could stand by itself upon purely economic and business grounds. It is also important to recognize that the seventeenth-century merchant was, on the whole, thoroughly opposed to war as injurious to trade, even though some trade might temporarily be benefited by it.

In the realm of economic fact the development of private banking is a matter of some interest and clearly helped the growth of a movement in favour of a State Bank. But the uncertain condition of Government credit made the creation of such an institution by the Protector impossible. Still the improvements in the administration of taxes and the steady advance in the successful and efficient organization of the excise and the monthly assessment helped to steady the transition from a system of public finance whereby the king was supposed to 'live of his own' to the system of the regular provision of supplies by Parliament. Here we strike the point of contact between financial and constitutional history, as we have above struck the contacts between the subjects of this investigation and foreign policy and military history.

But, on the whole, the ultimate significance of the six years' government by Oliver Cromwell lay in this: a gradual return to old ways. The restoration of the exchequer in 1654, the fiscal control over the Protector exercised by even the most subservient of Parliaments, the recognition of the necessity of regulating trade and shipping especially in war-time, all these things were the outcome of the stability given to the central Government by the formation of the Protectorate and the confidence felt in it by the trading classes. But as fine weather precedes the storm, so the trade boom which came at the end of the Anglo-Dutch war was the herald of an economic depression which was aggravated out of all proportion by the loss of confidence following on the death of Oliver Cromwell. The state of the public debt contributed to the difficulties of the new rulers. Cromwell himself might have borne the debt which had grown up during his Protectorate, and might have weathered the storm of the depression. As it was, the conservative system that he had helped to re-establish in matters of commerce and finance was left to fall into the hands of Charles II without any fear of violent upheaval.

APPENDIX A

Yields of Taxes during the Protectorate

THE list on page 185 of amounts derived from various taxes paid into the exchequer during the Protectorate, while not exhaustive, is practically complete. I have been fortunate in discovering some documents (Carte MSS. 73, f. 67 and Add. MSS. 32471, ff. 1, 15, 63) which almost fill up the gaps in the declaration books of the exchequer of receipt (E. 405/289, 390–1). These documents are clearly abstracts based on the missing declaration books, and therefore a collation of the three sets of figures is possible. There are a few minor discrepancies, but they are negligible.

APPENDIX B

The character of English exports and imports in the mid-seventeenth century

THE following summary lists of English exports and imports is based as far as possible on interregnum documents too numerous to quote. I have supplemented these to some extent by the complete list of 1662–3 (Add. MSS. 36785); the general nature of English trade did not change substantially between 1658 and 1662:

COLONIAL. *Exports*: cloth (esp. serges), tin, leather goods, lead, glass, earthenware, hats, shoes, stockings, raisins (re-exported), slaves (from Guinea), woollen goods, cattle, utensils for sugar-boiling, tobacco pipes, and provisions generally.

Imports: tobacco (Virginia), sugar (West Indies), ginger, cotton-wool, skins (a small quantity), indigo, fustic wood.

EAST INDIES. *Exports*: cloth, aqua-vitae, bullion.

Imports: pepper, ginger, saltpetre, calicoes, silks, cotton yarn, nutmegs, various spices and drugs.

EASTLAND. *Exports*: cloths (esp. Spanish), woollen goods, men's woollen hose, leather goods. To Poland, shortcloth; to Norway, bullion.

Imports: hemp, pitch, tar, potashes, tallow, masts, oars, deal.

NOTE. During the Protectorate, Whitelocke supported a proposal to secure a monopoly of Swedish copper.

FRANCE. *Exports*: cloth (esp. kersies and serges), woollen goods, hose, hops, refined sugar, wrought iron, butter.

Imports: wool, silk, wine (Bordeaux), beads, paper, olives, salt.

GERMANY. *Exports*: cloth (esp. bays and new draperies), lead, tin, corn, beer, gloves, stockings.

Imports: wine (Rhenish), copper, hemp, linen, canvas, flax.

	Mich. 1654–Easter 1655	Easter 1655–Mich. 1655	Mich. 1655–Easter 1656	Easter 1656–Mich. 1656	Mich. 1656–Easter 1657	Easter 1657–Mich. 1657	Mich. 1657–Easter 1658	Easter 1658–Mich. 1658	Mich. 1658–Easter 1659
	£	£	£	£	£	£	£	£	£
Customs and Subsidies .	116,638	151,245	150,963	166,189	156,399	152,615	159,217	166,420	154,566
							including separate London Farm		
Excise and New Impost	162,659	171,254	176,070	177,185	182,062	192,453	238,024	211,150	215,902
Prize Goods . . .	..	..	..	5,900	205,384	44,216	3,720	50	1,277
Rent of Delinquents' and Recusants' Estates .	12,539	25,761	17,144	19,589	29,746	19,953	27,111	12,645	22,977
Rent of other lands .	395	162	112	253	848	711	734	777	231
Fines for alienations .	2,000	2,000	2,000	1,950	2,500	2,100	2,200	1,800	2,200
Issues of Jurors . .	500	500	500	500	500	500	500	500	500
Composition of 12*d.* a chaldron on coal .	919	919	919	919	919	919	919	919	919
Aulnage of cloths .	499	499	499	499	499	499	499	499	499
Postage of Letters .	5,000	5,000	5,000	5,000	5,000	4,569	5,930	6,118	4,128
Probate of Wills . .	2,400	3,346	2,952	2,482	3,320	2,428	5,163	3,712	5,448
Sheriffs of Counties .	341	189	188	522	250	862	314	192	475
Sheriffs of Cities and Bailiffs of Liberties .	70	33	135	126	90	144	129	60	89
Fines of Leases upon outlaws . . .	12	19	15	8	12	15	9	..	19
Seizures and Extents .	4	..	360	2	2	62	108	2,570	80
Wine Licences . .	..	..	..	632	500	2,200	1,800	1,000	1,200
New Buildings . .	..	..	..	..	..	..	11,799	19,512	10,718

Guinea. *Exports*: cloth, provisions.

Imports: slaves (re-exported to West Indies), ivory, dyeing woods.

Levant. *Exports*: cloth (esp. light cloths) dyed and dressed, tin, bullion. To Italy; serges, perpetuanas, wax, tin.

Imports: cotton, galls, raw silk, currants (from Greece), hemp, mohair yarn, goat's hair, carpets. From Italy; wines, capers, beads.

Netherlands. *Exports*: cloth (mainly undressed), lace, red lead, skins, copperas (re-exported), hats, glass, earthenware, butter.

Imports: loaf sugar, flaxen goods, hops, tow, dressed hemp, indigo, cordage. From the Spanish Netherlands; Bruges thread, silks, tapestries.

Portugal. *Exports*: fish (esp. dried cod), cloth (esp. Spanish), shoes, stockings, silk and leather goods, gunpowder.

Imports: oil, sugar (from Brazil), fruit (esp. citrons), wine (port).

Note. The proposal was put forward by English merchants at the Restoration that the English should acquire a monopoly of the Portuguese salt trade.

Russia. *Exports*: dyed and dressed cloth, aqua-vitae.

Imports: furs (esp. sables and squirrel), skins, red hides, hats, potashes, caviare.

Note. There was very little trade between England and Russia during the interregnum.

Spain. *Exports*: fish, cloth (esp. bays, perpetuanas, Norwich stuffs), hats, stockings, gold and silver lace, bacon, hoops, glass, earthenware.

Imports: wine (Saragossa), raisins, wool (merino), silk, bullion (from Mexico), oil, indigo, iron, cochineal, tobacco.

INDEX